CW00694127

THE

UNDESIRABLES

Mark was born in Oxford, England in 1988 and his family immigrated to Australia by plane just one year later. His English father taught him to play cricket and football in the northern suburbs of Sydney; his Australian mother taught him manners, morals, and how to fold bedsheets properly.

Mark began exploring the world at a young age. When he was fourteen he travelled to Brazil and Argentina on a futsal tour. He backpacked around Europe in 2006, and worked as a London tour guide when he ran out of money halfway through the trip. Mark wrote his first manuscript, about the divine transient freedom of university exchange, while studying Spanish in Mexico.

Mark's farcical comedy *The Dark of the Matinee* was performed at the 2006 Short and Sweet ten-minute play festival. He graduated with a BA in Communications (Writing and Cultural Studies) and a BA in International Studies (Latin American Studies) from the University of Technology, Sydney. He also completed the Advertising Creative Award School in 2012. Mark has published social justice articles for Oxfam 3Things youth movement, and even a few articles for *The Daily Telegraph*.

Mark became impassioned by the asylum seeker debate after a visit to Villawood Detention Centre while writing for Oxfam. Months later, in October 2012, Mark was employed by the Salvation Army to work at the Nauru Regional Processing Centre. While in Nauru, Mark established the Recreations program and Oceans program for asylum seekers. He eventually resigned from the Salvation Army in June 2013 and spoke out publicly against the government's No Advantage policy.

Continuing his passion for humanitarian work, Mark is now employed as a case manager at an asylum seeker settlement agency in Sydney.

Surfing, football, sunscreen, shade, freedom, adventure and writing are a few things Mark loves.

THE
UNDESIRABLES
INSIDE
NAURU

MARK ISAACS

hardie grant books

MELBOURNE · LONDON

Published in 2014 by Hardie Grant Books

Hardie Grant Books (Australia)
Ground Floor, Building 1
658 Church Street
Richmond, Victoria 3121
www.hardiegrant.com.au

Hardie Grant Books (UK)
Dudley House, North Suite
34–35 Southampton Street
London WC2E 7HF
www.hardiegrant.co.uk

Cataloguing in publication data is available from the National Library of Australia
The Undesirables
ISBN 978 1 74270 833 1

Cover design by Josh Durham, Design by Committee
Cover image courtesy of Bob van 't Hul
Text design by Patrick Cannon
Typeset in Bembo 11.75/15pt by Cannon Typesetting
Printed and bound in Australia by Griffin Press

All asylum seekers referred to in this book have had their names changed
to protect their identities.

Sections of the introduction were originally published on Oxfam 3Things,
3things.org.au/blog/story/9281.

To Hattie, vivacious and witty, a lover of words and Yiddish and all things just; a bad present-giver but a consistent one. You were my biggest fan, and your soul will shine on in all that I write for now and for all time.

Contents

A four-fold Benedictine blessing

May God bless you with a restless discomfort
At easy answers, half-truths and superficial relationships
So that you may live deep within your heart.

May God bless you with anger
At injustice, oppression, and exploitation of people,
So that you may work for justice, freedom and peace.

May God bless you with tears
To shed for those who suffer pain, rejection, hunger and war,
So that you may reach out your hand to comfort them and
To turn their pain into joy.

And may God bless you with enough foolishness
To believe that you can make a difference in the world,
So that you can do what others claim cannot be done
To bring justice and kindness to all our children and the poor.

Sister Ruth Fox

Foreword

THIS BOOK MAY be the only chance Australian citizens have to learn what our government is doing to boat people held on Nauru. It shows how our government squanders four billion dollars a year of taxpayer funds in a conscious attempt to brutalise human beings who asked for our help.

It is a compelling account of the human reality of Australia's Pacific Solution.

The treatment of asylum seekers who arrive by boat has been one of the most divisive political issues in Australia's recent political history. It is worth knowing a few facts. First, asylum seekers arrive in Australia by two paths. They may come by plane or by boat.

Those who come by plane must have travel documents and a visa to enter Australia; if not, then they are put on a plane back to their point of embarkation, at the expense of the airline that brought them in. Asylum seekers who arrive by plane typically have a short-term visa (study, tourism, business) but when they clear passport control in Australia they apply for asylum. When their original visa expires (typically, in a matter of months) they are allowed to remain in the community on a Bridging visa, while their asylum claim is resolved. About 20% of this group are ultimately accepted as refugees.

Those who come by boat suffer several disadvantages. First, they come from countries that make it difficult or impossible for them to get travel documents. Second, they come from countries where it is practically impossible for them to get a visa to enter Australia. They come to Australia by boat because they can't come by plane. Typically, these people travel to Malaysia or Indonesia on forged papers. They do not pass through countries that have signed the Refugees Convention, so their position is very precarious when their people smuggler takes back the dodgy travel papers. From that time, they are liable to be jailed, or sent back to the country that has been persecuting them, if they are found. Asylum seekers who get to Indonesia live in perpetual fear of detection. In Indonesia, asylum seekers who are assessed as refugees may wait 10 or 20 years before they are offered a place in a safe country. In the meantime they cannot get jobs and their kids cannot go to school, for fear of detection. In countries that have not signed the Refugees Convention, they are truly 'illegal'. Not surprisingly, some of them – those with initiative and courage – place themselves in the hands of people smugglers, commit themselves to a dangerous boat trip and end up in Australia.

Over the past 20 years, more than 90% of boat people have ultimately been assessed as refugees legally entitled to protection. The tragic irony of their position is that they are the focus of political attack, while the larger number of plane arrivals create hardly a ripple of concern. But boat people are far more likely to be genuine refugees.

The majority view – to which both major parties have tried to pander in the last few years – is that boat people who come to Australia seeking asylum are 'illegals', 'queue-jumpers' and a threat to Australia's borders and thus to our sovereignty.

By fostering these views (or, at least, by not contradicting them) both major parties have succeeded in whipping up a kind of hysteria in the Australian electorate. The narrative started with 'illegals' and 'queue-jumpers', then it matured to 'smashing the people smugglers' business model', and finally evolved to 'Operation Sovereign

Borders' under the control of a military commander. From that point on, news about boat arrivals was restricted as 'an operational matter'. A promise to 'stop the boats' fairly swiftly became a process of denying information about the boats.

It is worth noting the trajectory of the public debate: people escaping horrors of a sort we can scarcely imagine are tagged as criminals; then the wickedness of the people smugglers is invoked to stir righteous indignation; and eventually we have gone onto a spurious war footing, protecting the country and shrouding the whole thing in the language of military emergency. It might soon be an act of treachery to say anything in support of boat people. But regardless of the trappings of the public debate, from first to last it is about frightened people who seek protection: often enough, protection from people identified as our enemies!

What is interesting is the fact that the public (or at least a working majority of the public) accepted without hesitation the tags applied to asylum seekers. This, despite the fact that boat people are not 'illegals': coming to Australia the way they do to seek protection is not an offence against any law. To the contrary, seeking asylum is a right promised by the Universal Declaration of Human Rights: a document Australia helped create, and to which Australia is a signatory.

And the public accept the increasing vilification of boat people despite the fact that the language of 'border control' and 'border protection' is completely misleading.

Each year there are about four million visitors to Australia. Each year about 150,000 people migrate permanently to Australia. At any one time, there are about 60,000 who have overstayed their visa and stay in Australia in breach of the law. By contrast, over the past 20 years, the number of asylum seekers arriving averaged about 1000 per year. The biggest number in one year was just over 25,000 and that was at a time when mandatory detention had operated for two decades (so much for its deterrent value). Even so, these figures mean that border control works in about 99.4% of cases, which would generally be regarded as pretty good.

Protection implies a threat. It is ridiculous to suggest that we are 'threatened' by a handful of women and children fleeing the Taliban or civil wars. Our capacity for compassion might be challenged, as our response to Tampa showed; but our borders were not threatened. When 60,000 backpackers and students from Europe and America stay on for years, there is no mention of border protection. When a much smaller number of terrified people seek our help, it is absurd to believe that they represent a threat to our borders.

To put it in context, Australia received about 25,000 Indo-Chinese boat people each year in the late 1970s. It happened with bi-partisan support and created no significant social division.

The arrival of Indo-Chinese boat people after the end of the war in Vietnam offers some useful insights to Australia's present behaviour. The use of Nauru and Manus Island is often referred to as 'off-shore processing'. Those who remember their history will recall that Indo-Chinese boat people were processed off-shore: mostly in Malaysia. This is used, rationally enough, as an argument in support of a new regime of off-shore processing.

Let me make one thing plain. Most refugee advocates are not opposed to the concept of off-shore processing: it all depends on what that means. Refugee movement is about resettlement in a safe place. From the refugee's point of view, it does not much matter where the processing takes place. But the processing has to be fair and efficient, and resettlement has to be swift.

In the late 1970s, off-shore processing in Malaysia met these criteria. While refugees undertook a dangerous boat voyage from Vietnam to Malaysia, they were processed and resettled swiftly. This, despite the fact that Malaysia has not signed the Refugees Convention. But a group of Western nations, including Australia, undertook the task of helping clean up the mess that was left after the end of the war in Vietnam and the genocide in Cambodia.

What we call off-shore processing now is a different thing altogether. The people who are warehoused in Nauru come (typically) from Iran, Iraq or Afghanistan. They make their way to Malaysia and then Indonesia. None of the countries they pass through have signed the Refugees Convention. The other group held in Nauru are Tamils escaping from Sri Lanka, where they are the target of a genocidal government. For the most part, they sail directly from Sri Lanka to Australia.

When boat people get to Australia, some of them are sent for 'off-shore processing'. That is, once they have survived the perils of the sea we take them by force to Nauru, in order to save them from the risk of drowning. But 'off-shore processing' is not what it used to be. Australia has made two things plain: first, those who come to Australia this way will gain 'no advantage' over those who simply sit in Indonesia and wait. In practice, we are told, they will be held up for five years before being resettled. Second, none of them will be resettled in Australia. These two features stand in marked contrast to off-shore processing in the late 1970s. They present several immediate difficulties, and several predictable consequences.

The most obvious difficulty is to find some place where the refugees might be resettled. Nauru is a very small country: 21 square kilometers; population about 10,000. GDP: immeasurably small. It does not have a supply of food or water or electricity sufficient for its own people. It has been reported that Australia intends to send up to 10,000 refugees to Nauru. Nauru has made it fairly clear that it does not intend to resettle *any* of the refugees there: it is available as a place for processing and warehousing, but not for resettlement. Other countries have shown no enthusiasm for taking refugees who have arrived in Australia. Australia is seen from overseas as large, sparsely populated and rich. Other countries, less well-endowed, cannot see a compelling moral case for helping us.

The strangeness of Australia's position is obvious: 10,000 refugees would represent a 100 per cent increase in Nauru's population; it would represent an increase in Australia's population of less than one hundredth of one per cent. The public does not seem to recognise the incongruity of the position.

When the Pacific Solution v1 was introduced in 2001, it took between 12 and 18 months for people to lose hope and sink into despair. Their hopelessness was marked by self-harm and suicide.

Under Pacific Solution v2, self-harm started within 6 months. The reason is not hard to find: refugees taken to Nauru see fairly quickly that there may be no escape from the misery in which they are held. Their sense of hopelessness is increased when they are handed a piece of paper by the Australian Department of Immigration when they arrive in Nauru. It says 'You will … need to wait and see how the "No Advantage" principle applies to your case'. Australian officials have told them that they may have to stay in Nauru for as long as five years.

Mark Isaacs relates a question asked by an asylum seeker quite early on:

> 'How long will we be here?' one man asked.
>
> Nobody could answer him. Nobody knew. The intention was clear: this was the No Advantage policy. Take them to a distant island, lock them away, punish them, forget about them. Criminals were given a sentence to serve; these men were not even given that. Lost hope ebbed out of the men in uncontrollable sobs and tears.'

Most Australians are decent people, who would find an encounter like that unbearable. But the harsh realities of Australia's Pacific Solution are hidden: if bad things happen there, news will not likely reach the Australian public so as to disturb the complacent belief that the government's hard line on asylum seekers is in some way a good thing for Australia. But most Australians will never be able to get to Nauru. Some Australians visit detention centres within Australia, and they do what they can to let the community at large know what goes on there.

But their only news of what happens in Nauru comes from the Department of Immigration. And the Department hides Nauru behind a firewall, just as it does with practically everything concerning boat people these days. We learn only what the government wants us to learn.

It has always been difficult and expensive to get to Nauru. In late 2013 it got more difficult and more expensive: Nauru increased the visa application fee to $8000. The fee is not refundable even if the visa is refused. This is a positive disincentive for journalists, except those who are friends of the Australian or Nauruan governments. But in any event, any journalists who manage to get to Nauru will not have real access to Topside Camp.

Access to Nauru became even more uncertain in January 2014. At the time of writing, the Nauruan government had just deported its only magistrate, despite an injunction from the Supreme Court ordering Nauru not to deport him. When the Chief Justice of Nauru tried to fly from Melbourne to Nauru, the Nauruan government cancelled his visa. It is no exaggeration to say that the rule of law has broken down in Nauru. It is not the first time, and it will not be the last time.

*

When the Gillard Labor government revived the Pacific Solution in August 2012, it decided to send a group of care workers to Nauru whose sole function would be to watch over the mental and physical health of asylum seekers detained there. It chose the Salvation Army. Mark Isaacs is one of the people who went to Nauru in that role.

This book gives a finely-textured account of the realities of life in the detention centre on Nauru.

Both the physical remoteness of Nauru, and the practical difficulties associated with getting information about conditions there, make this book all the more important. It gives an inside view of what is being done to human beings in our name. It also gives some insight into the sort of people who are being treated this way. While it may be comforting to think that dangerous criminals are being pushed away from our shores, it is very different when you recognise that we are spending vast amounts of money demonising and mistreating human beings who have done no wrong and who do not represent a threat to us or our way of life.

The fragility of the Nauruan legal and political system emphasises the importance of the role of the Salvos. Detainees there cannot rely on the rule of law to protect them.

It is an unhappy coincidence that, late in 2013, the Abbott government decided not to renew the Salvation Army contract. At the time of writing, there has been no announcement of any organisation to fill the role formerly carried out by the Salvos. Until another organisation is found that can watch over the treatment of detainees in Nauru, we will have to rely on the judgment of those NGOs that have managed to get to Nauru to report on our operations there.

In late 2012, Amnesty International reported on detention in Nauru:

> Amnesty International has found a toxic mix of uncertainty, unlawful detention and inhumane conditions creating an increasingly volatile situation on Nauru, with the Australian Government spectacularly failing in its duty of care to asylum seekers.
>
> Following a three-day inspection of the facility, Amnesty International researchers found the facility totally inappropriate and ill-equipped, with 387 men cramped into 5 rows of leaking tents, suffering from physical and mental ailments – creating a climate of anguish as the repressively hot monsoon season begins.

'The situation on Nauru is unacceptable. The unlawful and arbitrary detention of these men in such destitute conditions is cruel, inhuman and degrading,' said Amnesty International's Refugee Expert Dr Graham Thom.

A year later, not much had improved. In late 2013, the UNHCR presented a report on detention in Nauru. The Report observed:

> UNHCR was disappointed to observe that the current policies, conditions and operational approaches at [Topside Camp] do not comply with international standards and in particular:
>
> a) constitute arbitrary and mandatory detention under international law;
> b) despite a sound legal framework, do not provide a fair, efficient and expeditious system for assessing refugee claims;

c) do not provide safe and humane conditions of treatment in detention; and

d) do not provide for adequate and timely solutions for refugees.

The Report added:

> ... the harsh and unsuitable environment at [Topside Camp] is particularly inappropriate for the care and support of child asylum-seekers. UNHCR is also concerned that children do not have access to adequate educational and recreational facilities.
>
> In light of the overall shortcomings in the arrangements, highlighted in this and earlier reports, UNHCR is of the view that no child, whether an unaccompanied child or within a family group, should be transferred from Australia to Nauru.
>
> ... UNHCR is very concerned about the physical and mental health of the asylum-seekers at [Topside Camp]. Overall, the conditions ... if left unaddressed, will inevitably have a detrimental impact on the physical and psycho-social health of asylum-seekers, particularly vulnerable individuals.

Amnesty and the UNHCR were reporting on conditions they found at Topside Camp despite the presence of the Salvos, and despite all of their endeavours (so clearly illustrated in this book) to make life bearable for the detainees.

It is not difficult to imagine how standards will slip without the Salvos to monitor human rights standards, and without any real prospect of journalists getting to Nauru to report, in Australian media, what is going on in Australia's Nauruan gulag.

Julian Burnside
2 February 2014

The Nauru Riot: Staff Condemn Cruel and Degrading Conditions

A statement by past and present Salvation Army staff members

23 July 2013

In light of the recent events that have taken place in Nauru, a collection of former and current Salvation Army staff who have spent the last ten months working with asylum seekers at the Regional Processing Centres in Nauru and Manus Island would like to make a public statement.

For those of us who work and have worked in Nauru, this riot, although shocking, was an inevitable outcome from a cruel and degrading policy. Since the opening of the Nauru Regional Processing Centre (NRPC) there have been incidents of unrest that have reoccurred in escalating seriousness. Salvation Army staff in Nauru have been predicting such a tragedy for a long time.

We have worked alongside these asylum seekers since the opening of the NRPC when the men were first housed in tents. Brought them pedestal fans when the temperature within their tents soared to over 50 degrees. Used buckets to empty rivers of rainwater when the same temporary accommodation flooded during the wet season. We comforted men who were brought to Nauru in handcuffs by the Australian government under false pretences. We watched their numerous peaceful protests against the uncertainty of their future. We saw the scars of self-harm, and suicide attempts. We tried to motivate the hundreds of men on hunger strike to eat again.

The asylum seekers have been given no idea of when their applications will be processed, or when they can leave Nauru. If they are found to be refugees, they do not know if they will be resettled in Australia or on the other side of the world. Meanwhile their families are left struggling in their home countries.

Countless men have suffered physically and psychologically. The mental health impact of detention in this harsh physical and policy environment cannot be overstated. The service providers in Nauru have been unable to prevent the marked deterioration in health and wellbeing. Previously healthy, resilient men have been worn down. We have witnessed a man scrabbling in the dirt, suffering a psychotic breakdown for several days without treatment, read another man's suicide note apologising to his family, and seen countless others suffer similar mental breakdowns. Thousands of taxpayers' dollars have been spent on flying asylum seekers to the Australian mainland for medical treatment on ailments suffered in detention.

The asylum seekers have voiced their concerns over and over again only to be continuously ignored by the Department of Immigration and Citizenship (DIAC). Despite this constant degradation and suffering, we have witnessed the strength, humility and resilience of these people. We have seen men from all cultures pour their energy in to keeping themselves and each other alive and hopeful. The support and kindness that the men detained in Nauru offered to each other and the staff never wavered, even in the face of increasing injustice and frustration. There are countless examples of their good nature, not withholding the Tamils indicted in this current unrest. The Tamils who were always the men who put their arm around you in a friendly gesture and assisted in labour with no thought of reward.

The most recent incident in Nauru was not borne out of malice. It was a build-up of pressure and anxiety over ten months of degrading treatment, and a planned peaceful protest that degenerated. It was a reaction to a refugee processing system that is devoid of logic and fairness. While we do not condone these actions and are horrified by what has happened, we can understand the frustration and the anger that led to such a demonstration. We would also like to offer our sympathies to the Nauruan people who have suffered during this period.

We have good reason to believe that those asylum seekers arrested and detained in Nauruan jail will not be provided with legal representation. It is likely that a large number of those men arrested in the riot did not in fact act criminally. As such we advocate for everyone to be treated as innocent until proven guilty in a court. This is especially pertinent given the comments of Minister Tony Burke already stating that visas may not be granted to those men arrested. We also believe that there are many injured men who are not receiving adequate medical treatment. We call for immediate action from human rights groups to be present in Nauru to assist those men in jail and those men who need immediate medical treatment.

We fear that their reputations and the reputation of all asylum seekers will be marred by an incident which was ten months in the making. For those people who sit outside of Nauru, who have never met an asylum seeker, it is easy to judge these men as dangerous, destructive or ungrateful. But anyone who has worked in Nauru will see them as the desperate souls they are. Fathers, sons, brothers, who are trying to forge a life for themselves and their family. Frustrated and down-trodden by the degrading bureaucracy implemented by our government.

For further information and interviews please contact:
Mark Isaacs, Jack Rabl, Amanda Lloyd Tait, Amy Marden, Darren Wyatt, Martin Reusch, Laura Button, Jennifer Dennis, Kai Noonan, 22 current and former Salvation Army staff members who wish to remain anonymous

Introduction

I DID NOT become invested in the asylum seeker issue from altruistic motives. My real reason for visiting an immigration detention centre was to become romantically involved with a girl I worked with at Oxfam, where I was doing an unpaid writing internship after graduating with an aimless university degree. The girl had told me her mother, Fabia, took people to visit asylum seekers at Villawood Detention Centre. I thought if I could get to know the mother, I could get to know the girl, so I valiantly put my hand up to join Fabia on a trip to Villawood. That trip changed my life.

Up until then the little I'd heard about asylum seekers was what was reported by the media and from politicians' speeches on television. Boat people were travelling to our shores illegally in droves. They were being conned into making dangerous journeys by people smugglers who packed them onto crowded boats not fit for making such a trip. Hundreds were drowning. Those who survived were being packed into overcrowded detention centres. We didn't have the resources or the infrastructure to take them all. We needed strict policies to stop the boats and save lives. We needed strict policies to protect our borders from potential terrorists.

Fabia drove me to Villawood in her beat-up old car. She was a single mum with three adult children; a part-time ESL teacher with bung knees. She described herself as one of the grandmothers of Villawood, and she told me how delighted the men would be to have someone young visit them. Fabia spoke animatedly about the men, referring to them by names that seemed so foreign to me: Rahmat Ullah and Srinath and Khalid. Fabia was not a social worker, nor was she visiting on behalf of any community group or charity organisation. She had no obligation to visit these men, yet she did often. It seemed that her only reason for visiting the men was because she cared about them.

On the way to Villawood, Fabia gave me a crash course in asylum seeker politics. She told me that Australia was one of 148 states that were party to the 1951 United Nations Refugee Convention to protect refugees. The convention, adopted on 28 July 1951, was originally developed to respond to the needs of displaced European refugees following World War II. Under this convention Australia was obligated to process refugees. Under the guidelines of the United Nations Refugee Convention, a refugee is defined as:

> a person who is outside his or her country of nationality or habitual residence; has a well-founded fear of being persecuted because of his or her race, religion, nationality, membership of a particular social group or political opinion; and is unable or unwilling to avail him- or herself of the protection of that country, or to return there, for fear of persecution.[1]

'An asylum seeker is not a refugee,' Fabia told me. 'An asylum seeker is a person seeking protection from persecution who has not had their refugee status determined.'

According to her, seeking asylum in a country that is a signatory to the UN Refugee Convention is not illegal, regardless of the manner in which the person came. She explained that if an asylum seeker could prove they had a well-founded fear of persecution and that their government could not protect them from this persecution then they should be awarded refugee status and could live in Australia with a protection visa.

Asylum seekers arrive in Australia by boat and by plane but the asylum seeker debate in Australia focuses on those who come by boat, who are branded as 'illegals' or 'queue jumpers'. Yet here was Fabia telling me that this wasn't true, that we had an obligation to protect them.

'Look it up,' she said. 'It's all on the internet, you've just got to dig deeper than the *Daily Telegraph*.'

With that in mind I entered Villawood.

*

To enter the detention centre, we needed to provide at least one name of an inmate we wished to visit, and a maximum of four. Fabia wrote down four names on each of our admittance forms. We passed through security checks and metal detectors, underneath barbed-wire fences, and into a yard with benches and a visiting area.

The first man I met was a Sri Lankan Tamil who had rope burns around his neck. Fabia told me he had been cut down just a few days before by the other asylum seekers. He didn't stay to talk to us. Another Tamil man chided Fabia for not bringing a pretty girl. He was twenty-four years old and had been in detention for thirty months. I asked him what he did for fun in Villawood and he told me he played ping-pong. When I asked him why he came to Australia Fabia answered for him, saying he came after his Tamil girlfriend was murdered in Sri Lanka. He bowed his head to the floor. An awkward silence followed until he got up and left.

Fabia told me that since the end of the civil war between Tamil and Sinhalese ethnicities in Sri Lanka, the Australian government had deemed the country to be safe and had stopped processing Tamil asylum seekers as refugees. My mind kept returning to the rope burns around the Tamil man's neck.

I talked to Hazaras from Afghanistan and Rohingyas from Burma. The stories of why they fled their home countries and how they arrived in Australia differed in detail and length but not in tragic circumstances. Mothers dead, wives lost, homes destroyed. There were men who had been detained in Villawood for several years waiting for a decision on their future. They didn't know when they could leave, they didn't even know if they would be able to live in Australia at the end of their sentence. Ishmael, a Hazara man from Afghanistan, told me they had two options: to wait or to commit suicide. The hopelessness was suffocating.

Fabia and I visited the maximum-security section of Villawood to meet an Iranian man, who had been imprisoned in Silverwater jail for two months for his alleged role in riots at Villawood. He told me he was sleeping during the riots. He was charged with witness evidence provided by the detention centre guards from SERCO. Fabia told me there was no video evidence of his involvement in the riot.

By this time I had spent five hours in Villawood and I felt drained. I was shocked that such misery could exist in my country—misery that I'd never known about; misery caused by a system we created. The shame of it all dragged me down. I was relieved to leave after five hours, but the relief was mingled with guilt. The thought of spending thirty months there brought me to tears.

I wanted to promise to help the men, but what could I do? *Free us*, they asked me. But how? I couldn't even promise them my time. Once I stepped outside of Villawood, how easy would it be to return to my old way of life and forget about these poor souls? They gave me their phone numbers and email addresses but what would I write to them about? Above all else, I was left wondering why. Why were we making these people suffer so much? It is a question I still cannot answer.

I went home and wrote an Oxfam article in an hour. I couldn't get the plight of these men out of my head. Fabia had described the asylum seeker issue as an octopus that takes over your life. Only now can I fully understand what she meant.

*

Seven months later I had the chance to be at the centre of the asylum seeker policy. Since that initial visit to Villawood I had begun full-time work with the state government. I still tried to write the occasional article for Oxfam, usually about asylum seekers. I followed the news when boats of asylum seekers crashed against the rocks of Christmas Island; when Julia Gillard requested an expert panel to formulate a policy to stop asylum seekers making the dangerous journey to Australia by boat. The panel, headed by former Chief of the Defence Force Angus Houston, recommended the urgent introduction of offshore processing on Nauru and Manus Island.[2] This would be one part of the No Advantage policy that would attempt to deter asylum seekers from arriving in Australia by boat.

Not long after the Houston report was released, I received a call from my friend Catherine. The Nauru Regional Processing Centre had been reopened. Julia Gillard had revived the Pacific Solution, a 2001 Howard government policy of deporting asylum seekers to remote Pacific Islands. I didn't know much about the Howard Pacific Solution, but I did know that it had been internationally condemned for its inhumane treatment of asylum seekers and that it had been scrapped by Gillard's predecessor, Kevin Rudd. The Salvation Army was hiring, Catherine said. She knew I would be interested because of my writing for Oxfam. 'Call this number,' she said. So I did.

'Ah, hello?'

'Yes?'

I didn't know what to say. 'I'd like to go to Nauru.'

'Great,' said the woman on the other end. 'Can you leave in two days?'

The abruptness of the conversation shocked me. Was I actually going to quit my job and move to Nauru? 'I have a job. I have to give them notice.'

'Well, can you go in a week?'

My mind went blank. 'Yes.'

*

It was difficult to fully comprehend what a major life decision I had just made. I had called out of curiosity, out of a sense of adventure.

I called because I wasn't satisfied working in an office, organising meetings and doing paperwork. I called because I wanted to help. I knew that the asylum seeker issue was close to my heart yet I abhorred the Villawood Detention Centre. I left heavy-hearted after just a few hours there. How would I survive working ten hour days in Nauru? The last thing I wanted was to be an accomplice to such a policy. At the same time, like many Australians, I didn't have any answers. I just hoped I could make a difference on the ground, in Nauru.

I quit my job the next day and left within the week. I had been offered a four-week contract by the Salvation Army. I didn't know what I would do after my contract expired. The government had started deporting asylum seekers to Nauru on 14 September, just two weeks earlier. The policy was applauded for turning around boats. The then opposition leader, Tony Abbott, claimed the policy wasn't harsh enough. A day before I flew out it was reported in the media that a group of Tamils had decided to return to their home country because the conditions at Nauru were unbearable. This was where I was going to live for the next four weeks.

*

I began writing this account of my time in Nauru for my own purposes. It was an attempt to come to terms with what I had experienced. It quickly evolved into a documentation of the men's stories. I was acting as a witness to Australian immigration history. I was a conduit for their stories, the story of the asylum seekers in Nauru, seen through the eyes of an Australian, so Australians could make sense of it.

---

1 United Nations High Commissioner for Refugees, *The 1951 Convention Relating to the Status of Refugees and its 1967 Protocol*, 2011, viewed 23 August 2013, <www.unhcr.org/4ec262df9.html>, p. 3.
2 P Aristotle, A Houston & M L'Estrange, *Report of the Expert Panel on Asylum Seekers*, Australian Government, Canberra, 2012.

PART 1

ROTATION 1

1 October 2012 to 1 November 2012

Chapter 1

THE HEAT IN Nauru is oppressive. The moment I stepped off the plane it infiltrated my clothes and left me slick with sweat. The air was thick with moisture. A brief coastal wind temporarily dried the sweat to a grimy substance. When the wind died, the sweat ran freely.

My first impression was that the Salvos had hired a collection of misfits. The Salvation Army recruitment policy was a knee-jerk reaction to the rushed establishment of the camp. *Get as many people out there as quickly as you can.* I joined a motley crew of seniors, eighteen-year-olds, university students, mothers, social workers, religious experts, atheists. Many of the staff, me included, were underqualified. Most had no experience working with asylum seekers. Some arrived in Nauru not knowing what an asylum seeker was. None of us had been interviewed for the job. Some of us received our contracts at the airport. I underwent a medical, received my vaccinations, undertook a brief psychological assessment, and then I was sent to Nauru. Prior to my departure from Australia I understood that my role as a Salvo would be to provide support to the asylum seekers in the camp. That was all I knew.

*

Four Salvation Army cultural advisors arrived on the same plane as me. Zulfigar and Mooji were Afghan Hazaras, Sadat was a Sri Lankan Tamil, and Azad was from Iran. All four men had been recruited from a refugee and asylum seeker settlement organisation in Melbourne. They came from the same countries as the asylum seekers in the camp, and were hired for their language skills and their cultural knowledge. They were expected not only to assist the men, but to educate Salvo staff as well. I spent the plane trip to Nauru mining them for information.

Zulfigar was a little man who spoke with an assumed authority. Like many Hazara men his appearance looked to me half Asiatic, half Middle Eastern.

'It is very dangerous in Afghanistan and Pakistan for Hazara men,' Zulfigar said. 'In these countries there is a long hatred against Hazaras. The government of Afghanistan have killed Hazaras for a long time. That is why we are all leaving. That is why we come to Australia for protection.'

Mooji was nineteen years old. He was a good-looking kid with a shock of black hair flecked with grey. While Zulfigar had arrived in Australia by plane with his wife and child, Mooji had come by boat. I asked him what detention was like. He seemed unwilling to talk about it.

'It was very scary,' Mooji said. 'I was there for a long time.'

Sadat had spent several years in Indonesia waiting for a visa to enter Australia. His family were still in Sri Lanka. It had been five years since he had seen them.

'Brother. The war is over in Sri Lanka. But it is not good for Tamil. Big problem, brother,' Sadat said.

Azad had moved to Australia on a skilled migrant visa. Despite being a computer engineer he had been working with settlement services, using his native language to get him work. He said there weren't any jobs in his industry and he needed the money. He was worried that if anyone found out his name in the camp the news may be fed back to his home country, endangering his family.

These were my introduction to the type of stories I would be confronted with in Nauru.

We were collected by a bus from the airport. There weren't enough seats for everyone so I joined the head of the Salvation Army Nauruan mission in a car. He was a white-haired man with a soft smile.

'Welcome to Nauru. I'm the operations manager. We'll drop your bags off at the hotels and then take you straight up to Topside. That's the camp by the way. Topside. It may take longer than expected, the ring road gets closed when there's a plane on the island. And unfortunately there is only one main road around the island.'

We moved slowly around the island. Large Nauruans maintained an easy pace on tiny motorbikes, their legs held wide so they wouldn't scrape the road, only the wheels emerging from beneath their bulky frames. It made me think of a circus act.

'The speed limit is forty-eight kilometres an hour for the whole island. And it's illegal to splash people,' said the operations manager, swerving slowly away from a puddle in the road.

The tiny island was rimmed with idyllic beaches and palm trees. According to the operations manager, the beaches were a temptation, attractive to the eye but dangerous to swim in due to the coral and currents. At low tide the water was sucked out to the ocean drop-off, and all that remained was an uninviting platform of coral. There was one boat harbour that was safe to swim in.

'Watch for feral dogs. They can be aggressive.' The operations manager pointed out a mangy pack, their ribs poking out and their heads bowed low to the ground, their eyes averted from our stares.

'You can drive around the country in thirty minutes,' the operations manager said. 'There are restaurants to eat at, mostly Chinese. The staff stick to a few sure bets after a few incidents of food poisoning. Please don't eat the raw fish. We can't afford to lose people.'

There was one main store, Capelle's, a two-storey warehouse of odds and ends. The Nauruan people lived in beach shacks.

The closer to the beach the house was, the poorer it looked. The poverty was startling: roofs falling apart, broken windows and doors, none of which looked like they were going to be replaced any time soon.

'It used to be a very rich country, thanks to the phosphate mines,' the operations manager said. 'Only now are they starting to see the environmental damage the mining caused.' I later learned Nauru had actually taken the Australian government to court in 1989 over the poor management of the environment, and the Australian government agreed to a $73 million settlement. 'About ten years ago the government lost all the money on bad investments and a corrupt president,' the operations manager continued. 'One day the banks just stopped dispensing money. The island was broke. Now the country relies on aid from Australia to survive.'

The abandoned infrastructure and barely functioning refineries were a reminder of Australian pillaging of Nauruan land. There were 10,000 local inhabitants, many of whom looked obese. A mural on a wall promoted World Diabetes Day. We passed a haunted house of a hotel, a three-storey structure that had visible construction taking place. It stood beside a hollowed-out, rusted boat shed of equal size.

'This is the Od-en,' the operations manager said. 'You won't be staying here. Lucky for you. It has intermittent electricity and water.'

The Menen Hotel was a much nicer option, overlooking the ocean. There was a bar, the rooms looked clean and most were air-conditioned, and the electricity and the water worked all the time. At least, the empty rooms looked comfortable. We were sleeping ten men to our room. Stretchers, mattresses, clothes, towels and rubbish were strewn throughout Room 161. This dump was going to be my sleeping quarters for the next four weeks. Azad and I left our bags at the hotel and got back in the car to go to Topside.

I was strangely excited to see the camp. All the build-up of the past weeks—quitting my job, the flights, the car ride around Nauru—had culminated in this moment. We drove up a steep shale-like incline called the Tsunami Track.

'Topside is run by a number of separate organisations,' the operations manager explained. 'Wilson provide the security personnel. They're called Client Service Officers.'

Wilson sounded familiar, and then it clicked. In Australia, Wilson Security was responsible for car parks. It appeared that in Nauru they had replaced the cars with men.

'Transfield is in charge of logistics. They order all the resources, cook the food, run the buses. We have IHMS, International Health and Medical Services, to provide all medical services. IOM, the International Organization for Migration, are responsible for transferring the men who volunteer to return to their home countries. What else? Oh, well obviously the Salvation Army. We provide the welfare and support for the men. You will also notice that the Australian Army are present. They have been called up to perform the initial construction of the camp. They are also responsible for the desalination plant that supplies the water for the entire camp—Nauru does not have enough water on the island to provide for the camp. Finally there is DIAC, the Department of Immigration and Citizenship.'

Once the car had climbed the rise the horizon levelled out again and we could see right across to the far side of the island. Excavated mine sites had created pinnacles of rock that covered the top section of Nauru. A dirt track took us up to the front gates of Topside. A boom gate and a Wilson guard were all that stood between me and my first step inside the Nauru Regional Processing Centre.

Chapter 2

IT IMMEDIATELY BECAME clear that the Nauru Regional Processing Centre was as disorganised as the pre-destination shambles had threatened. When we arrived at the front gate we gave our names and were passed through. No form of identification was requested and none was provided; there was no orientation to the camp, neither were there job descriptions or mission briefings for Salvo staff. The purpose of the Salvation Army's presence in Nauru was to support the asylum seekers, but staff were given no direction in how to do this. We were thrown right into the mix with an enthusiastic 'Go out and help the men'.

Thankfully I ran into a friendly face from Sydney. Amanda was a recent graduate like me and a friend of many years. We had made the decision to come to Nauru together, however, she had left a week earlier than me. It was comforting to know that Amanda was on the island with me.

She hugged me tightly. 'It's good to have you here,' she said.

We walked across the loose gravel that covered Topside and approached the entrance of the men's compound. A high fence surrounded the camp. From the outside looking in, all I could see through the gaps in the fence were tents. Rows upon rows of dark-green army tents.

'The only thing we have to do is supervise the internet and the phones, otherwise we're left to our own devices,' Amanda said. 'I spend most of my days running around trying to do stupid trivial tasks. Things that should be easy to do take hours to sort out. One of the men didn't have a stretcher to sleep on. It took me two hours to find one. We don't have enough staff, we don't have enough resources. It's been really tough.'

It was eight in the morning and I was already sweating. I decided it would be easier to not shower in the morning. If I had a shower I felt clean momentarily. The minute I re-entered the heat I began sweating again and it made me feel dirtier than before. Better to embrace the sweat and the invasive humidity and cleanse myself at night.

I signed my name on a staff list at a small pergola called Charlie 5 at the entrance to the camp. A Nauruan guard in an orange shirt that said *Sterling* on it opened the gate for us and we entered the camp.

'There are about one hundred men in the camp. It's difficult to say exactly how many because each week men leave and more men arrive. The majority of the men are Tamil. There are Iraqis and some Iranians just arrived, too,' Amanda said. 'They socialise in ethnic groups and there isn't much mixing. There are only single men here. That doesn't mean they're not married, just that they travelled to Australia alone. Apparently the camp was deemed unfit to house women and children by the Nauruan government. But there are always unfounded rumours going around the camp. Who knows what's true or not?'

We walked past high-roofed tents with wooden pallets for floorboards. Army stretchers with thin mattresses for beds were crammed in next to each other, six or eight to a tent. Some tents fit more. Dark-skinned Tamil men looked out at us. They smiled and wobbled their heads at me. I smiled back. We walked on to a long green marquee.

'This is the Green Room. Everything happens under here because it's the only real shady spot in the camp,' Amanda said. 'It's the dining room, living room, rumpus room, television room and classroom.'

It was situated in the centre of the camp, separating the living quarters and the bathrooms on the left, and the kitchen, the demountables and the open space on the right. The front section of the marquee had a concrete floor with white fold-up tables set up. Men sat at the tables playing card games with Salvos. A group of Arabic men sat around looking surly.

'They're the Iraqis. They're pretty intimidating,' Amanda said.

Off to the side of the Green Room Amanda gestured to a young male Salvo who was standing in front of a group of twenty Tamil men. He was pointing at pieces of paper that were pegged to a piece of string hung between two poles. The Tamil men were repeating words after him.

'That's Paul and the classroom. Paul set it up himself but it was difficult to get management on board. If you want anything to get done, do it yourself. And even then it's a real battle.'

'How has it been for you?' I asked.

Amanda sighed and rolled her eyes so far back all you could see were the whites of her eyes. She had a habit of making weird faces. She had only been there a week more than me but she already looked tired and stressed.

'There are rifts in the staff. Between young and old. Salvationists and non-Salvationists. There is sexism. Young women are restricted in what we can do. There is an assumption that the men could rape us at any point. We've been accused of flirting with guards and asylum seekers. It has been really frustrating.'

The flooring of the back section of the marquee returned to the gravel-like shale. There were men sleeping on cots back there. Mosquito nets hung from the roof, covering them. Wilson guards loitered close to these men, radios crackling.

'That's the new Iranian group,' Amanda said. 'They refuse to sleep in the tents because they're too hot.'

An Iranian with a thick beard looked at me angrily. 'Heil Hitler,' he shouted and saluted me. His intention was clear to me. This was a concentration camp and I was his jailer. My skin prickled with discomfort. I averted my eyes and we walked the other way.

'They've been really aggressive with everyone,' Amanda said, looking at me with concern. 'Don't worry about them.'

There were facilities to contact family and friends. A concrete bunker adjacent to the Green Room was the phone room; an air-conditioned demountable housed six computers.

'The small room next to the computer room is the multi-faith room. All the men within the camp are expected to share that room to pray,' Amanda said.

On the other side of the computer room was the store. As the men couldn't earn or spend money while being processed, the government offered them welfare. Clothes, shoes and toiletries were all made available from the storeroom. The communal welfare fashion served as a form of uniform. Men were suspected of hoarding clothing. They were arbitrarily judged on whether their requests for clothes were legitimate or attempted manipulation.

The canteen was situated in another demountable. 'Phone cards can be purchased at the camp canteen run by Transfield,' Amanda said. 'They use a points system. The system awards men a weekly quota of points that can be spent on anything within the canteen. Chocolate, MP3 players, phone cards, cigarettes. Supplies run out quickly and nothing ever seems to come in.'

There was an empty demountable next to the canteen, where apparently a gym would be set up. To the side of the Green House a group of Tamil men lay in the shade of the only tree in the camp, doing nothing. Barring this solitary tree, the camp was devoid of vegetation. The men had been sectioned off from nature.

A commotion arose at the front gate of the camp.

'Looks like we have a new intake of men,' Amanda said.

*

A white minibus pulled up at the front gate of the camp and offloaded its cargo. A group of Tamil men stepped into the heat of Topside, tired and confused. The camp must have been a shock for them. On the bus trip to Topside they would have passed palm trees and beaches promising tropical paradise. These would have been replaced by the dilapidated phosphate refineries that emitted a hazy smoke into the atmosphere. You could snatch last glimpses of the ocean before it disappeared behind thick green foliage. Trees died off. Arid rock moonscapes proliferated. Then the men would have arrived at the front gate of the processing centre. Their first vision of what would be their new home: temporary fencing, rows and rows of dark-green army tents, green-shirted security guards speaking English, all surrounded by rock. By now most of the men understood that they were not in Australia. Others still harboured hope that the Australian government had finally saved them. The reality was that they had been sent to Australia's Pacific island rubbish tip.

The men had previously been housed at the Christmas Island Detention Centre. Their journey, lasting seventeen hours, had taken them via Darwin. Not all of the men had known they were being sent to Nauru. Some of them told us that representatives of DIAC had told them they would be moving rooms. Others told us they had been persuaded to leave with promises that their visas would be processed within six months. Some men even claimed that DIAC had resorted to offering them future residency in Australia. Whatever was necessary to achieve the end goal. Those who had resisted alleged they had been deported from Christmas Island in handcuffs by the Australian Federal Police. Some of them had been given no chance to say goodbye to their friends. By the time they'd arrived in Nauru they were physically, emotionally and mentally exhausted.

The white-haired operations manager, wearing a blue Salvation Army polo shirt, introduced himself to the Tamils and welcomed them to Nauru. A Tamil DIAC interpreter translated his words. The interpreter sweated profusely in his designer clothes, a symbol of the success the asylum seekers aspired to.

'I work for the Salvation Army. It is our role at Nauru to protect asylum seekers and uphold their human rights,' the operations manager said.

The Tamils looked at the camp behind him, and I imagined they were wondering what rights they had left to protect.

'We are your friends,' he forced upon them.

The Tamils lined up in front of green-shirted Client Service Officers who were seated at tables. The men, called by Boat ID numbers, took turns to sit at a table with a Salvo.

'MAC016.'

Their meagre possessions were emptied out of generic blue bags onto the table. Each piece of clothing was publicly scrutinised. Underwear was held up before the client and the Salvo. Although it did not take long for individual clients to be processed, the procedure dragged on for hours in the hot sun.

The men were escorted by Salvos to a tent to collect their bedding packs and care packs before being shown their new living quarters, a green tent with wooden pallet floorboards where the heat congregated creating a forty-eight degree furnace. Stretcher beds cobwebbed in mosquito nets were crammed together to fit more men in. The care packages hadn't always been packed correctly. Sanitary pads were the more humiliating mistakes, but there were simple errors: no string to tie up the mosquito nets; no razors; no shampoo.

'Sorry,' I said to a Tamil man who had no string to tie up his mosquito net. An hour later I still hadn't found string for him. Eventually he fashioned a tie out of the drawstring from his pants.

A Tamil man stepped on his wooden pallet floorboard to reach his stretcher bed. The floor rocked beneath him, tipping this way and that, balancing on a large boulder. The seesaw mattress shuddered to the left or right with the slightest movement. I was appalled that this was his lot. This time I had to help. I found a shovel and set about digging around the rock. Thirty minutes later the Tamil and I rolled the rock away defiantly.

Many of the new arrivals had friends already stationed in the camp. The pleasure of an excited reunion was brief. Their eyes returned to their surroundings. The rows of tents, one large marquee dining hall, rock-strewn dirt tracks, a single tree, a bomb shelter phone room, three demountables. Despite all the speeches and the introductions, they had not fully realised the reality of their new home until now. They were in a construction yard. They had been taken under false pretences to a distant island facility that was purposely underprepared to meet their basic needs.

'How long will we be here?' one man asked.

Nobody could answer him. Nobody knew. The intention was clear: this was the No Advantage policy. Take them to a distant island, lock them away, punish them, forget about them. Criminals were given a sentence to serve; these men were not even given that. Lost hope ebbed out of the men in uncontrollable sobs and tears.

Chapter 3

THE DAYS STARTED slowly in the compound. The men rose at all hours. There were those who woke with the rising sun. Others slept long into the day until the heat was too much to bear. Many barely slept at all and picked themselves up at breakfast time purely to be a part of the routine. Sleep was hard to come by during the night. The trapped heat within the mosquito nets made rest a battle. The men waited until past midnight for the tents to cool down. Rain was the only reprieve from the heat, however, it brought torrents of water through the middle of tents. Flash floods within the compound soaked the men's belongings, and sideways squalls left stretchers damp and uncomfortable. One man was sectioned off from the rest of the camp for fear of spreading tuberculosis under the oppressive conditions.

Topside time was slower than normal time. One day in Topside was worth a week of normal time. Calendars lacked significance. Clocks froze. It was Groundhog Day without the limitless possibilities Bill Murray explored. The men had nothing to do. They had no jobs. No responsibilities. The lack of routine or order played havoc on their minds. Time, usually so cherished, became their fiercest tormenter. And yet every hour wasted brought them one hour closer to freedom. All they wanted to know was when they would be released from Nauru and all we could answer was, 'I don't know.'

Each man had demons to face. The nightmares of the past. The hopelessness of the future. The inertia of the present. What was there to wake up for? Another day in a camp with no answers.

Often it was the heat of the day that dragged men from their beds. Cold showers were the most common tactic to battle the heat. The camp used more water than the entire island of Nauru. The showers flooded regularly due to poor irrigation. The toilets were filthy. Footprints could be found on the Western toilet seats. Most of the men didn't use modern bathrooms like these in their home countries. The men shaved as well as one can without a mirror, then lined up for breakfast. *Wash your hands. With soap. Use the hand sanitiser. Like this.* A Salvo rubbed his hands together to emphasise his point. A big-bellied Iraqi called Sidque pushed his way to the front of the procession, roaring in Arabic. He stood head and shoulders above the skinny Tamils. They grudgingly allowed him to shoulder his way to the front.

The men entered the white kitchen tent then took a plastic plate and plastic cutlery. A hot breakfast was served by local Nauruans, with the option of cereal. They ate well when there was enough food for everyone. Fresh fruit and vegetables were in short supply. The food was eaten in the Green Room. Tamils sat with Tamils. Iraqis sat with Iraqis. Iranians sat with Iranians. Salvos tried to mingle. Once breakfast was eaten the men turned their attention to the day ahead of them and what they could do to pass the time and occupy their minds.

Interactions with the men were born out of trivial pursuits. Movies, volleyball, card games, Jenga, Connect Four. It was mindless living. It gave a new dimension to ennui. In these bursts of action the camp livened momentarily. As they passed, the atmosphere returned to its dormant state of oppression. It was impossible to entertain the men en masse; instead the Salvos worked in pockets of entertainment. What few resources we had quickly deteriorated due to overuse. Cards went missing, board games were broken, volleyballs would go flat, and DVDs would scratch. The frustrations of camp life would often boil over thanks to a missing card in a deck.

The computer room rostered the men's internet usage. Six computers; thirty minutes at a time on a slow connection. The opportunism that ran rife in the camp was evident here. Take as much time as you could even if it wasn't your turn. If there was a free computer, jump on it. The camp mentality was survival of the fittest. It wasn't important what your tactic was—stealing, befriending Salvos for favours, physical dominance, numerical dominance—as long as you got ahead in some way. Rather than banding together under the commonality of their situation, the men were divided by the desperation of camp life.

The English classes were attended by most men, excluding the Iranians. Monday to Thursday the men worked on grammar and vocabulary. Friday was singing class. It was endearing to hear from across the yard thirty Tamil men belting out, 'Please don't take my sunshine away'. These songs became the soundtrack of protest. The camp hummed 'You Are My Sunshine' for days afterwards.

The school provided a goal to work towards. English would help the men with their asylum applications. It also gave them something to look forward to during the day. Outside of classes they had homework to complete. The classes gave them a semblance of structure.

Lunch and dinner meant long lines. Sidque, the fat Iraqi, pushed to the front each time. A punctured scar ran down his right arm. Curried meats and vegetables, rice and bread. The men ate, illuminated by beautiful Pacific island sunsets. The end of the spectacle was heralded by a thick mosquito-repellent crop dusting of the camp.

Night descended but the camp did not cool until well past midnight. Tents shone under spotlights. Pockets of card games played out silently across the Green Room. Quiet songs from the Tamils underneath the tree drifted across the grounds. Endless DVDs. Eventually the men made their way to bed and the camp went silent. Hundreds of men on stretcher beds on wooden planks underneath army tents thought of their families, their wives, their children. Hundreds of men enclosed within the same nightmare waiting for sunrise.

Chapter 4

THOSE FIRST DAYS within the compound were confronting for many Salvos. We were thrown, without guidance, into a camp full of angry, depressed men. Their stories were intimidating, their situation frightening. I couldn't shake the feeling in the back of my mind that this was wrong and that by being in Nauru I was complicit in this wrongdoing. The induction of new arrivals only confirmed this for me. Watching men break down at the sight of Topside compounded the guilt I was suffering.

I knew I needed to break down the social barriers with the men, however, communicating with them had been difficult. Many of them couldn't read or write in English or didn't speak it at all. DIAC employed a handful of interpreters, however, it was made clear that they were to be used only in formal settings, such as interviews and speeches. Interpreters were severely limited by strict government rules. They could only interpret what was said between the two parties. They could not advise either party and were discouraged from building bonds or relationships with their 'clients'. To acquire the services of the DIAC interpreters you needed to book in advance and this meant dealing with DIAC, which was tedious. The Salvation Army cultural advisors were officially hired to educate the Salvos on their particular cultures, however, they quickly became unofficial interpreters as they weren't bound by the same restrictions as the DIAC interpreters. Even with our advisors, there were not many interpreters available and more often than not they were busy when we needed them most.

I had struggled through broken conversations using body language. Simple gestures of hand shakes and shoulder touches became so much more in a camp where most of the workers refrained from touching the men. Knowing their names was important. It individualised each man in a camp full of faces. When Wilson guards referred to them as numbers, a name gave them back their identity. When I didn't know their name I referred to them as 'brother'. *Thanks, brother. No problem, brother.*

I made it my goal to befriend at least one asylum seeker who had a good command of English from each ethnicity. This was what drew me to Devkumar.

Devkumar was a good-looking man, skinnier and taller than most Tamils. He looked about twenty-five years of age to me. He assured me he was over thirty. The first time I met Devkumar I had been at Topside just two days. He approached me with a request.

'Mark, I want to organise a cricket competition. Can you help me?' he asked.

'Of course,' I said.

Dev was a leader and an organiser. He was resigned to life in the camp and was determined to make it as bearable as possible.

'I was the first man to step inside Nauru Processing Centre,' Dev said to me with a sardonic laugh.

He went about his day with a smile and a casual head wobble. Nothing seemed to worry Dev. He was always ready to help the Salvos. His personal hygiene and appearance were impeccable. He showered three times a day, and changed clothes with each wash. His beard was neat and trimmed; his hair gelled. Meanwhile I walked around in my grubby Salvation Army shirt smelling like the inside of a toilet. It must have taken him some effort to maintain his image and I couldn't understand why he bothered. He wasn't the only one. The Iraqis detailed their facial hair to curve perfectly along their jawlines, and combed their hair back delicately. When I watched the care they put into their appearance I realised it was a way of maintaining their humanity. When all else was being taken away from them, even mirrors, they still had the dignity to care for their appearance.

'There is big problem for the Sri Lankan Tamil,' Dev said. 'Thirty years before, there was war in Sri Lanka. Tamil Tigers fight against Sinhalese government. Very bad war, many people killed. Many innocent Tamil who don't want war were killed. The war is over but Tamils are still being shot by the Sinhalese government. They are still stopping Tamils from having good education, good opportunities. The Sinhalese police take our money in bribes and fines and we cannot argue. Everyone knows the war is finished but still they do this and the media do not publish this. If someone publish about this, they kill them and everyone gets afraid.'

He looked at me intensely. *What should I say? What could I say?*

'Why did you come to Australia? Why not India?' I asked.

'In India we are illegal. We are put in prison and we will never leave,' Dev said to me.

'Did you know about Nauru before you left?' I asked.

'We start the journey in August. We did not know about this policy change.' Dev said this with a laugh and spread his palms up to the sky. They were being punished by a policy that was created after they had begun their journey.

'Twenty-two days we travel by boat,' Dev continued. 'The Sinhalese people run the boat and they did not give food and water to the Tamil people. They eat, but not the Tamil guys. The last six days we did not get food or water. We drink sea water. The police catch us and take us to Christmas Island. Our journey was like this Nauru situation. Very terrible, very dangerous. But we come here because we face the big terrible situation in Sri Lanka. We come here because we care for our life. We have nowhere else to go. But at the moment we cannot do anything because we want to obey the law.'

'What would you do if you get to Australia?' I asked.

'Be a good man,' he said with a smile.

Dev cured me of any hesitation about talking with the men. He was so open I couldn't help but feel comfortable with him. Looking back I wonder how I was ever intimidated by the Tamils. The majority of the Tamil men were affectionate. If you stood alone in the camp for more than five minutes a Tamil hand would usually find yours and grip it gently. They liked to put their arms around your waist and walk with you. Tamil men rested on each other in the hot shade. The older men lifted their shirts above their bellies, allowing the air to cool their paunches. Their standard response to a question, no matter if they understood English or not, was to waggle their heads to and fro and say 'no problem'. This could mean yes, or no, or anything in between. I never fully understood the gesture.

Once I had met Dev, I realised that many of the men within the camp did not need probing to tell their stories. Some were desperate to talk of their journeys, earnest when discussing with me the situation in their home countries. Every morning at six the Tamil Running Man, Aravinthan, could be seen doing laps of the camp. He was an old man, thickset, with white hair. He didn't run fast; it could've been mistaken for walking. Nevertheless, he powered away at a steady pace. He had created for himself a constant daily task, which was more than most of the men had achieved. One evening I sat and talked with him.

'What did you do in Sri Lanka?' I asked him.

Aravinthan smiled and put his arm around me in a fatherly gesture. 'I had a shop,' he said, smiling. 'Textiles—we made all clothes. It was good business, successful. At Christmas, nineteen staff.' He smiled. 'Government say I help Tamil Tigers, the LTTE. They tell me I put my money to fighting. Big problem, big problem. I left because my business have big problem, could not make money with government. I am old man, fifty years old. I have two children.' He smiled. 'Twenty-one years, eighteen years, boy, girl. Good children. I come to help them and now they have no father. No, I can not help them here. What can they do there? They miss their father.' He smiled. 'Here men come to me with problems, I am leader.

I help men here, but I can do nothing for my children. What kind of father am I? Big problem.' He never stopped smiling.

Raj was a forty-year-old Tamil man. He had white hair and a good command of English. His smile made me smile. His teeth stuck out at odd angles. When he played cricket he ran like a duck, arms held against his side with quick, duck-footed steps. He was missing the middle finger on his right hand. When I shook his hand I felt its absence against my palm. He was a social man, a leader among the Tamils. Whenever there was a problem in the camp with the Tamils, service providers went to Raj for help.

One day I found him sitting by himself under the tree, head in his hands.

'Hey, Raj. How's it going?' I sat down next to him.

'I think. Too much I think,' he said. 'Of Sri Lanka. Of my wife. And my daughter. She is seven.'

I nodded. I was beginning to understand that the best service we could offer these men was our silence and our ears.

'It is very dangerous there,' he said. 'In Sri Lanka, the Sinhalese are the majority. They do not speak Tamil and we do not speak Sinhalese. If you go to hospital or police, they do not speak Tamil. If you have a complaint with a Sinhalese man, they listen to the man they can understand. Imagine going to the shop and people don't understand you. They take the business. Stop the Tamils from making money. If you do not have money, you cannot have power. In every region the police count the Tamils. If you leave, they know. When you come back, they know. It is very dangerous to return there. If I do I will go to jail. Maybe I will be shot in jail.'

I was starting to understand that prejudice and oppression didn't necessarily mean fear of death or physical violence. It was a constant feeling of worthlessness. Being a lesser person. With no way of being able to change it except to escape and look for a place where you will be considered equal to all men.

'Every day I think,' he continued. 'I do not know what to do. Until your government tells me my future I cannot do anything. Give me my sentence. Tell me how long I have to wait here for.

Give me my choice. When I know this I can decide to go home or not.'

Indefinite. That was the key. These men had no way of knowing how long they would be kept in Nauru and they had no way of knowing if conditions would improve. They had lost control over their own lives. They were stuck in a limbo of uncertainty: they could not go forward and they could not go back, and they had no idea when this nightmare would end.

'What can I do?' he asked me.

I didn't know what to say. I stared at the space where his middle finger used to be. 'What happened to your finger?' I asked. I wasn't sure if I wanted to know the answer.

'It got ripped off by an engine while I worked,' Raj said with a grin. Maybe he had understood that I was expecting a story of torture.

*

Amnesty International's annual report on Sri Lanka summarised the issues of concern that remained in the country despite the end of the civil war in 2009. Much of what was raised correlated with what the men had told me. Amnesty International reported that the Sri Lankan government continue to arrest and detain people without charge or trial, including 'prisoners of conscience' and Tamils suspected of being affiliated with the LTTE, using the Prevention of Terrorism Act.[1] For those Tamils living in LTTE-controlled areas of northern and eastern Sri Lanka, this affiliation is hard to avoid. According to the United Nations High Commissioner for Refugees, the LTTE used mandatory military training and recruitment of men, women and children, and required that civilians provide financial support for LTTE activities, making it difficult for anyone living within LTTE territory to avoid some kind of connection with the LLTE and therefore avoid government suspicion.[2] Three years after the end of the war these territories were controlled by the Sri Lankan army rather than civil police, who used temporary roving military checkpoints, just as Raj had said, to control Tamil population movement.[3] Those Tamils detained by government or paramilitary forces on suspicion of LTTE affiliation faced torture, enforced disappearance, extrajudicial killings, and violation of fair trial rights.[4] The Sri Lankan government has faced heavy criticism by Human Rights Watch and the International Crisis Group for its failure to investigate war crime accusations. The government set up an internal inquiry, the Lessons Learned and Reconciliation Commission, which was described by Amnesty International as 'flawed at every level: in mandate and conceptualisation, in composition and in practice'.[5] This failure to deliver accountability or justice was combined with the harassment of human rights defenders, journalists, and members of the judiciary who spoke out against the government's practices. The United Nations Secretary-General's Panel of Experts on Accountability in Sri Lanka found that: 'the government sought to intimidate and silence the media and other critics of the war through a variety of threats and actions, including the use of white vans to abduct and to make people disappear'.[6]

The continuation of wartime security measures which have led to the arbitrary detention of LTTE suspects and incidents of torture, combined with a lack of accountability for human rights abuses, left me in no doubt that there was an absence of state protection for the Tamil population in Sri Lanka. No wonder these people were seeking protection in Australia.

---

1   Amnesty International, *Amnesty International Annual Report 2013—Sri Lanka*, 23 May 2013, viewed 10 November 2013, <www.refworld.org/docid/519f516c18.html>.

2   United Nations High Commissioner for Refugees, *UNHCR Eligibility Guidelines for Assessing the International Protection Needs of Asylum-Seekers from Sri Lanka*, 21 December 2012, viewed 10 November 2013, <www.refworld.org/docid/50d1a08e2.html>.

3   Home Office (United Kingdom), *Operational Guidance Note: Sri Lanka*, March 2011, viewed 10 November 2013, <www.refworld.org/docid/4d8328da2.html>

4   Amnesty International, *Amnesty International Annual Report 2013—Sri Lanka*, 23 May 2013.

5   Amnesty International, *When Will They Get Justice? Failures of Sri Lanka's Lessons Learnt and Reconciliation Commission*, 7 September 2011, viewed 10 November 2013, <www.refworld.org/docid/4e69a9969.html>.

6   United Nations Secretary-General, *Report of the Secretary General's Panel of Experts on Accountability in Sri Lanka*, 31 March 2011, viewed 10 November 2013, <www.refworld.org/docid/4db7b23e2.html>.

Chapter 5

THE NAURU CONTINENTAL CRICKET CUP was played in the camp in the narrow open area between the Green Room and the demountables. There were eight teams in the cup, each limited to eight men per side. The Tamils were the only ones to sign up. Men joined teams according to the boat they arrived on: MAC, PEP, OGN. Five overs per innings, one-day rules.

At the start of the tournament the captains of each team lined up in front of me. I addressed the need to play fairly, in good humour, to ensure that sportsmanship was the winner on the day. The captains agreed, shook hands and picked names out of a hat to determine the draw.

The matches were played on a hard, rocky pitch. The pitch was favourable to bowlers as you could earn a lot of bounce and significant movement off the pebbles and boulders. The stumps were child-sized, only reaching the tops of most batsmen's knees. A white plastic chair was placed behind the stumps to give added height, but this complicated matters as the chairs were an extra stump wide on either side. It was up to the umpire to make the final decision. The leg-side boundary was marked by the Green Room. Over the marquee was six; through the marquee was four. It was an extremely short boundary, which gave the batters back some advantage. The demountables on the offside boundary blocked the ball from being lost down the sloping edge of the camp into the rock abyss. Any sixes on this side would be immediately given out to discourage batters from hitting the ball in that direction. We only had so many balls and couldn't afford to lose them. Tennis balls were wrapped in blue electrical tape to give them some weight. The tape on the first ball frayed early on. Men started to prepare a new ball for each match. They kept the old ones in case a match ball was lost in the middle of play.

The atmosphere around the matches built gradually. The first games were watched more out of curiosity than any real interest. It was something different, an oddity that broke up the monotony of daily life in Nauru. The men involved in the competition scrutinised every game—tactics could play a large part in the final outcome of the Cup. The games passed quickly with much excitement. Sixes were easy to come by and always drew a crowd. Every time a six was hit the onlookers cheered and Amanda and Catherine started a set of Mexican waves that swept through the crowd. The Australian Army umpired at square leg; Wilson client service officers lined up next to the canteen at mid-off to watch. The Tamils under the tree at the far end of the compound drummed a fast beat with sticks on the base of the green bins that had men dancing and singing. It did not take long for the whole camp to become engrossed in the matches.

By the time the final was about to start the cricket ground was heaving with anticipation. Six matches had passed and the shadows were growing. OGN A Team faced off against PEP A. Krishna opened the batting for OGN A, continuing the magnificent form he had displayed throughout the competition. He rocked onto his back foot and punished short deliveries. Full deliveries were lifted down the ground over the heads of the cheering crowd. OGN A set a formidable target to chase.

PEP A went about their task with gusto but it was always going to be tough. By now the crowd was barely even watching—the dancing on the sidelines was more exciting than anything the cricket match could muster. Until a ball jumped up off a length and hit a batsman in the nose. He dropped to the ground and had to be carried to IHMS. PEP A's run chase faltered and never recovered.

The end of the day crept up on the camp. It was a day the men lived, rather than waited to finish. It was a day some of the men could look back on proudly. As the last rays of light faded behind the horizon, the Nauru Continental Cup was awarded to OGN A. The men lifted the 10-centimetre tin trophy above their heads and cheered.

Chapter 6

I FELL ON my mat on the floor of the hotel room, exhausted after another long shift. I knew I should shower but I was too tired. My legs were crusted in dirt, and my hands were becoming callused from moving pallets and stretcher beds all day. After working in the Nauruan heat the air-conditioned hotel room felt like a shower, anyway.

Paul, Catherine, Stuart and Amanda followed me into the room. Amanda and Catherine were friends of mine from Sydney; Paul was the English teacher I had seen on my first day. They were veterans, having been on the island a week longer than Stuart and me. Time warped in Nauru. So much new information was packed into each day that I felt like I had been on the island for weeks. I was amazed at how my life had transformed in just three days. I had become immersed in the work. I lived and breathed Nauru. Even my meal breaks were taken with the men in their mess. My departure date in four weeks' time seemed incomprehensibly distant.

'Are you okay?' Amanda asked me.

'Exhausted.' As physically tired as I was, my mind was racing. I couldn't have slept even if I'd wanted to.

'It'll take you a few days to get used to the heat,' Amanda said. 'Just keep drinking water and Powerade.'

'And make sure you check your pee charts,' Catherine said. Dehydration charts were plastered on the toilet walls of the centre. 'I got to grade four.'

'What happened today?' asked Paul, who'd had the day off. Once you were out of the camp you were cut off. The day's events were not recorded and staff meetings were rare. Information dribbled out to the staff—the operations manager had told us that 'ignorance is bliss'. As a result the camp ran on rumours and politics.

'Another intake of men,' Amanda said. 'Tamils. Thirty or forty, I think. We had to sit and rifle through their underwear with them. It was so humiliating.'

'What did you think of it?' Catherine asked me.

'I feel like an imposter. What are you supposed to say to them to make them feel better? How does a hand on the back help?' I asked.

'There's not much you can say,' Paul said. 'You just have to be there for them. They'll come to you when they need you.'

'Where are the rest of the guys in your room?' Catherine asked.

'Evening shift.'

We worked three different shifts: morning, from 8 am to 6 pm; evening, from 12 pm to 10 pm; and night shift, from 10 pm to 8 am. Waking up for a morning shift felt like pulling yourself out of the grave. You were exhausted before you'd even started. Gradually your eyes would break through the sleep-crusted seal during the forty-minute bus trip to Topside. Evening shift gave you a much needed sleep-in, but it meant your timetable revolved around work, sleep, sleep, work. Night shifts were a joke. The two Salvos who were rostered on worked until midnight and then slept through the shift.

'The room to ourselves for once,' Catherine said, stretching out to take up as much space as she could. Ten people to a room left you with very little privacy. It was nice to only have five of us in there.

'I hate this place,' Stuart said, pacing around the room. 'I'm sorry. But it took me two hours to get a man into IHMS today. Two hours. I had to deal with so many ignorant people. They constantly referred to him as "the client" or by his number. They never asked his name. All the while this obviously sick man was getting more and more frustrated. It just, it just … it made me feel helpless.'

'You get used to that,' Catherine said.

'You never stop getting angry about it though,' said Amanda.

'I need to email my wife,' he said. 'I don't care what they say.'

Before arriving in Nauru we had signed contracts and confidentiality agreements that prohibited us from talking to anyone—even friends and family—about our work. Not privately; especially not publicly. We were discouraged from talking about the camp in public spaces because journalists might overhear us. There was a complete media ban on camp operations. If you weren't associated with operations at the camp, you weren't allowed within the gates. The government was attempting to place an iron curtain between Nauru and the Australian mainland.

'Be careful what you write,' Amanda said. 'Everyone says the government is monitoring all emails out of here.'

'I haven't touched Facebook since I arrived,' Catherine said.

'So fire me,' Stu said. 'Let them try. Imagine that—Salvo fired for emailing his wife. It's bullshit.'

His brashness gave us all a bit of cheer at the end of another hard day. These wind-downs were important. I felt that if I went straight to bed without talking out my problems for the day, they would stay locked in my head for my mind to churn over all night.

I went to bed, but my mind was still in the camp with the men. I thought of Raj and Dev and their families. What would happen to these men? Would they ever get to Australia?

Chapter 7

THE IRAQIS ALWAYS sat in a large group, shouting at each other in the guttural Arabic that for so many Australians had become synonymous with terrorism. They were big and strong—and Amanda was right, they were intimidating. Yaqub appeared different to the rest of the Iraqis. He was a good-looking Arab of my age, who could have fitted in comfortably with my friends at home. He smiled a lot, walked with a swagger. He treated a tight Afro hairdo with vigilance. One day he waved me over to the group.

'Hey man,' he said in his American accent. 'I want to request an Afro comb and Converse shoes. Can you help me?'

'Sure,' I said, eager to get an in with the men. I brought a pen and a request form over to them.

'All I ever see of Iraq is bombs and war,' I said to the men while I wrote the request. 'What is it really like?'

The men around Yaqub broke into Arabic. He was the only one of them who spoke good English and was forced to act as an unofficial translator. Jabber and Kazem, with their slicked-back hair, grabbed his arm roughly. Mustafa pointed at me with his big hands, shouting, 'Gile, gile.' Jawad appeared aggressive and angry. Fayiz leant forward eagerly, pointing his dark goatee into the group, his dark eyes shining. Yaqub shouted for them all to shut up so he could speak. I thought I had offended them.

'Man, that is what it's really like,' Yaqub said. 'Ever since the Americans came to Iraq the country has become worse and worse. We used to have one Saddam Hussein, now we have one hundred.'

From 1979 until the 2003 invasion of Iraq by the US-led Coalition of the Willing, Saddam Hussein headed a repressive regime that targeted the major religious group in Iraq, the Shiite Muslims, as well as the Kurdish ethnic minority, and political or media opposition to his rule, enforcing terror tactics of disappearing people, placing people in arbitrary detention, and committing acts of torture and assassinations.[1]

'With Saddam Hussein you knew what not to say,' Yaqub said. 'It was bad but at least you knew how to avoid trouble. When Saddam was in power everyone joined his party because if you didn't you would get in trouble. When the Americans came they reversed everything. Anyone who was a member of the party was punished. Teachers, doctors, everyone. Now there is no order. There are so many groups of militia you don't know who to obey and who not to. People are scared of everyone.'

Since the occupation of Iraq, accelerated violence and growing political schisms between Sunni, Shia, and Kurdish militia have threatened the country's fragile stability, especially since the extraction of US forces in 2011.[2]

'Why did you leave?' I asked. Yaqub gave me a bitter look. As if what he had told me wasn't enough reason to leave, as if I was judging his right to come to Australia. That wasn't my intention—I just wanted to know his story.

'I was walking home from a friend's house one night. A group of men circled me. They hit me with a baseball bat and knocked me out. I don't know why they didn't kill me. We didn't get on the boat if we didn't have to. But we had to. I left when the militia threatened my life. I used to have a girlfriend in the neighbourhood and her family knew about me and they threatened me. They put the AK in front of my face. Why do I have to suffer like that? If someone ask you, you want your money or your life, what would you choose? They want to stop the boats, but the people don't have a choice.'

Amnesty International reported that in Iraq in 2013:

Thousands of people were detained; hundreds were sentenced to death or prison terms, many after unfair trials and on terrorism-related charges. Torture and other ill-treatment of detainees remained rife and were committed with impunity. Hundreds of prisoners were on death row. At least 129 people were executed, including at least three women. Armed groups opposed to the government continued to commit gross human rights abuses, killing hundreds of civilians in suicide and other bomb attacks. Harassment, intimidation and violence against journalists and media workers continued to be reported. Over 67,000 refugees from Syria sought safety in Iraq.[3]

I wanted to ask more questions but I didn't know what was appropriate to ask. I didn't know these men. Was it offensive to be curious about their journeys?

'What was Iraq like before the war?' I asked Yaqub. Mustafa replied in slow English.

'Iraq was a very beautiful country. You could do anything. You could go to your job, you had money, you had freedom. You could meet family, you could meet your girlfriend outside. You could go to cinemas, nightclubs. You could go on holidays, go to other cities. You could do whatever you wanted to do. But now you cannot. You are lucky if you can go to your job and make it home alive. Anyone could shoot you. Militia or army or whoever.'

It was hard to follow all that they were saying. Hard to empathise yet keep emotionally distant like Salvo management had told us to.

'You came here alone?' I asked Yaqub, trying to imagine just how frightening that journey would have been.

'I came with Mustafa,' he said. 'Tell him, Mustafa.'

Mustafa leant forward. 'We had to pay a lot of money to leave. We first moved to Indonesia. We had to pay $3500 for fake visas to get to Indonesia. Then we had to pay $6000 to get on the boat. We spent seven days at sea. You can't believe what happened. We see the death every minute. It was a very small boat, maybe twenty-five metres, and there were eighty-five people. We didn't have room to sleep, just to sit. We thought they bought the boat for its last journey. After this when we see the navy coming all the people prayed. Everyone on the ship was saying, "Big ship, I see big ship." We thought life had started again, that we were born again. There was only one working engine left when the navy came. There were seven leaks on the boat. We thought we were going to die. After this they sent us to Christmas Island and then to Nauru because we arrived after the thirteenth of August.'

'Do you know anyone in Australia?' I asked.

'I have a brother in Melbourne,' Yaqub said. 'He is Mustafa's friend.'

'Really? How did he get here?' I asked.

'By boat.'

I wanted to think that having a brother in Melbourne would help his application for asylum but I didn't think it would matter. I noticed Mustafa fingering a photo in his wallet. There were two boys in the picture. They were hugging each other in a green backyard. There was grass, and no bombs.

'My family,' he said with a sad smile. His ID card was sitting next to him. It said his birthday was 1988. I couldn't believe he was born in the same year as me.

'Is this correct?' I asked him.

'Of course not,' he said with a laugh. 'I am ten years older than this. None of the cards are correct.'

It wasn't the first time I had seen errors in the men's immigration files. Surnames and first names mixed up, incorrect birth dates, some names completely wrong. These were the official files kept by the agencies in the processing centre. Would these be the details they used to determine identity checks?

'The Tamils are first to the line every day. They take all the supplies,' Yaqub said. 'Today there were no phone cards for the Iraqis.'

The Tamils outnumbered the Iraqis four to one. They were first in line solely thanks to their number, but I knew this wouldn't be a good thing to say to the Iraqi men. The Iraqis were determined to fight for their rights, despite being a significant minority. Racial tension was building in the camp, not due to any animosity harboured between Tamils and Arabs, but as a result of the conditions they had to endure.

'I'll see what I can do,' was all I could say.

As I left the tent, Fayiz draped himself in a pink mosquito net to make it look like he was wearing a hijab. He pouted at me and said in a girly voice, 'I'm a lady.'

It was totally unexpected and made me laugh.

'Oh shit. Stop,' he said with a delicate hand flick. All the men in the tent laughed as he pranced about in his feminine attire.

While talking to the Iraqi men an idea had begun to form in my mind. Fayiz's brief cross-dressing episode crystallised that thought. I had come to these men intimidated by a social preconception of Iraqi people. Their 'angry' Arabic, their 'terrorist-like' appearance. It was all an illusion. I couldn't categorise them like that. I marvelled at how easy it was for me to brand them, and then how easy it was for me to dispel that myth.

I had one more ethnic group to meet. The Iranians. I had purposefully left them until last.

---

1   Human Rights Watch, *Iraq: State of the Evidence*, 4 November 2004, viewed 10 November 2013, <www.refworld.org/docid/42c3bd150.html>.

2   United States Congressional Research Service, *Iraq: Politics, Governance, and Human Rights*, 26 March 2013, viewed 10 November 2013, <www.refworld.org/docid/519cbb434.html>.

3   Amnesty International, *Amnesty International Annual Report 2013—Iraq*, 23 May 2013, viewed 10 November 2013, <www.refworld.org/docid/519f519518.html>

Chapter 8

IT WAS OBVIOUS from the day the Iranians arrived that they were not going to accept this incarceration as placidly as the Tamils did. They too accused the Australian government of lying to them, claiming government officials had told them that they would not be flown off Christmas Island, and had assured them they were just moving rooms. On the day they arrived at Topside the frustration of their extensive detention on Christmas Island compounded with the shock of their new destination boiled over. As was often the case, it was the Salvation Army workers and Wilson Security officers who bore the brunt of the asylum seekers' anger. One of the men grabbed a female Salvo. The men were immediately put on high risk, to be monitored by Wilson Security.

At the time of the Iranians' deportation from Christmas Island they had been on a hunger strike, which they continued upon arrival in Nauru. Using their one-blade razors the Iranians shaved their heads to show their grief. One of the men sat out in the open as protest. The equatorial sun beat down mercilessly on his bare head. Every time a worker passed through the front gate of the compound they couldn't miss his determined vigil. Wilson guards erected a gazebo to provide shade for the man. A game ensued. He would move to avoid the shade; the client service officers followed him. After more than fifteen hours he was taken to IHMS. These were the first visible methods of protest I saw.

The Iranians did score one win in their first days at Nauru. Instead of sleeping in the tents, the men set up their stretchers in the Green Room, out in the open where the wind could cool them.

My first dealings with the Iranians were hostile. When I approached them they greeted me with Hitler salutes and unwelcoming stares. Faced with such significant gestures I found it hard not to question my complicity in their detention. I felt that my work was legitimising this camp, that as a worker I was culpable for any wrongdoing.

The Iranians proliferated obscenities; they bullied the Tamils. They intimidated the Iranians who didn't do as they said. One of them threatened an Iranian cultural advisor's family. Many of the Salvos avoided them. They refused to be involved in the camp, refused to enjoy even a second of their time in Nauru, as if enjoying themselves was legitimising the camp in some way, betraying their stance against their oppressors. They were suspected of hoarding razors to cut tents with. As a result the razors became rationed. The men could only receive a razor if they brought back their old one.

The Iranians were deemed troublemakers. I heard some staff from the service providers state that the men who accepted their fate gracefully were the real asylum seekers. *They should be grateful to be here, safe from harm.* Those same commentators believed that because the Iranians were rich and educated they were not real asylum seekers. They believed that the Iranians were 'economic refugees', that they weren't in any real danger in their home countries but had come to Australia to seek a better life. Criticism of the pursuit of happiness, something most Australians strive for all of their lives. The term 'economic refugee' was spoken like an insult. It was the first time I'd ever heard the term. It was with this reputation in the forefront of my mind that I met my first Iranian men in the centre.

Farid was an extremely large Iranian man. He had silvery hair, even though he was in his thirties, with a fringe combed flat to his forehead. He had so much hair on his back that it poked out the top of his shirt. His eyes drooped and he spoke slowly in a deep voice, which made some people think he was a bit slow. Many of the Wilson guards called him Lurch. I called him the Big Friendly Giant, a Roald Dahl character from my childhood. Our friendship grew over chess games together when I worked the evening shift.

'I go home to Iran,' he told me while we played. 'I cannot stay here.'

'What will happen to you if you go home?' I asked.

'I don't know. Prison, maybe worse,' he said. 'But I cannot stay here. Here I go crazy.'

What do you say to a man who faces such a choice?

'Mark, can you go to Iran?' he asked.

'Yeah, I think I just get a visa.'

'No problem. You can come by boat. Very easy,' he said and out pealed a booming laugh. He then took my rook with his queen. Checkmate. I quickly realised that his slow speech was no reflection of his sharp mind.

This Iranian truck driver taught me how to play chess. When I finally beat him in a game he smiled and shook my hand. 'Now you are thinking,' he said. That was when the games got hard.

Farid could always be found with his friend Shahab. Shahab was a small Iranian Kurd with a thick moustache.

'*Dosh* Shahab,' Farid announced. '*Dosh* Mark.' He pressed his hand against my chest. '*Dosh* Farid. Brothers.'

We joked that I could transplant Shahab's lip hair to my sparse covering. Farid pulled his shirt up to reveal his rug of body hair and we all laughed. Shahab did not speak English. The only words he said to me were 'thank you'. It embarrassed me. No matter how many times I refused to acknowledge the undeserved gratitude, pleaded with him to stop, he always smiled at me, placed an arm on my shoulder and said, 'Thank you.'

As much as I liked Farid, I recognised that he was quite demanding. I couldn't tell if this was his normal personality or a reaction to his environment. He played pranks on the female Salvos, particularly Amanda. He liked to bear hug me when I wasn't watching, which from a man of his strength and size could have been quite intimidating. One time he filled in a request form for a sex toy. Despite his immaturity it was hard not to like him.

Pezhman and Rashid were two other Iranians I was drawn to. Rashid was a quiet man. He spoke no English so we spoke with our eyebrows. When he smiled his whole face lit up. Every day he wore the exact same dirty white singlet. Every day. He learnt one word, 'chess', and that was how we bonded.

Pezhman was Rashid's closest friend. Pezhman was an intelligent man, university educated, with expressive eyes. He was of a similar age to me and we spoke often.

'If they want to stop economic refugees, offer them disadvantaged work visas,' Pezhman told me. 'Half salaries, living restrictions that will stop the men coming here looking for money.'

'I think you're misguided in your opinions, Pezhman,' I said. 'The government aren't trying to stop economic refugees. They are trying to stop all asylum seekers. The government want to pick and choose those who enter Australia. What do you think the government would do if the asylum seekers were British or American?' Foreign Minister Bob Carr had recently announced more visa opportunities for Asian tourists and businessmen.

Pezhman looked angry. Was I helping him by telling him my opinion, by telling him that our government did not want him? 'The policy solves nothing then. It just punishes the desperate,' he said.

'The government believe that eventually the message will be disseminated across the world that to try to seek asylum in Australia will be met with cruelty and that this will stop the boats coming,' I said.

'In Iran you are scared about the guys who are next to you,' Pezhman said. 'If you complain about the government, or discuss the government with a man and he works for the government and you don't know about it, he sells you to the government for money and you are in big trouble. Because of that you can't trust anyone. Your neighbours, even your relatives. You can't talk about what you believe if you believe in something different to the government. You have to be silent, follow the rules. In 2009, there were peaceful protests against the government and the government killed the people. If you are gay, Christian, anything the government doesn't like, you have no rights. Nauru will not stop us leaving Iran. I believe Julia Gillard did this because she wants to keep power until the next election. We are not lucky if Tony Abbott comes too because everybody knows he does not like asylum seekers. If he comes to power this situation can be worse than this.'

Unrest had followed Iran's disputed June 2009 presidential election, which was won by Mahmoud Ahmadinejad. Ayatollah Ali Khamenei, Iran's hardline conservative Supreme Leader of twenty years, described the 2009 election outcome as 'divine assessment'. Subsequent protests and riots had been severely dealt with by Khamenei, who used Revolutionary Guards and security services to implement a sweeping crackdown on human rights and civil society in 2010.[1]

In 2013, Amnesty International reported that:

The authorities maintained severe restrictions on freedoms of expression, association and assembly. Dissidents and human rights defenders, including minority rights and women's rights activists, were arbitrarily arrested, detained incommunicado, imprisoned after unfair trials and banned from travelling abroad. There were scores of prisoners of conscience and political prisoners. Torture and other ill-treatment were common and committed with impunity. Women, religious and ethnic minorities, and members of the LGBTI community were subject to discrimination in law and practice. The cruel judicial punishments of flogging and amputation continued to be used. Official sources acknowledged 314 executions, but a total of 544 were recorded. The true figure may be considerably higher.[2]

Pezhman and Rashid shaved their heads too, but it was clear they were set apart from the other Iranians. Farid, Shahab, Pezhman and Rashid were approachable. The rest of them were determined to push us away.

I began hearing more of the Iranian asylum seekers' stories when I performed their Salvation Army induction tests. The tests gathered basic information about the men, and were designed to direct camp policy around what the men wanted to learn and to do.

The long-eyelashed Parshan sat before me. Usually very liberal with his Hitler salutes, he was quite polite and talkative in the interview setting, and I saw he had a beautiful smile when he cared to use it. He had fled the entire Middle East region due to racial prejudice.

'Kurds are second-class citizens everywhere,' he explained. Parshan was of Kurdish ethnicity and grew up in Iran. There are Kurds in Iraq, Syria, Turkey and Iran. Kurds in Iran have suffered discrimination over a long period of time, limiting their education, employment and political opportunities.[3] He told me that the Kurds were considered a stateless ethnicity, and were not recognised by any nation since the demise of Kurdistan. Parshan had no passport, no official home anywhere in the world. The Iranian cultural advisors, none of whom were Kurdish, told me that the Kurds were separatists and were viewed with distrust by the Iranian government because they strived for independence. They believed that the Kurds weren't as mistreated as they made themselves out to be, and were allowed Iranian citizenship.

Arman was next to sit in front of me. His soft face had withered in detention. He spent every day aimlessly wandering the compound with his hands behind his back. As he passed people he pretended to smile. He did not participate in the card games or the English classes. I asked him if the Salvation Army could provide anything for him in the way of resources, classes or training to make the camp bearable for him. He shook his head and sighed.

'This camp has nothing for me. I gave away everything I have to leave my country and make a better life for my family. How can I return to my family a failure? I am too ashamed. What can you do here for me to ease this burden? Nothing.'

Arman had not told his family he had been deported to Nauru. Lots of the Iranians had withheld this information from their loved ones. There was an element of pride in their position. They could not be seen as failures to their family. But there was also a significant fear of the repercussions of their failure. The hopes of the family were pinned on each man's success. The money of the family was pinned on each man's success. If he failed, maybe his wife would look to a new man to help support her. Some of the men were even accused of lying—their families believed that they were in Australia and using the money on themselves. The pride and fear of failure of these men were inconsequential compared to the anxiety that their wives would abandon them.

I thought back to the idea that asylum seekers should be grateful to be in Nauru. This attitude overlooked the fact that the majority of the men had left families behind in danger. It overlooked the fact that many of the men had spent all their money trying to get to Australia. Now all they had was a dim hope that their families could hold on for who knew how long while they wallowed in a Pacific jail. I didn't think there were many men grateful to be in Nauru, and I didn't think any man was safe from harm within those fences.

I thought back to the actions of the Iranian men since they had arrived and what had I learnt about them. They acted as a collective, however, within this Iranian group were a multitude of different religions, ethnicities and social groups. There were Kurds and Arabs, homosexuals, Muslims, atheists and Christians. They were proud men who refused to accept their situation in Nauru. Their actions were subversive. They were utilising the limited power they possessed, trying to uphold some semblance of autonomy. I was unsure if I agreed with the way they acted but I was at least beginning to understand them.

---

1   Home Office (United Kingdom), *Country of Origin Information Report—Iran*, 16 January 2013, viewed 10 November 2013, <www.refworld.org/docid/510136952.html>.

2   Amnesty International, *Amnesty International Annual Report 2013—Iran*, 23 May 2013, viewed 10 November 2013, <www.refworld.org/docid/519f51956b.html>.

3   Amnesty International, *Iran: Human rights abuses against the Kurdish minority*, July 2008, viewed 12 November 2013, <www.refworld.org/docid/489174f72.html>.

Chapter 9

I worked at topside for a week before I was given my first day off. I didn't mind, because I didn't want to miss anything in the camp. It didn't matter what days you had off because each day was the same as the last. Weekends had lost significance for me. As depressing and confronting as the work at Topside was, I was addicted to it. I went to work excited because I knew I was going to see something I'd never seen before or have a conversation that I'd never had before. I hated leaving the camp, let alone taking a day off. The first week in Nauru felt like a month had passed. In one ten-hour shift you experienced a range of emotions: anger, elation, frustration, depression, irrepressible guilt. I couldn't imagine ever getting bored of the work. I devoted myself to the role, heart, body and mind.

It wasn't until I took a day off that I realised how much I needed the break.

Amanda, Catherine, Paul, and I wandered down to the boat harbour for a swim. It was only a ten-minute walk from the Menen Hotel, but Salvo management insisted we carry large sticks in case a pack of dogs came. We walked along beaches lined with coconut-laden palm trees. The boat harbour was a small area of aqua water enclosed by high sea walls. We jumped off the sea walls into the water, we snorkelled, we lay in the sun and did nothing, we ate fish and chips, we relaxed.

'What do the Nauruan people think of the camp?' I asked.

'I think the workers don't mind the camp,' Amanda said. 'It's a job, after all.'

The employment opportunities for locals were one benefit to the centre reopening. Nauru had a high unemployment rate. Every day you saw people just sitting on the side of the road doing nothing. Transfield employed locals as kitchen hands, bus drivers and cleaners. Wilson employed them as security. Both Transfield and Wilson used a Nauruan payroll company called Sterling to hire the staff.

'But they pay them between four and six dollars an hour. That's slave labour,' Catherine said.

'I heard that this wage was set by the Nauruan government to prevent inflation, but also so people wouldn't earn more than the Nauruan public servants,' I said.

'The Nauruan workers I talk to get pretty annoyed about the asylum seekers ragging on Nauru,' Paul said.

'That's what I've heard,' Catherine said. 'One woman said to me, "They have good food, they eat better than us. They have roofs, they have water, electricity, televisions. What are they complaining about?"'

I could understand why some Nauruans would be confused. It appeared as if they were helping the asylum seekers, taking them off boats by giving them a place to stay. Maybe some of them didn't understand why the men were so upset or why the men made such disparaging comments about their country. The men's hell was the Nauruans' island home.

'The Nauruans I met outside of the camp didn't know what was happening at Topside,' I said.

I had met Nauruans hitchhiking. It was an easy way of getting around the island. Nauruans were as relaxed as you'd expect Pacific Islanders to be and were usually happy to offer a lift. After all, nothing was too far out of the way in Nauru.

'They said there was no public consultation about introducing the asylum seekers to their island,' I said. 'That there were no community development programs to introduce the locals to the asylum seekers. One Nauruan said, "If they're going to allow the men into our world, why can't they allow us to visit the camp?" She called it a *Revenue* Processing Centre.'

Catherine barked with laughter. 'That's hilarious.'

'What about when the camp becomes open and the asylum seekers are allowed to join the community?' Amanda said. 'How's an island of ten thousand people going to cope with hundreds of foreign men? It will change everything.'

I couldn't imagine the transition. Unaccompanied children wandered the streets until late into the night. How could the parents know that these men were safe? After all, they were imprisoned for a reason, weren't they?

'I met a Nauruan who complained that it was only the well-connected who were fortunate enough to work at Topside,' Amanda said. 'Those who knew politicians.'

'At least locals are being employed,' I said. 'One Nauruan told me that in 2001 during the Howard Pacific Solution, there were no jobs, even though there was a camp. There was no money, even though there was a camp. People relied on fishing to survive.'

Even on our days off our conversations revolved around Nauru. We managed to get a car that afternoon so we could drive around the island. As we travelled around the island I began to understand just how little there was in the way of infrastructure. There was not enough accommodation on the island to house all the incoming Australian workers. Most organisations remained understaffed until more housing could be found or built. I had heard that the Australian government had started to approach locals trying to buy land or rent out homes. Profiteering from land was not common in Nauru. Nauru was divided into districts of land owned by families. Topside was slowly changing this.

While it was still illegal for foreigners to own land in Nauru, those fortunate enough to be able to rent out their homes made a lot of money. I had heard that the president of Nauru was leasing his house to Australian officials. A Nauruan lady I had met was disgusted by this. She described it as 'the father of the nation making personal profit from the human investment of Topside.'

The Meneng district leased the land for Topside. No other district directly benefitted financially from the camp. The Meneng district also owned the Menen Hotel and received all the profits from it.

This was an opportunity to revive a nation, to provide people with employment—to make an ounce of good out of an awful situation—yet uncertainty and distrust were the most common attitudes towards Topside. The Nauru Regional Processing Centre was directly and indirectly producing revenue for the nation, however, this amount was difficult to quantify and it was unclear how much of the money was going back into the Nauruan community. What's more, the camp was also producing waste. The phenomenal use of plastic water bottles within the camp had created an environmental issue for the Nauruan community. Another major issue was water wastage, on an island with severely limited clean drinking water.

That night we ate at one of the few Chinese restaurants on the island that had been declared safe. Lemon chicken, fish curry, spring rolls. There was no local produce on Nauru. All food except fish was imported. All resources and stocks were limited by the arrival of ships and planes. The island suffered from stock shortages until new shipments came in. Earlier that week the loading crane on the ship had broken and the stock couldn't be unloaded, affecting supplies in the camp and across the island. Today there were no vegetables available at the restaurant.

'Tuesday is Paul's and my last night,' Catherine said.

The thought of them not being alongside us was devastating. On a personal level, we had shared a lot of experiences and had grown to rely upon each other. On a professional level, so much knowledge about the camp would leave with them, and their replacements would know nothing about the camp.

'We should do a music concert,' said Amanda, a vegetarian, sifting through her plain rice.

'Yes!' Catherine shouted.

'Let's do it then,' I said.
So we did.

*

Thanks to our enthusiasm Friday singing classes evolved into a concert. I was beginning to see that was how most ventures got off the ground in Topside. It didn't matter that we didn't have a sound system, or lights, or a stage, or musical instruments. We arranged a number of wooden pallets at the end of the Green Room as our makeshift stage. The moment chairs were placed into rows the men began to occupy them, curiosity drawing them to the stage.

The night began slowly. The Tamils, who were usually so generous with their dancing and singing, were suddenly suffering from stage fright. No-one wanted to be the first performer. The Salvos kicked it off with a warbling collection of baritones, tenors, altos and broken notes united to sing 'Lean on me'. It was a Friday singing class special and the men hummed along, tapped their feet, and even joined in on the chorus.

The song finished to heartfelt applause, but no-one was ready to stand up quite yet. The Tamils tried to force each other on stage, shouting and pleading with each other, then running away. The momentum was picking up though. It just needed another nudge. The Salvos stood up and sang another motivation-charged ballad, 'I Will Survive'.

The chorus did the job. A group of Tamils dressed in red shirts with yellow stars milled about on stage gathering the confidence to perform. A number of different bins became a drum kit: a black wheelie rubbish bin became a bass drum, a steel bin lid became a high hat, and the steel bin itself, a snare drum. One guitar would have to do.

The Lucky Stars announced themselves to cheers and stamping from the crowd. A rapid, complicated beat was struck and the men lost all their inhibitions. Big grins, flashing hands, gyrating crotches. The men danced up against each other, not caring that their homoerotic dance moves were making the other men laugh and the more pious Salvationists uncomfortable. A Tamil choir chanted and clapped, 'ah huh, woah ho, ah huh, woah ho'. The Lucky Stars began pulling Salvos onto the stage and suddenly fifty feet were bouncing the wooden pallet dance floor up and down. Improvised dance moves, hugs, high fives. As the beat crescendoed, sweat dripped off the dancers.

The next performer was an unassuming Tamil with hairy ears and pigment-mottled skin. He sang beautifully to a much softer, slower beat, wailing delicately on high notes. The crowd rested in silence, appreciating the beauty of the moment.

Next up was 'Que Sera Sera', sung by a white-haired Tamil in a high reedy voice. It was hard to tell if he was joking or not—it didn't matter either way. He had the audience holding their sides with laughter. By now the entire camp was watching, even the Iranians.

The Iraqis lined up on stage, six or seven large men, all giggling and pushing one another. They sang an Arabic song, Jabber overpowering their voices with his own tone-deaf contributions. They wouldn't win an ARIA for their performance but they received the biggest cheer yet.

The Lucky Stars came back for an encore and everyone joined them. There were more men dancing than watching. Yaqub showed off a few breakdancing moves. Sidque flashed his large paunch. The Tamils strutted about the dance floor like proud cocks. It was madness—the good kind, the kind that strengthens the soul. The kind that makes you smile and reminisce years afterwards. A collective, joyful madness.

At the end of the concert Paul and Catherine were swarmed by the men. There were hugs and tears and wellwishes. It was hard to have a happy moment in Topside without it being tinged by sadness. And then Catherine and Paul were gone, and camp life continued.

Chapter 10

EVERY PERSON HAS a breaking point. When you are pushed and prodded towards the brink, it is inevitable that eventually you will jump.

The DIAC public servants made themselves scarce around the men's camp. They only ever entered to make official decrees. The day of the riot DIAC was due to make an announcement to the Iranian asylum seekers. The Salvation Army was determined to have the Iranians' stretcher beds moved from the Green Room and back into their tents before DIAC arrived. It was a show of authority that the men did not appreciate.

'Salvation Army loves injustice. This is Guantanamo,' they shouted and waved their arms in the air, but in the end they complied.

Later that day a Salvo was caught attempting to instil hope in the Iranians. It was a risky game of trying to uplift downtrodden men without patronising them. The Salvo erred on the side of exuberant goodwill.

'How ya going, mate?' she said with a large smile.

'How am I going? What do you think?' Atash, one of the Iranian men, was spoiling for a fight.

'Oh, come on. It's not so bad. You have food, you can eat,' the Salvo cajoled, underestimating the tone in Atash's voice.

'We are treated like animals,' he said. 'Caged animals.'

'Do animals get to watch TV? Get to use the internet?' the Salvo responded. It was an attitude all too common in Australia. The existence of perceived luxuries was latched onto as an example of how these men were leeching off the Australian government. Television may be a luxury but it is used as a distraction, not a basis for life. There is only so much comfort watching television can provide when it is all you have to do.

Atash erupted. He kicked his chair across the Green Room. The camp was placed on high alert. By the time DIAC arrived the mood in the camp was volatile. The Iranians and the Iraqis congregated in the Green Room to hear their futures. A DIAC official announced that they would not have their visa applications looked at for at least six months. Processing could take three to five years to complete and even then there was no guarantee that their applications would be approved. For those whose visa applications were approved, there were no assurances that they would be going to Australia. In the space of twenty minutes, fifty men had their futures blackened with the knowledge that they faced years of incarceration. Mustafa asked permission to address DIAC.

'The conditions in this camp are violations of human rights. If you don't agree with this, you don't believe in human rights. If you do agree with this, it is your obligation to change this. So I ask you, do you believe in human rights?'

'We believe the camp provides sufficient amenities,' a DIAC spokesperson responded.

'Would you sleep in these tents?' Mustafa asked.

'I'm different,' said the DIAC spokesperson.

Atash stood up and screamed. One can not begin to understand the range of emotions that scream was born from. It tore through the people around him. A scream and then nothing more.

The DIAC staff returned to their office, 10 metres from the camp, and allowed the Salvos and the Wilson guards to deal with the fallout. To understand what exactly occurs during an anarchic event such as a riot is a difficult thing to do. In the days after the riot the Naurumour mill was working hard. Everyone had a story to tell about what happened to them during the night, service providers and asylum seekers trading information. Eventually there emerged common threads that pieced together made a story that everyone could agree upon.

That night a small group of the Iranians went wild. They jumped on tents, slashed roofs, kicked in fridges, smashed lights. The Tamils endured a frightening night of ghosts in the dark wielding weapons. The men entered the kitchen, laid waste to $10,000 worth of food and damaged the bain-maries.

The Salvation Army workers were evacuated early in proceedings. There were no emergency guidelines to follow. Salvation Army staff milled about at the Menen Hotel, worrying for the men inside the camp and wondering where missing colleagues were. Those Salvos who hadn't been at the camp, and therefore were not evacuated with the majority of staff, remained in their rooms unaware that a riot was taking place.

Wilson evacuated the camp and waited for the Nauru police to arrive. By the time the sirens approached Topside the men's energy was spent. The alleged ringleaders of the riot, identified by Wilson's intelligence, were arrested by the police and placed in jail cells overnight. The Salvation Army heads were present throughout the arrests and vouched that no physical harm was done to the men. How much of this process was legal was difficult to judge. Nauru's police commissioner, an Australian, stated that the police would enforce Nauruan law within the camp. It was said that the men had broken visa restrictions, however, it was unclear whether the men even possessed Nauruan visas. If such visas had been issued it would've been done without the consent or knowledge of the men.

In the same sentence the commissioner admitted that the Nauruan government was still working on the legislation that would legalise the camp. Nauruan law was still catching up with Australian policy. The Nauruan *Refugees Convention Act 2012* didn't come into force until 10 October 2012, one month after the first asylum seekers arrived in Nauru.[1] Had the Australian government brought the asylum seekers here illegally? Was there a Nauruan law that legally kept the men in detention? What law was keeping them in the camp? Did international law support the Australian government's detention of these men on the island? Why did Wilson Security evacuate the camp? Did it have any authority to physically stop the men? If the men walked out the camp's front gate, what would happen to them? Could the Nauruan police legally convict the men of crimes? Could the men be forcefully deported? The operations manager of the Salvos described the legitimacy of the camp as a game of smoke and mirrors.

Men without passports, without identities, imprisoned in a place that had no legal legitimacy. No men locked nowhere. The men were frightened. They feared that they would go crazy. They feared that they would die in Nauru, that they would be forgotten; that they would become non-people.

Intense negotiations followed the uprising to restore some kind of trust between the parties. It felt like your parents were getting divorced—you knew the relationship was doomed yet you pretended that everything was okay. Everyone stuck under one roof, pretending. During the discussions, the Salvation Army leader told the men, 'We work hard. We have left families behind for you.'

'You want us to be grateful? You want us to be thankful?' Atash asked. *Yes*, I thought, *that is what Australia wants*. Australians think we are providing a service to these men by giving them food and water, the basic necessities for survival. Some staff said that they had seen worse conditions in prisons, or refugee camps in Third World countries, as if these were our yardsticks.

'Food and water isn't enough to live,' Raj told me. 'Every time I eat, I think of my family who aren't eating. Every time I am given clothes, I think of my family who don't have clothes.'

He had left his family behind in Sri Lanka. They had no bread-winner, no way of supporting themselves. Yet if he had brought them with him on the dangerous journey, how many Australians would accuse of him of endangering his family members' lives?

Raj put an arm round me with a sigh and said, 'How much of our lives do we waste here without our families?'

In the aftermath of the riot, it was announced that the Minister for Immigration, Chris Bowen, would be visiting the centre. Many of us hoped that he would be so moved by the conditions in the camp that he would reverse the policy.

*

A humane person would have to question their judgement when faced with the reality of Nauru. The heat, the drenching rains, the men's stories, the hopelessness of the camp. In the days prior to his arrival it was all the men could speak of. They placed their hope in his hands.

Chris Bowen came to Nauru, he performed a swift examination of the camp, and then he left.

What little hope we nurtured in our hearts was swept away when the minister's retinue was overheard by a Salvation Army manager at breakfast repeatedly referring to the asylum seekers as 'the undesirables'.

There was no fallout from this statement. What could we have done with such information? Who could we have told? Our contracts prohibited us from speaking to the media. Even if we could have, such news didn't make headlines. Although the words were shocking, the attitude was not so different from that of the other DIAC officials I had spoken to in Nauru. It confirmed what we already knew: that the No Advantage policy and the people who implemented it did not recognise asylum seekers as people.

---

1   J Williams, 'The Nauru 10: The Habeus Corpus Challenge', speech, NSW Young Lawyers' Speaker Series, 2013, slides viewed 7 August 2013.

Chapter 11

THE INITIAL EXCITEMENT and enthusiasm of working in Nauru was thrust aside by the riot and all that was left was a camp with grave issues. For many of the Salvo staff, work in Nauru was a continual challenge. We were caught between two major driving forces: assisting the men, and working under a government contract. We spent ten hours a day working and talking with the men, hearing their stories, handling their complaints about unjust treatment and unjust incarceration. We knew we were assisting them and we knew they appreciated our presence. Our work felt valuable.

Yet some Salvo staff were accused of being 'on the side of the asylum seekers'—the wrong side, in other words. This didn't make sense to me. Our role was to care for the men, yet they were on the opposing side? We were expected to show allegiance to the Australian government and the organisations that worked on Nauru, ergo helping the men was a form of treason? The riot was a perfect example of this. We were expected to condemn the men for their actions, yet we understood their frustrations, we sympathised with them and their situation. Wasn't that our job, after all?

It was especially hard to show 'allegiance' to the Australian organisations when rivalry existed between them. Each agency wanted to be the lead agency, the head honcho of the island. The disorganisation of the Salvation Army meant that it was a long way down the pecking order and the staff suffered because of this. If you did something wrong, it was inevitable that a complaint would be filed by another agency, which would be followed up the next day by disappointed Salvo management. Then a group representing all of the organisations operating at the centre would claim that we were a team and that we needed a united front from all organisations.

DIAC staff rarely spoke to or looked at Salvo staff, yet expected complete obedience from us. One female Salvo, Brett Woods, was sent off the island for tweeting about Nauru. Fear-mongering of ASIO checking emails and phone lines spread through the camp. It was safer not to post anything on Facebook. We couldn't discuss our problems with anyone outside of Nauru, so we were forced to discuss them among ourselves. It was safer to talk only to friends within your organisation who you knew shared your views. Otherwise you could be accused of being 'on the wrong side'. As a result, our problems became internalised, and revolved around our small social network.

Despite these political games, the work with the men in the camp motivated us to wake up every morning.

*

Working at Nauru was a game of one step forward, two steps back. The arrival of a Salvation Army major saw the Salvos take several consecutive steps forward. When he arrived in Nauru, he swept a concerned eye over the state of the Salvation Army mission. The Major was a doer, a man who wanted to make things happen. He had dedicated his life to helping people. Before Nauru he had run street churches, youth programs such as Oasis, and countless other ventures for the Salvation Army. The staff, me included, were galvanised into action by his presence.

After the success of the cricket tournament and music concert I was beginning to understand that projects relied on the initiative of individuals rather than the organisations. I approached the Major.

'We need excursions out of the camp,' I said to him.

'I agree,' he said. 'Make it happen.'

So I did. The liaison between Wilson management and Transfield was swift. It was unanimously agreed that this opportunity for the men to leave the compound could release some of the tension in the camp and show them that progress was being made in improving conditions. DIAC approved the proposal with uncharacteristic haste. The introduction of excursions out of the camp was a bright step forward for everyone involved.

Twice a day, buses of fifteen men were taken on excursions out of the camp. The first excursions lasted two hours. The men signed up to excursions in advance, every ethnic group without fail attended. Fishing, beach walks, swimming, sport at the Aussie Rules oval. Like everything else at Topside the excursions were loosely planned and could be cancelled at any time, but to see this program get up at all was hugely encouraging.

When the Nauru Regional Processing Centre had first been pitched to the Australian people, the government had told us that the processing centre would be an open camp. The men would have free access to the island. Every week the deadline for the open camp was pushed back. Despite these setbacks, I saw the excursions as the initial steps towards an open camp policy. I discovered that in the previous camp, during John Howard's Pacific Solution, Nauruans were employed as 'lifeguard escorts' to chaperone the men around the island. I saw this as a perfect opportunity for the Salvos to begin employing Nauruans and utilise the pool of unemployed locals. It would assist the perennially understaffed Salvation Army. It would also promote interrelations between the men and the locals, which would hopefully cultivate harmony and understanding. It could show the Nauruans they didn't have to fear the men and it could give the men hope that they could build relationships with the local people.

I proposed my ideas to Salvo management and they agreed enthusiastically. It had been a week of action. I now had clear goals to work towards, goals that if achieved would help the men.

That week the Major returned to Australia and progress on my grand plans slowed dramatically.

Chapter 12

THE IRANIANS CROWDED around the bus, unforced smiles, the excitement palpable. Their faces were masks of white sunscreen. A gaggle of grinning Geisha girls. Quiet Rashid gripped himself tightly, Farid the BFG bounced on his heels. The bus filled with laughter.

We passed through the gates and into open space. The sky was a deep blue. Foreheads rested against windows, eyes were glued to the passing scenery. Barren, rocky landscape gave way to lush tropical forests as the bus wound its way to the coast. Half-open smiles.

By the time the bus arrived at the boat harbour the men were all standing, lifted by the enthusiasm within the confined space. The doors opened and the men broke out of the bus towards the jetty. It was a glorious day for swimming. The sun that had tormented the Iranians within the camp now glowed warm and comforting. Dark-skinned Nauruan children played near the water's edge, jumping in the water, laughing. It wouldn't have mattered if the sky had been black with storm clouds—the men had a chance to momentarily escape their prison.

Within seconds Parshan the Kurd was flying through the air, lit cigarette still stuck to his bottom lip. He entered the pool with a graceful dive and came up metres away, eyes alight, cigarette out. The others were quick to follow. Rashid jumped in, not caring that he was a weak swimmer. He struggled to the rocky edge of the water, coughing and spluttering. The enthusiasm of the few brave ones was infectious. The others drew confidence from the loud slap of Pezhman's belly flops and the yelps of long-eyelashed Parshan, and followed them into the water. Little corks bobbing in the ocean. Beautiful Mohammed swam out by himself to lie on his back and listen to the silence of the ocean.

The weaker swimmers edged down the algae-slick boat ramp, dragon ring floaties tightly hugging their waists. The more impatient men scooted down the ramp on their bottoms before the tide hit them flush in the face, spinning them around the ramp. Shahab and Farid eyed the water uncertainly, too afraid to go near the edge. They joined the crowd of security guards who oversaw the men's transitory freedom, the crackling of 'Charlie One' at the edge of every man's consciousness.

The mood dipped and swayed between jubilant liberation and relaxed peace of mind. Parshan was the most confident swimmer. He swam underneath the other men and pulled them under, laughing as he resurfaced. No-one was safe, least of all the security guards. For once he held the upper hand. Defiant and angry within the camp, his dark eyes appeared to have brokered some kind of calm. The Iranians laughed—unbridled and youthful laughter. They were showing themselves as men, rather than caged animals. For two hours the claustrophobia of the detention centre was washed away by the lapping tides.

And then all too soon it was time to return to the camp and that endless summer was cut short. The men returned to the bus and sat in their wet clothes. The sun faded from sight. The blow of the air conditioner was icy and uncomfortable. An old grey-haired Iranian man sat on the steps and held a young Nauruan child to him. He stroked her hair in a fatherly manner and kissed her cheek gently. Tears coursed down his salty cheeks into his grey-flecked beard. Security personnel wavered on the peripheries. The old man placed the girl down and his two friends escorted him gently to the bus.

The return journey was sombre. As we passed through the gates of the camp, the bus emitted an audible sigh. The gates clanked behind the men. Rashid's dark glare returned.

Chapter 13

As my stay in Nauru continued, more men were brought to the camp: Tamils, Iraqis, Iranians, Sinhalese, Hazaras from Afghanistan and Pakistan, Pashtuns from Afghanistan and Pakistan. There were so many men arriving it was impossible to know all of them.

The Hazaras were one group I came to know quickly. They lived in the tents closest to the front fence. Every time I walked into the camp I greeted them.

'Mohammad Asif,' I called out to a pimply-faced man in his early thirties. 'How are you today?'

He gave me an exasperated look and I groaned at him. 'Nauru scale, not normal scale,' I said. 'You know it's a greeting not a genuine question, Mohammad Asif.'

'Then I am good today,' he said. He was sitting at the front of the tent watching the other Hazaras play cards.

Salar, a long-haired man with a wicked smile looked out at me. '*Luchak!*' he shouted.

'What is this?' I asked, poking my head in their suffocatingly hot tent. 'How you can sit in here?'

'Where else will we sit, *Luchak*?' Salar laughed loudly. 'Everywhere is too hot.'

'What is *luchak*?' I asked.

'"Loafer",' said Sher, a slight man with olive skin and almond-shaped eyes.

'No,' Hussein said. He was a young Bruce Lee look-alike who rolled up his sleeves and shorts and was rarely seen without a football at his feet. 'It means "junkie".'

'None of these are good,' I said.

'That's you, *Luchak!*' the boys shouted.

Mahbob approached me. He rubbed his hands together nervously.

'I am a very good shepherd,' he said to me. 'I want to be a shepherd in Sydney. Can I find a job like this?'

I hugged him to me and said, 'Sure. You could work in agriculture. Why not?'

Ulla sidled up to me. The little gremlin had hunched shoulders and an old face. He was twenty-five. A lot of the Hazaras had weathered faces, aged beyond their years. Ulla put his arm around me and whispered in my ear.

'*Luchak*. How much is your girlfriend?'

'What did you say?' I pulled him to the floor and pretended to punch him. 'How much is my girlfriend?'

The men began laughing and Ulla shouted out, 'How many girlfriend you have? How many girlfriend?'

Ferhod was sitting by himself on a step nearby. There was something not quite right with Ferhod. His eyes were vacant. He never looked people full in the face. He always sat by himself in a corner listening to his headphones. He saw me and waved, so I sat with him. It was something one of the cultural advisors had taught me. Always sit with the man who sits with no-one. He is the one that needs you most.

'Can. You. Help. Me. Please?' Ferhod said. He stopped after each word, as if it took supreme effort to remember what he wanted to say. He offered an earpiece from his headphones. I took it, wondering what I was getting myself into. It was an English language class. He fiddled about with his broken MP3 player and finally got the track he wanted. He gave me a pen and gestured for me to write in his book. I scribed what the person was saying while Ferhod spoke it. He knew it off by heart. The problem for most of these men was that their languages—Arabic, Farsi, Dari, Tamil—don't use the same alphabet as English. Most of the men were illiterate in English. The signs in the camp, the forms, they made no sense to them. I looked back through the book briefly and saw that Ferhod had the same lesson written out over and over again throughout the book.

Salar was the first to explain to me the Hazaras' situation in their homeland.

'In Afghanistan, my race are killed for the way we look. That is all. This is an old hatred,' Salar said. 'Two hundred years ago the king of Afghanistan killed sixty per cent of our people. When the Taliban came to power in Afghanistan the situation was very bad for the Hazara.'

The Taliban was formed by a group of Islamic clerics and students and former mujaheddins, guerillas, of the Pashtun ethnicity. Led by Mullah Muhammad Omar, the Taliban came to power in Afghanistan in 1996 promising stability and peace, however, its rule was quickly characterised by strict Islamic customs and anti-Western doctrines that were enforced by tyrannical punishments including public executions that civilians were forced to attend.[1] They were particularly ferocious towards Shia Muslims and the Hazara people.[2]

'There were many killings but in four days in January 2001 they killed over 150 people,' Salar said. 'Many Hazara decide to flee from Afghanistan and the Taliban.'

The Taliban held power in Afghanistan until 2003, when the United States and the Northern Alliance, a combined force of Uzbek, Hazara Shiite and Pashtun militias, overthrew its regime. Despite the Taliban's demise, oppression and violence towards the Hazara ethnicity in Afghanistan did not abate, forcing many families to flee to neighbouring countries such as Iran and Pakistan where they remained an oppressed people with no legal recognition.[3]

'My family moved to Pakistan many years ago, and now the Taliban is in Pakistan,' Salar said.

Salar placed a printout of a Google map of Quetta on the table in front of me. Markers on the map identified shootings and bombings of Hazara people in the city. The markers were clustered in two main areas. They piled on top of one another, too many to count. Roads that led between the two areas were covered with more markers.

He pointed at the area with the most markers on it. 'The militia target all Shia, but Hazaras are easily identified by our faces. Pashtun can pass as any religion, we cannot. This is a big market for Hazaras. These roads lead to another market. These two areas are targeted. The road is targeted. Here, these are the attacks.'

He placed a stack of papers in front of me. Each marker had a description of what had happened. Pages upon pages of violent attacks against Hazaras, attacks that dated back to 2010.

August 31 2011: thirteen died and twenty-two were wounded when a suicide bomber blew himself up near Hazara Eidgah. Four women and two children were among the dead.

September 20 2011: a bus carrying pilgrims to Taftan was stopped in Mastung near Quetta. After Hazara passengers were identified they were massacred, leaving twenty-six dead. Three more were shot dead when they were on their way to collect the bodies.

May 15 2012: two brothers were killed when unidentified gunmen opened fire on them while they were standing in the line outside a passport-issuing office on Joint Road, Quetta.

'These are just the attacks from 2010 to 2012,' he said.

'So how did you get out?' I asked him.

'I was lucky two times to escape from the targeting. Then I decided to come to Australia. I heard you are safe there, you are protected there. I spoke with the smuggler and he arranged my journey. It was too dangerous. Many people died in this way.' He sighed deeply after each sentence and shook his head over and over again. 'From Pakistan I came to Thailand, then Malaysia, then Indonesia, and then to Christmas Island. From Thailand I went illegally to Malaysia. From Malaysia to Indonesia it was too dangerous as well. When I think about that really, really I am scared. From Indonesia, when I got into the boat I wasn't sure if I would reach there alive or not. When I saw the condition of that boat it was terrible, but I am alive. Most of the people died this way, drowned in the ocean.'

'If you were in Pakistan now and you knew how dangerous it was, would you still come?'

'If you live in Afghanistan or Pakistan you wait for your death. It is something real. The Hazara people have to move to find a safe place for their family and their future. There is no other choice. If you come and see from my side, all pain. From the day you are born you are just hearing about fighting, war, killing. You are lucky to remain alive until you are sixty. When I was born I just heard the sound of guns and bomb explosion.'

We stood in silence watching the Hazaras play cards.

'Thank you for listening,' he said. 'You are the only ones in here that treat us like humans.' And then he walked away.

I felt embarrassed that, after telling me such a heartbreaking tale, he would thank me for my attention. Their world inside Topside was security guards, rules, restrictions, spotlights, fences and tents. The Salvos provided the men with humanity, dignity. We were their connection to the outside world.

The Hazaras appealed to me greatly. They had a dignified manner. They were polite and respectful and yet they had suffered such hardship. We had experienced vastly different upbringings, but with them I joked most and loudest.

Interactions with the men irrespective of their ethnicity were feeling less and less like work and more and more like conversations with friends. I thought back to my first days in the camp, when I was anxious about socialising with the men. I had wondered what to say, what to talk about. All I needed to do was talk to the men like I would any other person. Strangely enough, the majority of my conversations consisted of joking around and discussions about daily life in the camp. Eventually our socialising would come full circle and their minds would return to their daily trauma: *How long will we be here?*

'How do you deal with such a question?' I asked Nasir, an Iranian cultural advisor who worked for the Salvation Army. He had been detained on Christmas Island as an asylum seeker only a few months before.

'I talked to a group of Hazaras today,' Nasir told me. 'I wanted to help them see their situation. I asked one of the Hazara men, "How old are you?" "Thirty-five," the man replied. I asked him, "In thirty-five years, how many days of happiness can you remember?"'

Hundreds of memories flooded into my mind. The family dinner before I left, my house-warming party. I imagined the men doing the same, filling their souls with worthwhile moments.

Nasir continued. '"What do you mean?" the man asked me. I replied to the man, "How many days have you truly experienced freedom in your life? If your life was like mine, I can only think of five or six days in my entire life where I felt happy."'

I suddenly understood what Nasir was trying to do. He was attempting to give them perspective.

'In Iran, every day is suppression and control. To the very clothes you wear, the colour even. If men wore short sleeves, the army would paint the bare skin on their arm to humiliate them. You cannot express yourself. You are controlled by the government and their desires. Every day of your life. For men in Afghanistan of thirty-five years or younger, they have never lived with peace. They do not understand the concept of peace.'

I had not comprehended this kind of oppression before. When people think of asylum seekers, they expect to hear stories of massacres, genocide, violence. Not this subtle kind of oppression: the restriction of identity, the suppression of happiness, the denial of peace.

'That is why I talk to them like this,' Nasir said. 'They need to be patient. Five years in Nauru or life in their home country. It is not easy. But when your alternative is a world that does not offer you a real life, Nauru is your best option.'

1   United States Congressional Research Service, *Afghanistan: Post-Taliban Governance, Security, and U.S. Policy*, 3 June 2011, viewed 11 November 2013, <www.refworld.org/docid/4e4239832. html>.

2   Human Rights Watch, *Afghanistan: Massacres of Hazaras in Afghanistan*, 1 February 2001, viewed 11 November 2013, <www.refworld.org/docid/3ae6a87c4.html>.

3   Refugee Documentation Centre (Ireland), *Afghanistan: Treatment of Hazara by government forces, November 2009—November 2010*, 7 December 2010, viewed 11 November 2013, <www. refworld.org/docid/4d05d1992.html>.

Chapter 14

AFTER SEVERAL WEEKS in Nauru I was finally rostered on a night shift. I stayed up all night, determined to make the most of my allocated time with the men. Night shift was a different world to day shifts. Once the staff went to bed, the mood of the camp switched. Night shift meant spotlights and insomnia. Flashing torches in sleeping quarters from Wilson patrols. The zombies of Nauru roamed the grounds, evading the torment of their tents until the dark horizon began to turn grey. They engaged in inane activities to pass the time. Computer games, movies, cards, coffee, biscuits, children's morning television. It was in the dead of the night that past traumas came back to haunt the men. The fading memories of families hammered at their sanity in recurring torrents of regret and yearning. A time when not even sleeping pills helped them forget. And then suddenly it was a new day. Aravinthan the Tamil Running Man began his morning circuits of the camp while the air was still cool. The camp stirred to life again and the zombies had survived another night.

On night shifts you weren't caught up with requests and jobs. Everyone was quiet, worn out. You could talk to the men.

'Why aren't you sleeping?' I asked Dinesh, a round Tamil man with red eyes that he continually rubbed with his knuckles. It was five in the morning and he had been sitting by himself in the shadows of a tent.

'I don't sleep,' he said. 'I cannot in Nauru. No sleep in Nauru. My wife, my children, here.' He tapped his temple. 'Too much thinking.'

I often wondered why I asked such questions, knowing that the answer would most likely be upsetting, traumatic for both of us. It was such innocuous questions that often led men to voluntarily open up, as if they had been waiting for someone to listen. Dinesh spoke slowly. After each sentence he paused and breathed in deeply. He blinked a lot.

'I am thirty-two. Twenty-two years refugee. When I was ten, I move from my home. I live in Liberation Tigers of Tamil area. The government they come and they shoot all Tamils. They come with guns at night. Too much fear. I move six times, always war, always killing. I now have family. Wife, children, and still too much fear. I come by boat. Too much fear. Small boat, wood, eight lengths, eighty people. Too much small. My brother on same boat. He is in Australia. I am in Nauru. Not good. Nauru not good. Too much thinking. Why my brother in Australia and me in Nauru? Nauru not good. Too much thinking. Every night. The rocks. Crunch, crunch. It is like Sri Lanka. The soldiers. They come to our village. Shoot people. The rocks. Crunch, crunch. No sleep. Too much thinking.'

I shivered with horror. Every time I walked past his tent, my feet crunching gravel, I was retraumatising him, transporting him to the nightmares of Sri Lanka. How many times did I walk past his tent on the main thoroughfare every night? Twenty times? Thirty?

That night a Pakistani man was promised an extra fifteen minutes in the computer room. This was against computer room policy, which held that men had their allocated internet times and no adjustments could be made to this roster, no matter what the circumstances. It seemed a harmless promise, a promise of compassion in an attempt to placate the man. But often the smallest promises resulted in unforeseen repercussions in Nauru. The man was told calmly by the Salvation Army support worker that he would not be given his extra fifteen minutes because it was against policy.

The Pakistani man became agitated. He had been promised fifteen more minutes. Two Wilson guards loomed on either side of him, their presence magnified by the claustrophobic computer room. This only served to heighten his discomfort. Another Pakistani tried to calm the man, soothing him in Urdu. The man who had been allocated the computer offered his fifteen minutes up, everyone sensing an incident in the making. It seemed to work and the mood calmed down.

'Can we see your ID card, please?' the Salvation Army worker asked. They needed to write down the time details for the records. Suddenly the man became agitated again. He started speaking rapidly in Urdu, gesturing wildly. The guards tried to calm him. Imran, another man from Pakistan, spoke to him in his own language. Two more guards entered the computer room and suddenly it was hard to breathe in there. The man was trapped in the corner. He looked about wildly, knocked his chair back, shouted, picked up the keyboard and began bashing it against his forehead, over and over again. Two guards were onto him in seconds. They held his arms to prevent him from hitting himself. Instead he careened into walls, kicked his legs against tables. Bashed his head against the table while they struggled to stop him. The other two guards grabbed him and he screamed. It wasn't a scream of anger. It was a scream of desperation. A scream of an angry child being picked up by his father. The man looked so helpless, so pathetic. It was embarrassing. A grown man resorting to a violent and frightening tantrum to express himself. They dragged him outside the computer room and sat him on a ledge to calm down. The guards cleared a wide berth for him. Eventually they escorted him to IHMS, avoiding the front gate to give him the decency of temporary anonymity. All that remained of the outburst were a broken keyboard and hushed voices.

Night shift left me with a new understanding of the men. In the daylight hours you could pretend to be okay. At night, everyone was vulnerable. There was no tomorrow or yesterday for these men. It was all one long day.

Chapter 15

THE COMPUTER ROOM wasn't always the stage for such dramatic scenes. For staff, computer room supervision was usually the most inane hour of the day. However, monitoring the computer room did give you a bizarre insight into the asylum seekers' private lives and to the pettiness of camp life.

The computer room was always full. It was odd to see these men, who were portrayed as being so different to Australians, using Facebook, Hotmail and YouTube. The most popular use of the computers was to Skype family at home. The men's loved ones looked into cameras in Sri Lanka, Pakistan or Iraq, and their images were transported across the world to the computer screens in Nauru. Sadly, the men could not reciprocate the gesture. No cameras were allowed in Nauru. Their families would not be able to see their faces. They had to be content with a blank computer screen and a faceless voice.

Originally six computers were shared by all asylum seekers in Nauru. The number of computers was limited by the Nauruan internet connection, which buckled under heavier use. Eventually two more computers were introduced, but this took some time and was accompanied by a dramatic increase in the number of asylum seekers in the camp. Men were allocated an hour at a time in a roster system that ran almost twenty-four hours a day. This meant they were allowed a total of approximately three hours per week to use the internet, each session scheduled at a different time to the last. For the majority of the men, that hour equalled contact with their family and any disruption to this caused them distress. Often these disruptions were outside of anyone's control. Broken computers and the unreliable internet connection would often prevent the men from getting their time.

The rotating internet roster did not cooperate with the global clock. Men would do anything to get the time that would fit in with their country's time difference and when their family was available to talk. These methods could be as innocent as swapping their times, or as sinister as bullying and intimidation. Men would appear at the computer room door with another man's card, saying he was asleep. Maybe the man had stolen the card. Maybe he had used physical force to obtain it. Or maybe the man was telling the truth and he had permission to use the card.

The computer room was administered by petty rules to battle attempts at stealing time. One person per computer. Friends could not join. No-one could enter using someone else's identification. Swapping of rostered times was allowed but only once a week. This was to be recorded in the computer room book and spreadsheet. If there was a computer spare, another man could use it but only one extra hour was allowed per person per week. This was to be recorded in the computer room book and spreadsheet. There were another three computers with no internet connection, to be used for movies and music and games. The men were allowed ninety minutes maximum on these computers per week. This was to be recorded in the computer room book and spreadsheet. Another computer was used for printing. The men were allowed five pages per weekday. This was to be recorded in the computer room book and spreadsheet. No-one could enter the room unless they were using one of the computers, except for those on the list of approved helpers. It was not uncommon to be accused of 'injustice' when you enforced one of these rules.

Yet another petty rule was for the distribution of washing powder, which was kept in the computer room. The men could collect one allocation of washing powder for the washing machines. This was distributed in reusable bags, recyclable coffee cups, whatever was at hand.

There were no download restrictions on the computers, which the men took full advantage of—downloading movies, songs, television shows, even pornography. The computers quickly contracted viruses because no antivirus programs had been installed. One of our duties in the computer room was to stop the men looking at videos that they weren't supposed to. One of the banned materials was pornography. It felt odd to monitor men in such a way. Mind you, it was also odd catching men watching sex scenes in a public space. One day I was watching *Game of Thrones* over the shoulder of a Tamil man. When a nude scene came on he freaked out and closed the clip. Then he put on a movie about a tsunami. He had replaced breasts with a horrifying global tragedy. When the Tamils watched *Titanic* in the Green Room they deliberately skipped Kate Winslet's nude scene every time.

Pornography wasn't the only banned material. More worrying was the graphic material of deaths, massacres and assaults. One time I saw a man looking at a photo of a crushed head on railway tracks. I don't know why they felt the need to watch such things.

The oddity of the computer roster was Abbas, a tall, wavy-haired Iranian. He had been nominated as the men's representative to manage the Nauru asylum seeker Facebook group. He was allowed several hours per day to update their international media presence.

A Wilson guard was stationed in the computer room at all times. During these mindless hours in the computer room the Salvo and the Wilson guard were usually drawn to conversation out of mutual boredom.

'What do you think of the work?' I asked.

'Boring,' he said. 'It's just babysitting. Do nothing for hours and then an incident. It's not so different to working in jail.'

'So why do you work here?'

'It pays the bills,' he said. 'I've gotta support my family, you know? And this pays well.'

'How long will you do it for then?'

'Until I can put a deposit on a house.'

'What do you think of the camp?' I asked. 'Do you think it's okay to do this?'

'I couldn't care less. I just want to get paid.'

*

Wilson staff came from a range of backgrounds and past careers. They came from the police force, the defence forces, intelligence, private security, prisons, mental health care; there were bouncers, professional fighters, nurses, gym junkies, steroid pumpers and alcoholics. No one Wilson was the same. This gave them an interesting array of talents and perspectives, but it also made for some ideological diversity among the Wilson staff. The former defence force workers wore all the accompanying paraphernalia and insisted on using military terminology; other Wilson guards thought this was laughable.

At first glance, you would think that it was a selection criterion for a Wilson employee to be taller than six foot and wider than three. There was a disproportionate ratio of male to female workers. As with all the organisations Wilson had good and bad staff, hard workers and lazy staff, guys that treated the men like prisoners and guys that spoke to the men as equals.

They worked twelve-hour shifts for two weeks straight, with no days off. The shifts changed at 6 am and 6 pm. Some men worked two weeks on, one week off; others worked two weeks on, two weeks off. In the middle of their work fortnight, teams had a changeover day where they would move from nights to days, or from days to nights. This gave them a day that, for a large proportion of them, was spent boozing up. It wasn't uncommon to see an off-duty Wilson employee cracking on to a female Salvo at the Menen Bar. For a period, Wilson staff were banned from talking to Salvo girls. This didn't stop some female Salvo staff members documenting sexual harassment claims against male Wilson guards. The Wilson boys had a fondness for passing on grand tales that ranged from war stories and old fighting careers to drunken antics, blurring the line between truth and fiction.

When I arrived in Nauru, Wilson Security was fulfilling those case management requirements of the Salvation Army contract that the Salvos weren't meeting. They monitored the men's habits, their eating, their sleeping, their emotional and psychological wellbeing. Wilson welfare teams were responsible for keeping the men from killing themselves. They carried knives to cut nooses. When men were suspected of hoarding razor blades, the Wilson guards performed searches of their rooms. If the men were involved in violent altercations, Wilson guards were expected to step in between. If Salvos were threatened, Wilson guards were the first point of call. When you were seen sitting in tents alone with the men, it was a Wilson guard who reported you. When you talked for too long with one man, a Wilson guard was there to eavesdrop and record your conversation.

Over time we began to realise that the Wilson guards monitored all people within the camp, not just the men. They monitored Salvos, listened to our conversations, recorded our interactions, and tried to catch us out. It was a Wilson guard who reported a Salvo for secretly providing the men with legal support. To my knowledge, none of the men had been provided with access to legal advice by any authority in the camp despite numerous requests for legal representation. That Salvo was sent home from the island and was forced by Salvo management to have her SIM card cut up. When journalists arrived on the island, Wilson Security kept photos of them on their guard house wall so they could be easily identified and prevented from entering the camp. It soon became obvious that the fences and the Wilson guards weren't just there to keep the men in. They were there to keep other people out.

On one hand, you trusted the Wilson guards with your safety. On the other hand, you knew that for some of the guards their own agency's interests were much more important than the men's welfare or your ability to do your job. It felt like we were constantly being monitored, judged on whether we were helping the men too much. I was starting to see that although we were in Nauru to help the men, we would be restricted in doing it.

IHMS provided the medical services for both the asylum seekers and the staff of the service providers. Ever since I'd arrived in Nauru there had been a long list of complaints from men of all ethnicities against the medical services provided by IHMS. There were daily complaints that IHMS prescribed water for a variety of ailments. Farid told me that while being treated for a personal injury that he had wished to remain private, the staff had left the door open, allowing all the men to see. Several men complained of feeling ill days after being injected with unknown substances. One man received nine injections. He didn't know what any of them were for. One man received thirty pills a day. When asked why, he replied, 'I don't know'. Men complained of skin conditions that weren't treated. Many of the men needed dentist and optometrist appointments, but services like these were limited in Nauru. Some men told me that they refused to go to medical appointments because they didn't think they were being treated properly.

Testosterone and sexuality within the camp caused a lot of controversy. Men complained of eating too much meat, which they told us made them fat and horny. One of the men asked for pills that would stop his erections. A few men went to IHMS with testicular pain and were told they needed to masturbate more. They came away feeling extremely embarrassed and offended. One of the cultural advisors told me that at Christmas Island they put desensitising formulas into the food to make the men less virile. In the Nauru camp, it was expected that the men would have sex with each other. IHMS promoted safe sex practices by providing condoms to the men. It was rumoured that more condoms were being used in Nauru than at any other detention centre in Australia. Some of the men were homosexual. An Iranian cultural advisor told me that some of the Iranian and Iraqi asylum seekers left their countries due to homophobic oppression. With no women to sleep with, some of the heterosexual men chose to sleep with each other. Wilson guards told stories from their night patrols when they caught men in the act. Those who chose their fate were lucky; some weren't given that option. There was talk in the staff mess by Wilson guards of a few incidents in the showers and the tents. There was also speculation that phone cards were being used as currency to barter for the younger men. I guess I had known sexual violence would occur. It was an inevitable part of prison life. But it didn't make it any easier to stomach. I began looking at the smaller men in the camp differently, wondering if they'd been victims.

The homosexual activity was too much for one geriatric Salvo. He came blustering into the office one day, head and neck wobbling like Harold from *Neighbours*.

'Condoms,' he muttered. 'Condoms.'

'What's wrong?' I asked him.

'Did you know that there is homosexual rape in the camp?' he said to me. I nodded.

'Worse, some of it is consensual,' he said and stormed off.

*

One day I was offered a lift by the IHMS psychological health team. It was inevitable that we would end up talking about work—conversation between Topside staff revolved around the asylum seekers.

'What do you think of the work here?' the psychological nurse in the front asked.

It was an interesting question to ask in Nauru but I always answered in support of the men. 'I don't think these men should be subjected to these conditions.'

There was a moment's silence. No words of agreement.

'What about you?' I asked.

'Well, I don't like talking about politics,' the man replied. 'But I agree with offshore processing. We have to protect our borders. Of course, I feel sorry for the real refugees. But if they're not coming by the correct channels, well, they deserve to wait. As for those acting up, they should be punished. There is no excuse for that kind of behaviour.'

The other nurse in the front agreed with him. The psychologist next to me didn't say anything. I held my tongue. I knew that the opposite view was held by other members of the IHMS staff, who had told me that it is clearly documented that indefinite detention damages an individual's mental health. One study by the Physicians for Human Rights found clinically significant symptoms of depression were present in 86 per cent of detainees, anxiety in 77 per cent and post-traumatic stress disorder in 50 per cent, with approximately one quarter reporting suicidal thoughts.[1] Suicide Prevention Australia cited extensive academic research spanning a decade showing numerous and unambiguous conclusions that detention corrodes mental health.[2] One study estimated that the rates of suicidal behaviour among men and women in Australian immigration detention centres were approximately 41 and 26 times the national average, respectively.[3]

It also must be acknowledged that many of these men were victims of torture and trauma. According to the Service for the Treatment and Rehabilitation of Torture and Trauma Survivors (STARTTS), victims of torture and trauma continue to suffer a range of debilitating effects from their experiences such as insomnia, loss of memory, flashbacks, nightmares, anxiety, depression, chronic pain and loss of self-worth, to name a few. The effects of torture and trauma are widespread and can damage societies, nations and cultures. Victims of systematic state terrorism lose trust in government, in authority, and have trouble readjusting to 'normal' society. Imprisoning them in a camp that further erodes their trust of governments and compounds the trauma they suffered in their home countries seems counter-productive to any kind of rehabilitation or healing process.[4]

The fact that some IHMS staff didn't know these facts or chose to ignore them made me doubt their judgement. It wasn't the first time I'd had reason to question the IHMS staff. It turned out that one of the IHMS nurses had worked at Darwin Detention Centre when Nasir, an Iranian cultural advisor, was an asylum seeker being held there.

'I don't like her,' Nasir said. I could see him holding back a lot of emotion. 'No man liked her. She was rude. She looked down her nose at us. She thought she was better than us. She had no care for our personal space. She was the one who left the door open every time we had an appointment. Now she won't look at me.'

There was something satisfying about knowing that this nurse, who had treated Nasir as a cockroach, now had to face him as an equal. And she wouldn't. Couldn't.

One day I talked to an IHMS doctor who gave me another perspective.

'I won't be coming back to Nauru,' he said. 'I have hardly slept in six days because of all the medical emergencies. We are expected to do too much with no resources. We can't prescribe what we need to prescribe. I want to help the men but I can't. I won't come back.'

It was easy to criticise IHMS staff but their job was thankless. There were two psychologists on the island at any time. One psychiatrist made intermittent visits. I never saw more than three doctors on the island at once. A lot of the medical issues were results of stress: kidney problems, stomach-aches, grey hair, hair falling out. How could IHMS treat the men's stress-related medical conditions when they couldn't remove the source of their stress?

Once again I faced my greatest concerns about working at Topside as one of the support units. How much good could we do in a camp designed to treat men poorly, under a policy whose goal was to give these men 'no advantage'? I was becoming more and more convinced that the government didn't want us to help the men—we were purely there to keep the 'hippie left' happy.

While the men suffered in Nauru, the Australian government paid the International Organisation for Migration, IOM, to perform the repatriation duties, offering asylum seekers the opportunity to voluntarily return to their home countries. The reintegration packages offered passage back to the asylum seekers' home countries and financial assistance, or incentives depending on the way you looked at it, when the men arrived. IOM told us that the only way this financial assistance could be accessed was by using it for small business planning or vocational development. DIAC and IOM told the Salvation Army to encourage the men to meet with IOM and sign up for the repatriation packages. The presence of IOM made the camp's purpose much more obvious. The Australian government's justification that it was protecting people by dissuading them from taking boats across dangerous seas didn't fit. Our government was attempting to create an environment in Australian-approved centres that was worse than the oppression the men suffered in their home countries, and then used IOM to offer them 'voluntary' repatriation.

A small number of men took IOM's offer and went back to the very countries they had fled from. When the news of voluntary repatriations reached the public in Australia, people saw this as proof that these men were not genuine refugees. It justified the No Advantage policy. That may very well be true for some of these men—maybe they arrived in Nauru and decided it wasn't the easy entry they'd thought it would be. But there were men who had left families behind. Their families were suffering with no source of income, while their journey stalled. Some of these men believed they had no choice but to return.

Many of the men found promises of safe repatriation hard to believe. Rumours spread around the camp that a group of Tamils who were returned to their home country by IOM were met at the airport by government officials with five-year prison sentences. It shouldn't come as a surprise to us if they were taken by the government. A plethora of reports detail the abuse of Tamils who returned to Sri Lanka once the war was over; allegations of missing or disappeared people, of beatings, of arbitrary imprisonment, of interrogation of Tamils by Sri Lankan armed forces. IOM's services seemed too good to be true.

---

1   Commonwealth of Australia, *Joint Select Committee on Australia's Immigration Detention Network*, 2012, viewed 24 August 2013, <www.humanrights.gov.au/australian-human-rights-commission-submission-joint-select-committee-australia-s-immigration>.
2   Commonwealth of Australia, *Joint Select Committee on Australia's Immigration Detention Network*.
3   Commonwealth of Australia, *Joint Select Committee on Australia's Immigration Detention Network*.
4   STARTTS, *Learn About Torture and Trauma*, STARTTS, viewed 14 November 2013, <www.startts.org.au/resources/refugees-asylum-seekers-and-trauma/learn-about-torture-and-trauma/>

Chapter 16

THE CAMP WAS built on a culture of paperwork. If a man had a complaint, he filled out a form and waited. If he had a medical request, he filled out a form and waited. As the requests needed to be written in English, the men were forced to depend on Salvos to help them. Forty-year-old men were dependent on 21-year-old men and women to help run their everyday lives.

The effects of institutionalisation were becoming evident. The men were losing their independence. They had no responsibility, they had no jobs. They sat around doing nothing all day. They waited for everything. When the rains came and their tents had holes and the water rushed through they had no other option but to wait for the overworked Transfield staff to help them. Some issues they could fix themselves but they'd lost the drive to solve problems.

When the men felt powerless it wasn't uncommon for them to react with short tempers. *I will never talk to you again, Salvos never do anything for us.* Their responses were born out of their inability to take ownership of their lives. Empowerment of the asylum seekers became one of the biggest goals for the Salvos. The more we could inspire them to self-manage the camp, the better for their health and the easier it was to help them.

The Salvation Army set up leadership meetings with the men. Each ethnic group voted in a leader to speak for the good of the rest. Many of the men refused to partake in the voting—for some, cooperation could be seen as acceptance of the situation. Many had grown tired of the continual broken promises, and these leadership meetings smelled suspiciously like a waste of time.

The one meeting I attended had been intended to discuss involving the men in positions of labour: chefs, carpenters, electricians. The idea was to implement their skill sets, keep them active. Yet the meeting was dominated by questions regarding their processing. All the men wanted was to know what the government intended to do with them. The meeting ended with a sombre address to the men from the Salvation Army leadership.

'You can choose to live with hope or you can choose to die here.'

The longer I stayed in Nauru the harder the fight got. The supply of resources and the recruitment of staff didn't match the arrival of asylum seekers. The weeks were punctuated by intakes of men: two intakes a week for weeks on end. Upsetting and traumatic and personal and tiring. By the end of my first trip of four weeks there were more than three hundred men in the camp. More men arrived, more problems mounted, until the very act of walking through the gates of the compound felt like pushing back a tidal wave. In fact it seemed as if we had less of everything the longer the camp stayed open. One walk down the length of the Green Room left you with a list of complaints:

No milk.
No cups.
Holes in the tents.
No fans in the new tents.
What happened to the excursions?
I have a headache.
The internet is down.
The store closed early.
There are no mirrors.

You did what you could, trying to balance personal requests with maintaining policies, programs and services. To ignore personal requests was as bad as saying *No-one cares about you*, yet a personal request usually meant facing the stalling bureaucracy of the camp and could take an hour or more to complete. There wasn't enough time in the day to help everyone, and this only served to undermine our relationships with the men. I became an errand boy, spending the majority of my time trying to solve issues that shouldn't have been difficult to solve.

Mohamed, a squat Hazara, asked me to help him transfer money back to his family. The usual process was to help them complete a request form. Mohamed wanted to count his money, though. So I took him to the front gate of the camp, where all the asylum seekers' valuables were kept in safes. Walking past the front gate always brought some kind of confrontation.

A Pashtun man approached me, angry. His head was bowed, and he winced when he spoke. His eyes were bloodshot.

'I have a headache. I need Panadol, but they won't let me get one. They say I need an appointment. I just need Panadol.'

I nodded. It was a story I'd heard before.

'IHMS won't let people get Panadol without an appointment,' I replied, hating having to refuse the man his simple request.

'I make a request. They don't give me an appointment.' He sighed with frustration.

'Okay. I'll talk to the guard.' Every day the men had the same complaints.

Pezhman was sitting at the gate when I walked over to talk to the guard. A Wilson security guard was standing on the other side of the gate, asking him for his appointment slip. Pezhman was visibly upset.

'What's wrong, Pez?' I asked.

'Every day they make me wait. Every day for one hour in this sun. Twice a day. Twice a day I need to get pills, twice a day I need to come here with a medical slip. And I wait, every day. Every day they ask me, "What are you here for? Have you got your slip?" And then I wait. Why must I wait? Why can't I have my medication here? Why must I wait every day in this sun?'

The Wilson guard offered a patronising barb into the tense silence. 'Just calm down, LIC029.'

'He has a name,' I interjected.

The guard put his face up to mine and whispered, 'When we go in there they are numbers. That is all.'

'Today I come twice in the morning. And they send me away,' Pezhman said, his voice rising incrementally.

'No you didn't,' the guard interjected.

'You ask her,' Pezhman shouted, pointing at the female guard at the gate. 'The nurses were busy, she said.'

This was what sent them crazy. Compounding frustrations, daily humiliations. A flesh-eating infection that slowly devoured the men day after day. Each little interaction with guards, Salvos and Transfield workers stripped them of their ability to fend for themselves. They relied upon us for everything: food, clothes, medication, bedding. Each little item they needed they had to follow procedures to get. They had to fight to understand these procedures and then they had to wait. Then procedures would change and they'd have to fight again, and then wait. They couldn't even write the request forms themselves; they had to ask a Salvation Army worker to do it for them.

Need shoes. Go to shop. Wait. Shop has no shoes. Shop is closed today. Come back another day. Have a complaint? See a Salvo. Fill out complaint form. Hear nothing.

Need medication. Go to gate. Wait. Come back in one hour when the nurse is free. Have a complaint? See a Salvo. Fill out complaint form. Hear nothing.

Need a phone card. Go to shop. Wait. Phone cards are sold out. Come back another day. Have a complaint? See a Salvo. Fill out complaint form. Hear nothing.

Calm down. Don't get angry. Act rational. Act like a human being. You number.

By the time I had calmed Pezhman down, Mohamed and the Pashtun had left. They couldn't stand waiting in the sun while we argued.

Rather than let them demoralise me, I used moments like these to motivate me. Who would advocate for the men from within the camp if we didn't? Who would fight the little battles for the men when everyone else treated them as guilty before being proven innocent?

Chapter 17

'STUFF ME UP a bloody gum tree, are you coming or what?' Joel shouted out in his broad Queensland accent. 'Inca and Roach are waiting.'

'Yeah, gimme a sec,' I shouted back. I rushed out the door of 161, struggling to hold my flippers and snorkel. I found Joel outside sitting on the back of Inca's postie bike. I jumped behind Roach and we sped off into the night. Joel and I were both barefoot and bare-chested, just wearing boardies. I rested my ankle against the exhaust and yelped when I felt my skin sizzling.

'What are you doing?' Roach shouted at me, the words whipped away by the wind. I didn't bother replying.

Joel was a Salvo of my age. He was a real Australian cowboy: he wore boots and an akubra, and spoke in Australian slang that made me think he was dumber than he actually was. We were employed on a rotating roster of short-term contracts, so by my third week on the island the majority of colleagues I considered friends had returned to Sydney. Paul, Amanda and Catherine had all gone home. When friends left, you made new friends. It was impossible not to. You worked together, ate together, lived together. We were expected to shoulder a heavy burden by working in Nauru, and we relied upon each other to share the load. Your coworkers became your brothers and sisters.

Joel's and my friendship grew out of diving. Roach and Inca were our Nauruan dive partners. They showed us the best places to dive in Nauru, or at least the parts that didn't have too many sharks or currents that could wash you far from shore. Usually these routes avoided the coral pinnacles. Usually.

Inca and Roach led us onto a natural rock jetty with only the light of our torches to guide us. Heavy waves crashed into the rocks, all the more intimidating in the half-light.

'Where are we getting in?' I asked.

Inca gave me a funny look. 'There,' he said, and pointed at the frothing water. Inca was a man of few words. He slipped his flippers and snorkel on, took his torch and spear in either hand and jumped into the water. I didn't like the look of this.

'Come on, you kangaroo dog,' Joel said, and disappeared into the water after Inca.

I fumbled with my gear on the rocks, then dropped my flipper in the water, then jumped in after it, leaving my spear behind. Once in the water and geared up I settled. The water was calm; the sound of my breathing filled my head. Topside was forgotten and the underwater world became everything. No trauma, no politics, just fish.

The nature of the short-term contracts made work there feel like a gap year, albeit a traumatic one. The high turnover rate meant a lack of consistency for the staff and for the asylum seekers. There was something exciting in meeting new people every week, but each time good people left everyone felt it. The continual break up of three- and four-week relationships resulted in a growing distrust between the men and the Salvos. The men quickly learned that to trust a Salvo would only end in betrayal. The constant turnover also resulted in a loss of corporate knowledge. The Salvation Army kept no record of past events at the camp; there were no handovers. The history of the camp was being lost by staff but not by the asylum seekers, the people with the least amount of power. Justice within the camp followed the cycles of work rosters.

The pervading emotion of Nauru was frustration. There weren't enough resources, weren't enough staff. Resources were ordered but never arrived. Every time new staff arrived, good staff left. Our answers for the men alternated between *I don't know* and *It's been ordered*. Information changed daily; no plans could be relied upon. Everything was susceptible to last-minute alterations: flights, bus timetables, intakes of asylum seekers, policies, laws, contracts, rosters. In some ways we should have been grateful for the disorganisation of the camp. Efficiency would have implied some kind of professionalism. An expertise in oppression and degradation.

Diving allowed me to momentarily escape the pressures of the camp, and after three weeks I was starting to cherish my time away from the men. It gave me time to think outside of the vacuum that was life in Nauru. I was weighing up two possible futures: continue working in the camp with the men, or go home and publicly advocate for them. I knew that by staying in Nauru I could make life better for the men: advocate from within, set up programs that would provide them more freedoms. Yet the camp would still be open and the main source of the men's stress and depression would never go away. I thought that if I went home and spoke out then maybe people would see just how awful the camp was. I didn't know what would happen to me if I did speak. I didn't know if the government would go after me. I didn't even know if the public would care. What shocked me most was how I had got into this position. Five weeks earlier I had been enjoying a placid life in Sydney. Now I was faced with dilemmas that could change my life and the lives of hundreds of men.

*

It wasn't until Nauru that I realised a person has several breaking points. Steps that mark their descent into madness. As you get closer to the bottom the steps get shallower. We were forced to watch these men slowly crumble before our very eyes.

Abbas sat in a chair and, using pen ink, tattooed chains in meticulous detail all over his body. Namdar sat staring at the television with wild eyes.

'I am going crazy,' Namdar said, looking at nothing.

It is a truly disturbing experience to hear a man admit his own mental frailties. How do you respond to a man who knows his sanity is teetering on the edge? We weren't just dealing with the traumas of their past, we were watching trauma in action, inflicting it upon them. We held their lives in our hands and there was nothing I could do to unclench the government's fist.

'Soon Nauru will be the biggest exporter of crazies in the world,' Namdar laughed to himself.

Farid the BFG received a medical appointment slip that had 'adjustment disorder' written on the back of it. His inability to adjust to this surreal experience was diagnosed as an inability to adjust to all situations. Farid shrugged his shoulders and said, 'I have a headache, IHMS say drink water. I have a knee problem, IHMS say drink water. I have adjustment disorder, I drink water.'

According to Zulfigar, one of the Hazara cultural advisers, suicide attempts were the ultimate surrender of hope, the gravest insult a Muslim could commit against his God. Parshan, the long eye-lashed Kurd, was the first man to attempt to take his life in Nauru. He tried to hang himself with a bedsheet. He had been in Nauru for three weeks and already his mind was starting to crumble from within. He wasn't the only one. There were worrying signs from a lot of the men.

There were times when the Iranians' solidarity as a group began to wane, leaving one Salvo in tears. 'They sat there for thirty minutes,' the Salvo told me. 'No-one spoke. Not even a joke, not even a comment, not even a sound. They are broken. How can they expect to last years here?'

Parshan and his friend Yashar were placed on suicide watch. They were followed by a guard everywhere they went, twenty-four hours a day. The guard became their second shadow, a spectre of suicide. A constant reminder of their instability. Yashar went for runs around the camp to help the fat guards lose weight.

'Come on,' he shouted back at the heavy-breathing green shirt, 'Come on.' At first this was amusing. Then it became tragic. Yashar started taking his clothes off, blowing raspberries at the guard, slapping his bum, jerking his penis, and eventually he broke down and cried.

One of the Wilson security guards had worked as a carer for mentally ill patients. He told me that the men who are monitored as high-risk patients have a high level of care and are at less risk of doing something serious. 'The quiet ones, they're the ones I worry about,' he said.

I thought of the Tamils. Their dignified public acceptance was hiding an internalisation of the same thoughts and fears that plagued the Iranians. Just because they smiled and waggled their heads didn't mean they were happy.

I had often sat with Pez in his tent over the past four weeks. In my last days before going home, I sat with him and he stared intently into my eyes.

'I studied a class at university in suicide,' he said to me.

I hesitated slightly, acknowledging to myself that this conversation could lead somewhere peculiar, and then I nodded for him to continue.

'Each method of suicide can be seen as having a statement. A hanging is a show. Someone has to find you.' Pez paused to emphasise his point. I nodded again, this time to show my understanding.

'Jumping off a building can be seen as trying to be free. Cutting your throat or wrists is an emotional hurt. A fire, that is desperation. That is a sign of deep political hurt. It is a protest of the gravest extreme.'

I tried to examine Pezhman's face but he was obscured by shadow. A chill accelerated down my spine, leaving me cold inside and out. He began singing in a beautiful voice. It was a sad song that resonated in the hot tent. Without knowing the words, I knew it was a sad song. When he finished I asked him what the words meant.

Candle and butterfly I am,
The wine's cup loved friend, I am
Disgraced by life I am,

Mad I am,
Stranger to myself I am,
Beloved friend of wine tavern I am,
Disgraced by life I am,
Mad I am,
Oh my lord,
Listen to my weepings,
Your earth and sky are shaking under my feet,
Your moon and stars are burning from my weepings,
Disgraced by life I am,
Mad I am.

Chapter 18

THE OUT-OF-CAMP excursions were a win for the Salvos and for the men. Access to the outside world was a refreshing shower after the humid camp atmosphere. Yet it seemed inevitable that the Salvos would take their two steps back. The excursions had been deemed a priority to camp safety and the mental wellbeing of the clients, but as a result they were rushed through as soon as possible without following usual risk-assessment procedures. Men ran into the coral-infested waters on beach walks and cut their feet. IHMS were inundated with trivial injuries to treat. A new policy decreed that men must wear shoes into the water. The agencies were on edge. Where I wanted to give the men as much freedom as possible on excursions, the other agencies demanded more control. It would only take one serious incident to jeopardise all that progress.

The lead-up to the injury was innocuous, so much so that at the time I did not even realise there had been an injury. The men cavorted by the water's edge at the boat harbour for their allotted two hours. Backflips, dives, slides on the boat ramp, and general tomfoolery that didn't exist within the confines of Topside. At the end of the trip, as the men were boarding the bus, a Tamil man approached me. Sadat, a Tamil cultural advisor, translated.

'He has hurt his shoulder,' Sadat said. The man did not appear in too much pain—more discomfort than anything else.

'How?' I asked.

'Jumping on the floaties in the water,' Sadat translated.

'Is it serious?'

The man waggled his head at me with a grimace. I didn't know what this meant exactly.

'Okay. We'll take you to IHMS when we get back?' I asked.

'Okay, brother,' Sadat said.

Within five minutes of leaving the boat harbour, Sadat called me over.

'He is in a lot of pain, brother,' Sadat said. 'He has pain in both arms.' He motioned up and down his arms quickly. The man was grimacing and arched his back every time a bolt of pain accelerated through him.

'Not a problem,' I said, swallowing the ball of anxiety that had stuck in my throat. 'We've got a situation here,' I called out to one of the Wilson guards, trying to remain composed. The Wilson guard radioed in to Wilson control and IHMS was put on standby. Within five minutes the Tamil man's fingers had curled up and he had lost sensation in his hands. He said he could feel burning in his arm from an old shrapnel injury. Water sprang out of his clenched eyes as the bolts of pain became more frequent.

'I think we should call an ambulance,' I said. The thought of this man suffering a spinal injury swirled around my head and into my stomach. I felt ill. Selfish guilt about personal repercussions inter-mingled with fear that this man might never walk again. Another Wilson guard took the man's neck in both hands and held him steady. The bus bumped and rattled its way up the rocky path to Topside, the man feeling every shudder. When we arrived at Topside I was met by a nose-flaring nurse.

'You'd better understand the gravity of this situation.' She shot me a furious stare. I was shocked by her aggression. Did she think she was the only one who understood the severity of a spinal injury?

'Of course I do. You think I'm not worried about the guy?' I replied.

'Well, you should have been worried before accidents like this happened. You'd better write a statement right now.'

I walked away feeling wretched. If the man had sustained a spinal cord injury, I had no confidence that the government would support me or the Salvation Army. It would hang me out to dry. I gave my statements to security, IHMS and the Salvation Army. By the time I walked away from the scene I was exhausted.

That night the situation in the compound was volatile. The pressure cooker had been turned on. Two of the new Iraqis were strong, proud men, Arabic warriors. They stood off against a group of Tamil men in the line for food. Sidque flew off the handle. He kicked chairs, broke plates, knocked a Salvo out of his path, all the while shouting in Arabic. A Tamil man bashed another Tamil in his tent. It was the first time we had had an incident of violence among the men, other than against themselves. Three times the Salvos were evacuated out of the camp. I could feel the atmosphere in the camp building.

*

That night Shahab attempted to commit suicide. I walked past him out the front of IHMS lying motionless in the back of an ambulance. My mind began to unravel.

I found the Iranians sitting in their tents. The mood was a storm cloud of anger and sadness. I sat next to Pez and Rashid.

'He received a phone call from his family in Iran telling him not to come back. That he had taken their money and achieved nothing,' Pez said. 'His wife said he was a failure. He took a cord from one of the tents and hung himself from the tent pole of his room. Mohammed Reza found him. You all did this to him. You did this,' Pez said, pointing at me. 'You lied to him. You told him you would get him pants and you didn't. You told him you would take him fishing and you didn't. There is no hope here. You have taken everything from us.'

It wasn't a fair statement, but I had no arguments. Every moment I exercised power over this man, whether it was involuntary or not, was a turning of the screw. I was a jailer and he was a prisoner, and no matter how I believed I was his friend, there had always existed an imbalance of power.

'We thought he was one of the safe ones, the stable ones. To be rejected by your own family, this is the worst. Nothing can bring you back from that. He really wanted to kill himself. Look at this cord. Look.'

Pez pulled at one of the thin, rough cords. It looked like it would cut through a man's flesh. I imagined Shahab dangling from the roof and held back a mountain of grief.

'It is our destiny here,' Pez said. 'We cannot change this now. We are stuck here and we have no options. You are killing us.'

The rain came down.

'God is crying for us,' Pez said.

One white bird flew over our heads and out of sight. I thought of the freedom that little bird represented and wondered if Pez was thinking the same thing.

Pez pointed at Farid, who was sitting in the next tent, head bowed. 'They were best friends.'

I sat beside Farid and held him. My left arm barely reached his other shoulder. He shuddered silently. The rain teemed down while Farid cried. I wanted to cry with him, to cry for *Dosh* Shahab and share his grief but it wouldn't be fair. I had no right here, not within these fences. Shahab was not my friend, he was my client. They were his friends and I was a worker within the walls of oppression.

I willed myself to be that support. For one hour, just one hour of support, just one more. And then what? Then I could leave the compound and escape from the overwhelming hopelessness while they were stuck in the suicide camp.

Farid looked at me, eyes rimmed with red. 'Thank you.' He hugged me, his big arms wrapping around me and dragging me into his body. 'You are my friend.' Then he walked to his tent and lay down on his bed. I returned to Pezhman.

'Look at Rashid. He never cries. I am worried about him. He could be next,' Pezhman said with accusing eyes. Beautiful Mohammed and angry Pezhman picked up Rashid despite his refusals to leave, and led him out of the rain. I was soaked by now.

Abdul walked past. He was not walking to go anywhere, he had no aim, he was just walking. I put my hand on his shoulder. He looked at me and then past me. We stood in silence until he began talking.

'In Iran, to eat, to drink was not a problem. The government was a problem. I come here, the government is a problem. If I go back, I have big problem. If I stay here, I have big problem. I come here. Why? Why? First Parshan, then Yashar. Now Shahab. Then?'

In each of these men you could see fear. They recognised the pain that Shahab was feeling and they wondered when their limit would come. The turmoil inside them was pulling them apart. The regret of leaving their families, the heavy decisions weighing on their minds. To return to Iran and face a vengeful government, or to stay here and endure years of psychological torture? The only way they could hope to survive was to battle the demons in their own heads, but how could they do that in a place so devoid of hope?

IHMS asked Mohammed Reza if he would like to talk to them. He shook his head. 'I told you they would try to commit suicide.' And he walked away. *They knew*, I thought, *we all knew this would start happening. How could we not?*

A Wilson guard informed us that Christmas Island had two attempted suicides a day. That's what we had to expect. We were working in death factories. The camp was built around destroying men, breaking them down so far that they would take their own lives. Grind them into the dust and force their hands to pull the nooses and knives on themselves. I rode a wave of anger, frustration, grief, guilt and hate. The moment I stepped out of those gates I felt free. It was an awful sensation.

Chapter 19

AFTER SHAHAB'S SUICIDE ATTEMPT the mood settled, as if the attempted hanging had taken the lid off a boiling pot. It was the cycle of violence. One Salvo predicted that it would only take a few weeks for the pressure to build up again.

All excursions since the neck injury had been cancelled until full occupational health and safety procedures were developed. It felt cruel to take away the little freedom the men had. I was hounded by the same questions every time I walked through the camp.

'When will be the next excursion?' Dev asked.

Rashid had learnt a new English word. 'Swimming?' he said with a grin, motioning with his arms.

Every day I had to respond the same. 'Not yet. Soon.' I was mindful not to make promises I couldn't keep.

During this calm period the ethnic groups joined together to protest peacefully against the camp. After all the racial tension within the camp, a united front was a welcome change. The men agreed to sit out on the cricket pitch, unprotected from the sun during the hottest part of the day. They made banners from sheets and drew murals on wooden boards. In one mural, chained doves had padlocks through their wings, and Australia was the key to their bonds. In another, a group of men in Australian bins. A red eye crying a tear. A tear made of 1 per cent water, 33 per cent hope,

33 per cent feelings, 33 per cent dreams. They had found a way to express their pain outside of self-mutilation.

Not everyone participated in the protest. A group of Tamils sitting in their tents said they were happy with the camp.

'It has good food, good shoes.'

Salvo staff were evacuated from the compound for the majority of the day. Some of the men were disappointed that the Salvation Army hadn't witnessed their protest. It was frustrating. We knew, we saw, but we couldn't be there.

'Were you scared of us?' they asked. Of course we were not, but because we were evacuated every time there was trouble, that was what it looked like to the men. Instead, the media falsely reported that there had been conflict between Tamils and Sinhalese. This only served to demoralise the men. They had done nothing wrong and they still received bad press.

Prior to the protest the Australian workers at the camp had told the men, 'This is the way to voice your displeasure. The Australian people will respect this.'

I disagree. Would the Australian people ever see these peaceful protests? Even if they did, would they care? The men were told that peaceful protests would be viewed more favourably in Australia than violent ones. The truth was that only the violent protests would be reported by the media. Some of the men within the camp were already aware of this.

'We only see the Nauruan government when we act badly. When we perform a peaceful protest, nobody listens.'

*

Shahab's suicide attempt changed everything in Nauru for me. I could see good men being broken down and there was nothing I could do to help them. I knew the work we were doing was important, but it wasn't enough.

The Australian government had approved this policy; Tony Abbott wanted harsher measures. The Australian people did not oppose it. Yet we, the workers, were the poor few who had to deal with the day-to-day realities of the camp. We were the ones who made excuses for DIAC's policies; we were the ones who attempted to calm angered men; we were the ones saying *I don't know* and *I'm sorry*; we were the ones crying. We were the ones questioning our complicity. We were the ones trying to instil hope in broken men.

Too often the stress overwhelmed the staff and resulted in break-downs. Azad, one of the Iranian cultural advisors, was escorted out of the compound screaming, 'I can't think anymore.' Another of the cultural advisors had previously been detained at Christmas Island for eighteen months; Nauru triggered a relapse of his past traumas. I often thought of the eighteen-year-old Salvos facing atrocities committed by a government they hadn't even been allowed to vote for. Did they fully comprehend the enormity of the situation? How would it affect their outlook on life? A year ago they hadn't had the legal right to drink a beer, now they were working within a detention centre communicating with traumatised men.

It was obvious that the government had no sense of justice for the asylum seekers, yet what simmered beneath the surface was the level of the contempt the government harboured for its own people. Among all this confusion, frustration and bureaucracy there was one goal. Our job was to create hope out of the ashes of these men's dreams. But at times it felt like we were being employed solely as sounding boards for their grievances.

Chapter 20

'WE'RE MOVING,' Stuart announced. He was already packing his uniform into his suitcase. Moving rooms was not uncommon for Salvation Army staff, but those of us in Room 161 had been lucky enough to maintain a permanent residency while all the other Salvos were rotated through rooms.

'What? What is this? Moving? No,' Azad said. His sentiment was shared by all of us in Room 161. As much as we hated sleeping ten men in two small rooms, we had bonded over the experience.

'We're moving into tents at Topside,' Stuart said, 'DIAC need these rooms.'

'Tents?' we echoed.

'That's not fair,' Azad said. 'We have ten of us in this room. They will not put ten in here.'

'Of course they won't.' Stuart said. 'But when DIAC says jump, everyone asks how high.'

We all knew it was true. Once DIAC made a decision there was nothing we plebs could do to change it. An example of this was the prohibition of hair dye in the camp. DIAC deemed it too dangerous as 'it could result in dry, rough hair'. These men had seen so much trauma, the danger of dyed hair could easily be the last straw.

We packed our bags and moved out of the icy air-conditioning of 161. Arriving at Topside with all our luggage was odd. We had always arrived for work in the morning and left for the hotel in the evening. The Salvation Army lectured us on separating private life and work life, yet here we were about to live, sleep and breathe Topside.

We slept on creaky stretcher beds in steamy humidity that night, entangled in our mosquito nets. We knew the army tents were hot—we had been in and out of them for the past few weeks—but trying to sleep in them was a different matter. The heat was suffocating, the mosquito nets clung to sweaty bare skin, the stretchers squeaked. The tents were bearable only in the way a camping trip is comfortable. The knowledge that this arrangement was temporary was the saving grace. Once you were awake there was no place to relax. The tents became saunas after nine in the morning and suddenly we were turfed out into Topside, a bus ride away from the ocean.

'This is outrageous,' Stuart said. 'I'm not sleeping here another night.'

He investigated the sleeping options and came back to us with an intriguing piece of news. 'One-six-one is empty.' We weren't sure what to say. If the room wasn't being used, why had we been moved?

'I don't care what they say, I'm sleeping in 161 tonight,' Stuart announced. No-one disagreed with him. We squatted in the room for four days without anyone noticing. On the fourth day I became ill and had to be taken to IHMS.

'We need to pick you up,' Salvo HR said. 'Where are you?'

The ruse was up.

*

In my fourth week on the island gastroenteritis spread through the camp, leaving the afflicted with loose bowels, fever and dehydration. IHMS nurses held emergency hand-washing meetings. If you entered the mess hall without cleaning your hands you were named and shamed. IHMS was so concerned with the rapid spread of illness it feared an epidemic. The consequences would be devastating. If the illness spread quickly enough it had the potential to shut down the camp. I began formulating master plans of germ warfare to infect the entire camp with my illness. I dreamed of wiping my snotty fingers on all the cutlery in the mess, taking extra care for some of the ruder IHMS nurses' spoons.

The epidemic started on 'our' side of the fence. I don't think that's what the DIAC official meant when she told Mustafa that she was 'different' from him. With just a week left before I was due home I was quarantined with a bout of gastroenteritis. I was placed in an air-conditioned room that was covered in ants. Sick asylum seekers were quarantined in tents. There were three soldiers already lying on stretcher beds in the room when I arrived.

'What's the army still doing here?' I asked.

'Fucking who knows, ay? It's bullshit. Just doing the desalination plant for eight weeks now. I say get you fuckers to do it so we can get back to our jobs,' the blond soldier next to me said with a grin.

'I wouldn't know where to start.' I returned his grin. 'What do you normally do?'

'I'm a combat officer,' he said. 'Explosives unit. I served in Afghanistan. It was my job to fight against guys like these.'

'But these aren't the soldiers,' I said. 'They're the men running away from the soldiers you're sent to Afghanistan to fight against.'

'Yeah, but they're all the same.'

'What do you mean, they're running away?' one of the other men asked.

'Well, most of the Hazaras fled Afghanistan because the Taliban were trying to kill them,' I said.

'Fuckin' ay?' The second soldier whistled.

'Yeah, but they're just as bad. They're coming here illegally and making us work here. It's bullshit,' Blondie said.

'They don't come here illegally,' I said. 'The men are seeking asylum. Australia signed a United Nations Refugee Convention to accept asylum seekers fleeing from danger.'

'Aren't the Tamil Tigers like the Khmer Rouge?' the second soldier asked.

'No. The Tamil Tigers were a rebel group fighting their government,' I said. 'More like the IRA. But these guys are Tamil, not necessarily Tamil Tigers. A lot of these men will have been persecuted purely because of their race.'

The blond soldier came back at me. 'But why do they get on the boats? I just don't get how these people can risk their families' lives. They're fucked.'

'I've talked to a lot of the guys in the camp. They told me that they fled their countries looking for freedom. They picked Australia because they heard it was a great country. So they flew to Asia. Places like Indonesia and Malaysia aren't signatories to the same UN convention we are. In these countries, asylum seekers are illegal immigrants. Indonesia will put them in prisons or detention centres worse than anything in Australia. Once they are in Indonesia or Malaysia their best option is to come to Australia by boat. I don't know if they realised just how bad the boats would be, or just how dangerous the journey would be, when they left their home countries, but now they've got nowhere else to go. Some of the men have told me that even if they'd known how bad the journey would be they would still have come.'

We mulled over the men's desperation in silence.

'I worked for the navy, ay?' the blond soldier said. 'And I picked up the boats when they smashed on the rocks. It wasn't a pretty sight, ay? Those cunts chucking their kids into the water, ay? They'll do anything to get into Australia. It's not human.'

I didn't know the truth of what he said, but I couldn't imagine the men I had worked with doing that. Could I believe that asylum seekers valued their children less than we did ours? Did these soldiers think asylum seekers were so different from us?

'I'm going to the toilet,' I said.

The quarantine toilet was situated on the other side of the camp. Stepping out of the cold, air-conditioned room into the humid heat played havoc with my fever. I stumbled across the rocky ground to the toilet. The men's quarantine and the boundary to the men's camp were adjacent to the staff quarantine toilets. There was a man sitting in the asylum seekers' quarantine talking to a friend who was standing on the other side of the fence in the compound. Where I was standing, the three sections were divided by one pole.

'Hello,' I called out. The two men approached me. They were Pashtun men from Pakistan. We talked between the gaps in the fence. Green mesh hid their faces from me.

'Don't get too close,' I said to the non-quarantined man. 'I don't want you to get sick.'

'It's okay,' the man said.

'Are you sick with gastro too?' I asked the quarantined man.

'No. I asked to be left alone for mental health reasons.'

The idea of anyone being alone in this camp concerned me. 'What do you do all day?'

'Think.'

'That's too much thinking,' I said. All day, every day, thinking about the future, the past, the present. It would be too much.

'When will we be let out of here?' he asked.

'I don't know,' was all I could say.

'Why were we brought here?' he asked me.

'I don't know.'

'Will we be processed? Where will we be sent?' They asked me questions only a politician could answer.

'Where did you live in Pakistan?' I asked, keen to move the conversation along.

'Parachinar, on the border with Afghanistan,' the self-quarantined man said.

'It's very dangerous there?' I felt stupid the moment I finished my sentence.

'Yes, of course.' He pushed his hand up against the gap in the fence. He was missing two fingers on his right hand. 'I was a computer engineer until a bomb blew up my house.'

We stood in silence, faces resting against the fences that divided us. Too often I felt inadequate in Nauru.

'You know what "Nauru" means in Pashtun?' one of the men asked. I shook my head. 'Don't cry.' We laughed sadly among ourselves. I left the pair in silence.

*

While I was in quarantine, Yashar attempted to cut his throat and his stomach with a razor in the shower. Farid feigned gastro problems, and was placed in quarantine. While in isolation he threatened to hang himself.

I couldn't wait to go home.

Chapter 21

BY THE END of the month I felt cold to the harsh reality of the camp. I no longer noticed the sweat dripping off me. I joined the men at voiceless tables and offered no words of encouragement; the conversation hung still in the hot air. I no longer pushed the men into the heat of the day to keep them active. One month in Nauru and I was tired.

I joined the Iraqis in the shade of the gym block. Assad, the hairdresser, took me into a chair and performed threading, a technique of plucking facial hair using two pieces of string. He ripped the hair off my cheekbone without mercy. Tears popped into my eyes and I yelped loudly to the men's merriment until the sting became numb.

A Hazara man collapsed in the yard with a cry of despair. I looked across at the commotion.

'Is it a suicide attempt?' I asked the Iraqis, aware that in my first week I would've been in the first row of onlookers.

'He is dehydrated,' Yaqub replied.

We returned to the plucking. I had become numb to the sting of the camp. After the threading, my cheeks remained red raw and smarting for the rest of the day.

*

In the final days of my first rotation Yashar tried to hang himself in the Green Room, despite being under twenty-four hour watch. Another Iranian tried to swallow razor blades. Such violent ways to express their pain. One of the Tamils had claimed he was under eighteen years of age. Every week more men came and the camp had run out of space to house them all. The men had stolen knives from the kitchen; we were told to be vigilant. It was divulged to us that the 35-year-old army tents, originally soaked in kerosene as a waterproofing tactic, were highly flammable. The men were believed to have lighters in their possession. We were sitting on an army-supplied bomb.

It was impossible to keep track of everything that was happening within the camp. Every day a new crisis rocked the staff: a new self-harm incident, a new medical emergency. Small everyday inter-actions between men and staff were forgotten. It washed over you and you absorbed it. You heard these stories, you met the people, and you knew the truths of the camp. Yet it was ephemeral infor-mation. How much of it could we prove? You never had the full story in Nauru. Just when you thought you had all the facts, some-one else would arrive with a new insight, a new bit of information, that turned what you knew on its head. Anything and everything could be swept away by a dismissive denial from the government. The camp was built on lies, secrecy, illegalities and denial. We knew all that we had seen were truths, but when we returned who would believe us?

I had been offered another short-term contract but I had refused to sign it. I didn't want to make any decisions until I was outside of Nauru. I wasn't sure if I wanted to return. Since I commenced my employment with the Salvos I had received comprehensive psycho-logical care. I was told it would take me time to process and recover from the traumas I witnessed. As long as I'd spent in Nauru, that was how long it would take for me to feel 'normal' again. These men weren't receiving adequate psychological care. They didn't get psychological preparation before entering the camp. They wouldn't get a psychological debrief when they eventually left the camp.

They had to expect to spend years in Nauru and would suffer far worse traumas than I ever did. How long would it take for them to recover? How many years had we stolen from them? Time is one of the most precious commodities we have and we were going to rob them of years.

*

On my final day at Topside I said my goodbyes to the men. Farid, Shahab, Pez, Mustafa, Yaqub, Dev, Salar, all of them. Handshakes, hugs, wellwishes. I wrote them a letter, sure that it could express my thoughts better than anything I could muster on the spot.

> *My brothers,*
>
> *This month has taught me a lot about this world, about the injustices and about the beauties. Your journeys have been long, you have endured atrocious conditions, and suffered oppression that I can not begin to understand. And yet now an Australian has hundreds of new brothers from Iraq, Sri Lanka, Iran, Afghanistan and Pakistan. And we all met in a small island in the Pacific.*
>
> *You have humbled me with your exceptional spirit and undying optimism. Maintain these attributes, they are your most powerful allies in the face of all adversity. I recognise you as men. I see your worth. You have as much right to freedom as the Chris Bowens of this world. However long you stay here, don't allow the system to take away your humanity.*
>
> *Your future relies upon your involvement in this camp. Salvation Army workers will come and go, but this place will stand. Do not let it become the hell that it could so easily be. Take ownership of this community, make it as good a place as it can be. Write, contemplate, plan. Take care of each other.*
>
> *Be kind to yourselves.*
> *Strive to be happy.*
> *Survive.*
> *Your brother.*

Yaqub walked me to the gate. It closed behind me, and I walked away from him. I walked towards my family, a trip to Australia, my future. While my brother of the same age, with the same hopes, and the same dreams, was stuck behind steel fencing, fingers curled around his incarceration.

PART 2

ROTATION 2

8 November 2012 to 19 December 2012

Chapter 22

WHEN I RETURNED to Australia I felt disconnected, numb. My first social interactions were at a house party. It was crowded, the music was blaring, people were drinking heavily. Friends accosted me and asked, 'How was Nauru?'

How could I begin to explain the enormity of the experience?

'Good,' I replied and hoped they wouldn't ask any more about it. Yet when people nodded their heads and changed the subject I was surprised, annoyed even. I couldn't understand why they didn't care about it as much as I did. When people pressed for a real answer, I caved. A torrent of words rushed out of me and overwhelmed the questioner. Prison, depression, hopelessness, self-harm, suicide attempts. This was usually enough to scare most people away.

My gut feeling after having experienced Nauru was that the Pacific Solution was a cruel and unjust policy that punished innocent people based on an unfounded fear that they were a threat to our way of life. Everything I'd ever been taught, by my parents, at school, about the Australian values of equality and justice, were the opposite of what I witnessed in Nauru. Worse, it appeared that the Australian people were in favour of these policies.

I found it hard to associate with people who hadn't been to Nauru. I couldn't stop dreaming about the men. I couldn't stop thinking about them in the middle of social situations. The majority of my respite time I spent with my colleagues from Topside. One Salvo was finding it particularly hard to readjust, and suffered from nightmares, insomnia and panic attacks. He was diagnosed as suffering from vicarious trauma.

My writing made it easier for me. When people read my writing, they understood. They began asking different questions, more pertinent ones. This encouraged me to keep at it.

Before I left Nauru I asked Yaqub if he would prefer for me to campaign publicly or to return to Nauru. The reality was I couldn't do both. Whistle blowing was a breach of contract and DIAC would not allow a vocal denouncer of its human rights abuses to work in its detention centres.

Without hesitation Yaqub said, 'Come back.'

With him in mind I made my decision to return to Nauru. The Salvos had offered me a six-week contract. I was home for a week before heading back over. I hardly had time to process everything that I'd seen and done before I was gone again.

I was anxious about returning to Nauru. The naivety of my first trip had been squashed by the reality of the camp. The excitement of round one was now nervous adrenaline. The belief that I was about to have a 'character-building' experience had been replaced by the knowledge that I was entering a traumatic and depressing jail. It was possible that I would see more riots. It was possible that I would see a suicide. It was possible that this person would be a friend of mine. While I was in Australia the media reported that the men had started a mass hunger strike. It made me feel sick in the stomach.

The earlier encouragement of my friends and family, the reiterations of *It will be so rewarding*, were replaced with one question: *Why are you going back?* The answer was simple. For the men.

Chapter 23

STEPPING BACK INTO Topside and seeing the amazed grins of the men justified the return trip for me. Hundreds of hugs, warm handshakes, gracious *thank yous*, ironic *welcome backs*, teary eyes.

'It's good to see you, I missed you,' I told them and I meant it.

The hundreds of reunions revived in me the joyful moments of the previous trip. I remembered furious soccer matches in the fading light, late-night conversations in the Green Room, chess games, card games, Tamil dancing, off-key singing. I remembered walking through those gates every day and feeling that my presence was needed, appreciated. I saw gratitude in the men. The Salvos had not abandoned them. They had remembered them, cared enough to come back for them. Trust was slowly being restored.

Dosh Farid bear-hugged me. 'My friend,' he cried out.

Shahab's ribs poked into me when we hugged. 'Thank you, Mark. Thank you.'

Yaqub and the Iraqis dressed me in their Arabic robes and paraded me around the compound.

Dev's warm smile. Raj, Salar, Pezhman. 'My brother. It is good to see you.' They looked older and skinnier.

I immediately noticed hollow cheeks and curved bellies, evidence of the mass nine-day hunger strike that started while I was in Australia. Even though I'd heard about it through the Australian media, no article could truly capture the horror of the hunger strike. Those not eating were weak and thin. They had moved their stretcher beds into the Green Room and lay there all day. When the strikers did move, they passed through the thick heat like zombies. The atmosphere in the camp was dead—no-one was doing anything.

Those who were eating did not want to flaunt it in front of the others. They abstained from physical activity and they ate in their tents. Thanks to this the rat population was growing. Excursions out of the camp were barely running. The official number of hunger strikers reported by the media was 260, but that number seemed hyperbolised. Some of the men weren't checked off when they ate, some of the men were coerced into joining in. The Iranians, ring-leaders of the strike, were caught smuggling food into their tents to eat. Having said that, there were still more than a hundred men forgoing food.

Namdar was a Kurd in his mid-thirties. He had a hooked nose, a frowning brow and intense eyes. He shaved his head like the rest of the Iranians. He was bull-headed, defiant and proud. His hunger strike had reached thirty days. Before the strike he had possessed the lean and languid body of a kickboxer. After thirty days without food he looked like a skeleton. He was too weak to leave his tent, yet his brain remained sharp enough to negotiate with the organisations. Their requests for him to start eating again were met with scorn.

'Are you going to offer me anything?' he asked. When it became clear that the Australian organisations had come to the negotiation table with no incentive for him to eat except his own welfare, he sent them away. I thought of Nelson Mandela, who once said, 'Only free men can negotiate; prisoners cannot enter into contracts.'

Namdar's personal Wilson guard did his utmost to convince the Kurd to eat. Every day he talked to Namdar about eating, he brought him food, he cooked for him, he even tried bargaining with him. Namdar politely refused all his efforts.

The tents were beginning to look more like houses among little communities. The Afghan quarter comprised three tents at the front gate. They had cardboard rugs and played cards on a square table. High-powered fans had replaced the cheap pedestal fans. The Iraqis placed water on the floor in front of their fan for a makeshift air-conditioning unit. They had strategically hung purple drapes at the front of their tents to allow the warm air to escape while trapping the cold air. Empty water containers that Shahab had taken to the front gate to be cut up were now hanging from the roof of his tent and used as toiletry storage units. Tamils were now leading their own English classes within tents. There was a mosque tent, and a gym was running in the previously empty demountable. The classroom had shelves, books, a whiteboard, computers. The storerooms had shelves. All this progress but still no housing for the men and still no word on their processing.

Stories of the previous week trickled down by the usual unreliable methods. At least the gossip of Topside was more reliable than the news reports back in Australia. In Australia I was on the wrong side of the iron curtain.

Boorish Sidque had returned to Iraq. A gravestone had been erected in his honour. It was a poignant moment for me. As obnoxious as Sidque was, he had been a character of the camp. His loud bellowing across the yard was more frequent than any bird call. He was the first man I knew personally who had returned to his home country. I wondered what would happen to him.

While I was in Australia Yashar had tried to hang himself from one of the spotlights in the camp. When he climbed the spotlight, shouting and berating people, he drew a large crowd. Then he crawled off the light and dropped. The crowd surged around him, overwhelming the Wilson guards. In the confusion of Yashar being cut down a Tamil had been knocked to the ground leaving him with blood pouring out of his nose. The men were convinced that a Nauruan security guard had punched him. The Wilson guards unanimously claimed that the man had punched himself in the face in an effort to frame the guard.

The Salvation Army had undergone a restructure, the previous management being replaced. I was given the opportunity to meet the new management on my first day back. Just before my return to

Nauru it was reported in the media that the Gillard government was attempting to excise the Australian mainland from the migration zone. If this bill passed, Australia technically would no longer exist to anyone trying to claim asylum without a visa or travel document. More importantly, it would retrospectively legalise the Pacific Solution, a policy that had been in operation for two months. In 2006, Chris Bowen had led a scathing Labor Party response to John Howard's attempts to pass the exact same bill. Bowen had called the policy 'a stain on our national character'.

I was given an official warning by the new management for posting the above quote on my Facebook page. It didn't matter that at the time I posted the comment I was not under contract with the Salvation Army. The message was clear: we were to have no public political opinion whatsoever. Sit down and shut up.

New management brought some positives. There was now an induction upon arrival, and there were teams of staff determined by duties: a recreations team, an education team, a team of cultural advisors, a supplies team, and a social welfare team. Since the Salvos had taken over the canteen, complaints had stopped and the line was non-existent. New rostering for men to collect goods at the store meant no fights and few injustices. There were team meetings at the beginning and end of each shift and a weekly team meeting that all staff were expected to attend. A strict uniform policy had been introduced. Management were intent on restoring professionalism to the Salvos. Meanwhile, some staff were still expected to sleep on site in tents.

While the changes were welcome, my first impression of the new atmosphere in the camp was worrying. Every Salvo had set duties that kept them busy, but where were the Salvos playing cards with the men? Where was the Salvo sitting with the lonely man at the back corner of the camp? Where was the laughter, the fun? All staff were expected to begin taking case notes of their conversations with the men. I understood the need for monitoring the men's wellbeing, but having not come from a case management background I felt it was obtrusive and disloyal. The welfare team had made it their duty to approach all men in the camp at least once a week, but there were not enough staff to implement a comprehensive plan. They had hired two case managers for four hundred men. When they did get the time to find a man, was there a connection? Or was it one more rushed interview among hundreds in an attempt to fulfil contractual obligations? It was a facade of competence.

Survivors of Torture and Trauma Assistance and Rehabilitation Service (STTARS) arrived in Nauru, employed for torture and trauma counselling within the camp. A counsellor for STTARS confessed that torture and trauma counselling within detention centres was ineffective because the men were constantly being retraumatised. She said that the organisation's involvement in the camp was a box-ticking exercise; the best they could hope to do was keep the men alive.

Salvos were expected to travel around the camp in pairs. Women weren't allowed to walk among the tent lines. Male staff were discouraged from sitting in tents with the men for fear these friends of ours would suddenly attack us. Hugging was illegal, touching was discouraged. One Salvation Army HR officer advised new female staff that one of them would most likely be raped within the camp. We were no longer the men's friends. We were their case workers, their professional care, assisting them in their battle by recording their grief. Not by touching them, not by connecting with them. We were providing more services than ever before but I felt that we were losing touch with the men. The more structured the Salvos became as an organisation the more the men became prisoners, patients, clients. When previously Salvos had fought to maintain the men's reputations, now it seemed we agreed with Wilson staff that we had to fear them. The Salvation Army used to celebrate its differences from the other organisations, and I feared that this time round they were conforming to the others' strict regimes.

I was amazed by how much had changed in the camp after just one week. But that was the nature of Topside in the early stages. Despite my misgivings with the Salvation Army mentality, coming back to Nauru felt oddly comforting. I had a job to do, I had a purpose. I was back among people who understood what I had been through. I had received a promotion: I was now the team leader of the new Recreations team. I was excited to get stuck in to my new role and implement some ideas I had been working on. Maybe I should've been concerned about accepting a six-week contract, two weeks longer than my previous rotation, after just one week's respite, but I wasn't. It didn't even cross my mind. It was good to be back.

Chapter 24

THERE WERE JUST three of us in the Rec team, all aged in our twenties. Laura and Chris were both university students, both new to Nauru. Like me, they did not have any experience in social work. We hosted our informal team meetings in a water-stained demountable.

Before the end of my first rotation excursions had been re-introduced to the camp, with limitations on any water-based activities. Risk-assessment procedures had to be followed and any excursion with a risk of drowning was off limits. That meant no swimming, no fishing, not even beach walks in knee-high water. Swimming would not be reintroduced until we had appropriately checked off all risk-assessment suggestions. First and foremost, that meant training qualified lifesavers to supervise the excursions.

Before the Rec team tackled the swimming problem, we focused on establishing an excursion roster for the existing activities we could run. Every man within the camp was given the opportunity to register for excursion groups with their friends. Groups were limited to a maximum of seventeen men, in accordance with the seating limit on the bus. Once registered the group would then be listed in the excursion roster, which gave groups one and a half hours outside the camp at a time. Excursions were restricted to a few locations we had permission to use by the local land owners, but we were scouting more locations to be approved.

In theory the schedule ran perfectly; in reality something always went wrong. One morning when I arrived at the gate of the camp, there was a group of Tamils waiting but there was no bus. I called Dave, the Nauruan bus driver.

'Ah yeah, I'm, ah, just around the corner,' Dave said. It sounded like he'd just woken up.

'Outside?' Suji asked me. Suji was a Tamil with furry ears who loved yoga. *Outside* was his way of asking me if I was taking the excursion.

'The bus is late,' I said.

'Okay. No problem,' he said but I knew he didn't understand me. He turned back to his friends and shook his head. They looked at me and pointed at their watches. Buck-toothed Rasni approached me.

'We are ten minutes late,' he said, speaking in good English, 'so we come back to camp ten minutes later. Okay?'

How many times did they have to try this? 'Come on, Rasni, you know I can't do that. That's not fair on the next group.'

He wobbled his head at me. 'Okay, no problem. I just ask.'

I could understand their annoyance. They were only allowed out once or twice a week—they didn't want their time outside the camp cut short for any reason. I was worried, though. If the men had to wait for too long in the hot sun they might become irritable and leave.

Finally the bus lurched around the corner and drove up to the gate. It parked inside the fence so the men couldn't leave the compound unless they boarded the bus. I gave the Wilson guards a list of the names of the men who were going on the excursion. The men lined up, the Wilson guards took their IDs, examined their faces and then allowed the men to step onto the bus. A few of the men were not on the list. One of our aims for the excursions was to see as many men get out of the camp as possible. Often the buses would not be filled by one group: men would be sick, have English classes, not want to leave that day or at that time. So rather than have empty seats on the buses, we encouraged men to join the bus trips of other groups. This was fine, depending on the Wilson team on duty.

'Wait,' a guard commanded the man in front of him, putting a hand up in his face. Then the guard turned to me and said, 'We can't let them on. They're not on the list.'

Wilson teams rotated every few days and each team had a different view on how excursions should be run. Some were more lenient than others. They wanted to see the men enjoy themselves and allowed anyone on the bus. Some adhered strictly to the rules to avoid getting in trouble and would only allow the prepared list of men to attend. A small minority treated each excursion like a military operation. It was confusing for both the Salvos and for the men.

'The last Wilson team allowed us to fill the bus even if the men weren't on the excursion list. Can you call control and check?' I asked.

'They're not on the list,' the guard repeated. 'We can only take people who are on the list.'

It didn't matter that the Salvo Rec team were the ones who ran the excursions. Security always had the final say.

'Sorry, guys,' I said, turning to the men. 'There's nothing I can do.'

'But there is space,' Sibilraj said. 'Yesterday, no problem.'

I looked at the guard, wanting him to explain why they couldn't go. The guard looked blankly back at me and then at Sibilraj.

'We have to do security checks on every man that leaves the camp,' he said to Sibilraj.

'I am not bad man,' Sibilraj said with a smile. 'I don't make trouble.'

The guard looked at me. 'Are we going?' he asked.

Sibilraj gave the guard a hard stare, then said to me, 'This is no good, no good.' And he stalked off.

Abdul was the last man to arrive. The rest of the Iranians boycotted the excursions, which meant Abdul had no group to go with, and I had to slip him onto another group's list. When Abdul got on the bus I could see that the Tamils were angry. He walked to the back of the bus, sat by himself and looked out the window.

'We do not want him on the bus,' one of the older Tamils said.

'There's space on the bus,' I said.

'We don't want Iran on the bus,' he said. 'Only Tamil. Iran no good.'

Men fleeing from racial prejudice, practising racial prejudice against other men fleeing from prejudice. If men who had experienced oppression could not accept one another irrespective of race or religion, how could they expect the rest of the world to? Their inability to understand the hypocrisy of their views made me tired.

'Too bad,' I said.

Thankfully the Tamils' discontent was quickly forgotten. Once the bus began to move the excursion erupted into life. The restrictive mentality of the hunger strike made living in the camp even more oppressive than usual. Men were discouraged from enjoying themselves in any way. Any show of skylarking was an insult to the starving men. The excursions gave those not hunger-striking the opportunity to escape the gloom. The Tamils, so downcast within the camp during the hunger strikes, blossomed on the excursions. The trips around the island became their outlet. A few bongos and a guitar turned the tour into a music concert. The Tamil men danced in the aisles and serenaded anyone who would listen.

> *Why this* kolaveri kolaveri kolaveri di
> *Why this* kolaveri kolaveri kolaveri di.

'What does it mean?' I asked Rasni.

'It is a song about love, and killer rage,' Rasni said. The singing grew louder still.

'Where to?' I shouted over the roar of Tamil singing.

'Anywhere,' Rasni said.

Right now it didn't matter to the men where they went. It was enough to be given the opportunity to sit on green grass, by the beach, feel the ocean breeze; not to be surrounded by tents, fences and gravel. A chance to experience a touch of real life.

'Tour is very good,' Francis told me. He was a chubby twenty-year-old Tamil with a chicken pox scar in the middle of his forehead.

'We like tour. But we don't like to come back.' He giggled like a schoolgirl.

'I know, buddy.'

I told the bus to pull over at a shop, not waiting for approval from the Wilson guard this time. Francis and his Tamil friends looked about curiously as I got off the bus. *Why had they stopped? They never stop.* I came back with seventeen ice creams in my arms. The men were dumbfounded at first.

'Whose money?' Francis asked. 'No money.' The men showed empty pockets.

'My money,' I replied.

They couldn't believe their luck. The men sat on the bus dripping raspberry Splice ice-creams into their laps, happily sucking on their treats like a bus full of schoolchildren.

The guard pulled me aside for the inevitable talking-to. 'You can't stop the bus. It's a security risk.' Then I heard him radio in to Control at Topside. It was worth it.

Palm Cove was a small area of grass that overlooked a beach. There were palm trees the men weren't allowed to climb. Coconuts that the men weren't allowed to eat. A beach that the men could look at but not walk on. An ocean that the men could look at but not swim in. The road behind them was their border. The locals looked at them but the men were not allowed to talk to them. Sometimes it felt like the harder we fought for their freedom, the more enclosed they became.

The men stood at the edge of the beach, where the grass met the sand. One step away from the sand, not permitted to progress any further. They watched the waves roll in and out.

'Seventeen of us came from the same village in Sri Lanka,' Rasni told me.

I wondered what had happened to their village once they had gone.

'We have one friend not here. He is in Australia,' Rasni said.

'How did that happen?'

'They split us up at Christmas Island.'

'You think he's lucky?' I asked.

'We do, he does not. He wants to be with us.'

'What did you do in Sri Lanka?'

'We are fishermen,' Rasni said. They were all watching the sea. I wasn't sure if I should tell them how beautiful it was underwater in Nauru. 'How long do you stay here?' he asked.

'I'm going home to see my family for Christmas.'

'Your family are on Christmas Island?' he asked, wide-eyed. I started laughing, then stopped myself. It was ridiculous to imagine my family on Christmas Island, wasn't it?

Rasni sat with me to talk about his frustrations. The Tamils believed that the loudest and most confrontational men in the camp were rewarded with attention. There were rumblings from some Tamil men, talk of rising up like the Iranians had and making the organisations listen to their grievances. The majority, however, bore the injustices of being ignored with mild-mannered acceptance like they always did.

'There are many injustices here, small things. But they are injustices,' Rasni said. 'The Iranians always get the best television. They always push in for the food line. Just like this. We are not complaining, just telling you because you are our friend. These things are not big problems. We have dealt with this in our home countries. We have dealt with much worse in our home countries. In Sri Lanka, we could not speak in groups of more than two in the street. Sinhalese police would come and hit us on the head and we would go home. Here we can speak to whoever we want. We can do whatever we want without being told we are bad men, only because we are Tamil. These things in the camp, they are nothing. Sri Lanka was much worse.'

One of the men walked to a tree to urinate. I moved to stop him, knowing that this could aggravate the locals, but one of the large Wilson security guards was there before me.

'What are you doing?' he screamed. 'What are you doing, you dog? Are you a dog? Do you do this in your own country, you dog?'

I was too shocked to defend the man. Everyone looked embarrassed at the guard's reaction.

On the bus back to camp, Jimmy Barnes sang about the choir girl 'crying like a refugee'. None of the men could understand the lyrics. As we arrived back at the gates Rasni looked at me and said, 'Back to hell.'

Chapter 25

PHILIP ZIMBARDO's 1973 Stanford Prison Experiment made revealing observations about the psychology of imprisonment.[1] Zimbardo attempted to test the belief that your environment has a greater influence on your behaviour than who you are. In other words, powerful situations can overcome internal behavioural tendencies.

Zimbardo simulated a prison scenario for a two-week study in which twenty-four volunteers were assigned roles as prisoners or prison guards. It was recorded that within a day of the start of the experiment the true identities of the guards and prisoners seemed to vanish and the roles they were being asked to play took over. Real life and experiment blurred. Zimbardo wrote in his original study that:

> In less than a week the experience of imprisonment undid (temporarily) a lifetime of learning; human values were suspended, self-concepts were challenged and the ugliest, most base, pathological side of human nature surfaced. We were horrified because we saw some boys (guards) treat others as if they were despicable animals, taking pleasure in cruelty, while other boys (prisoners) became servile, dehumanised robots who

thought only of escape, of their own individual survival and of their mounting hatred of the guards.[2]

The experiment reported that guards abused prisoners using degrading and humiliating language. Used tactics of sleep deprivation to torment the prisoners. Punished prisoners with physical tasks such as push-ups. Implemented solitary confinement. Used toilets as a privilege not a right. Stripped prisoners naked as punishment for planned escapes. Quelled a rebellion by turning a fire extinguisher on prisoners. It was noted that the guards enjoyed their sadistic control over the prisoners and were creative and inventive in finding ways of breaking the prisoners' spirits. Furthermore the other guards did not stop them. Even Zimbardo assumed the role of the prison superintendent and forgot his role as a scientist.

The student volunteers could have quit the study at any time but they did not. After several days the men asked to be paroled, but when they were denied they returned to their cells without any more fuss. They obeyed, even though they didn't have to.

The emotional breakdown and stress reactions of five of the prisoner–participants were so extreme that they became depressed, were unable to think clearly and stopped eating. They had to be released from the study within the study's first several days.[3]

Furthermore, it was reported that the prisoners suffered uncontrollable crying and rage, and disorganised thinking. They showed early signs of trauma. They formulated escape plans and rebellions. They eventually gave up all attempts at rebellion and solidarity, assuming an attitude of every man for himself. After six days all the prisoners became completely passive and dehumanised. Robotlike.

The experiment was called off after six days because the mock prison situation was so powerful it had morphed into reality. Zimbardo confessed that he had become more worried about the running of his prison than the needs of the young men entrusted in his care as a psychological researcher.

---

1   RR Hock, 'Chapter X: Social Psychology. Reading 37 A Prison By Any Other Name', *Forty Studies that Changed Psychology: Explorations into the History of Psychological Research*, Pearson, New Jersey, 2012, pp. 286–94.
2   Hock, p. 291.
3   Hock, p. 291.

Chapter 26

THERE WERE ONLY five men on the excursion bus, an intimate affair. I sat next to Jabber. He was a skinny Iraqi with yellow teeth and a goofy grin. He was often around, but rarely spoke. The men made fun of him because he was from the south of Iraq and they couldn't understand his accent. His appearance gave the impression that he could have been a bit slow, but I had learned over time that he understood English even if he didn't speak often. He had a talent for bone-breaking massages that cracked every joint in your body. I attended his parlour every so often, but I didn't tell anyone because it would have been deemed as inappropriate touching and unprofessional. I'd never had a one-on-one conversation with Jabber before this excursion.

'How are you, Jabber?'

'Good. You?' he said, leaning forward earnestly and grinning.

'Very good today,' I said. 'Yesterday I was flat. Too many self-harms yesterday.'

Jabber put his hand on my shoulder in a friendly gesture.

'What did you do in Iraq?' I asked. 'What was your job?'

'I was truck driver,' he said. 'And I work on farm.'

'What kind of farm did you work on?' I had always thought of Iraq as a dusty Middle Eastern desert. I didn't know they had farms.

'A tomato farm.'

'Really? What types of farms are there in Iraq? Do you have crops?'

'Yes. They grow all vegetables in Iraq.'

'Where are you from in Iraq?' I asked.

He named a city I'd never heard of. 'In the south,' he said. 'The British army were there. I used to work for them. That's why I left.'

'Because of your work for them?'

'Yes.' He didn't offer more than that so I didn't ask, but his suddenly downcast look was enough to suggest something bad had happened.

Another Iraqi on my left, Mohammad, began talking. He was older and had a round, pock-marked face.

'I also worked for the US army. I had to flee because of my work for them. Before the US and British armies came, Saddam Hussein was restrictive. There was no freedom of speech, freedom of religion. The US and British came to stop him, but when they pulled down the statue of Saddam Hussein all the soldiers ripped off their uniforms and became civilians. When Iraq became occupied all the terrorist groups like al-Qaeda from the surrounding areas came to our country. They were attracted there by the foreign soldiers and they caused a lot of trouble. Now you can't even cut your hair like that.' He pointed at the razor cuts in the side of Jabber's hair. 'So I fled to Syria. It was good there for a bit, but then came the Arab Spring. Egypt, Libya, and then Syria. In Syria it was a very bad time, very dangerous. So I fled from there as well.'

There was a silence as I mulled over their stories. We had fought Saddam Hussein in Iraq and the Taliban in Afghanistan on the basis of democracy. These men had risked their own lives to assist our armies. They had fled the anarchy, terror and instability that followed the regimes' collapse. And now we placed them in indefinite detention. It didn't seem just.

'What is Sydney like?' Jabber asked.

'Very beautiful,' I said. 'A city of water, boats, parks, blue skies. You can enter Sydney Harbour by boat, pass the Opera House, the

Harbour Bridge, and let the river take you all the way to Parramatta. You can go bushwalking. You can go surfing at the beach. There are animals. It is safe. You can believe in any religion you want. No wars, no bombs, no conflict.'

They were both smiling by the end of my mini speech.

*

I liked running the excursions at Nauru. They gave me time with a small group of men, uninterrupted by requests or complaints. I could see immediate results in my work. The moment a man exited those gates I could see a little bit of tension go out of his body. IHMS staff touted it as the best thing to improve a man's mental health while in detention. I attacked my work with fierce determination—I not only wanted the excursions to run smoothly, I wanted more activities, new activities. The bus tours were never going to be enough for the men. After the initial excitement of leaving the camp wore off, the men wanted more. Inevitably the men's excursion requests reverted back to their greatest desire.

'Swimming?'

I had made contact with John Short, a representative of the Nauru Surf Club. He was an Australian mechanic living on Nauru. He came to our meetings covered in grime. He spoke rough and to the point, 'no bullshit'. Between us it looked like we had the situation with swimming resolved. Fifty Nauruan lifesavers were being trained by an Australian surf lifesaver. Now all the Salvation Army had to do was agree on a financial contract with the Nauru Surf Club.

Meanwhile I battled with Wilson Security management on excursion policy. I saw the excursions as an easy way of improving interaction between the local people and the asylum seekers, and my hope was to foster understanding between the two groups. Yet it was a constant struggle with Wilson Security, who feared that the asylum seekers would approach the local women in an unsavoury manner, cause fights with the men, or associate inappropriately with the children. Considering Topside was supposedly on the verge of becoming an open camp, these kinds of fears and restrictions appeared to be a hindrance to social cohesion.

During one of the trips a Nauruan youngster approached the Hazara men.

'Hi. How ya going?' he asked one of the men.

'He doesn't speak English,' I told the boy.

'What does he speak?'

'Hazaragi. Say *as-salamu alaykum*,' I suggested.

'*As-salamu alaykum*,' the boy repeated slowly, finishing with a smile.

The Hazara smiled broadly. '*Waalaikum as-salaam*.'

We sat down together in the grass.

'Where are they from?' the boy asked me.

'They are from Afghanistan and Pakistan but they are an ethnic group called Hazara,' I said. 'They fled their country because people were trying to kill them.'

'Why were people trying to kill them?' the boy asked.

'Because of the way they look, because of their religion,' I said.

The boy looked at the men sadly and they smiled back at him. 'That's really bad.'

'Yes. It is,' I said. 'Now they are looking for new homes for their families so they can live in a country without the fear of being killed.'

'They can live here,' the boy said immediately. 'Nauru is a very good country. No-one will try to kill them here. And there's lots of good fishing.'

One of the Hazara men with good English thanked him. If only it were that easy.

*

On one trip to the beachside park a few of the Iraqis leaned out of the bus window and began wolf-whistling at women on the side of the road, something the Nauruan people found insulting. It proved that Wilson's fears were not unfounded and it highlighted some of the dangers of introducing the men into the local community. They had little to no connection with women in the camp; sexual frustration was bound to be an issue. The Nauruan community was angry and the Australian organisations were outraged.

As much as the men's actions were inappropriate, these reactions frustrated me. I had observed Nauruan men sleazing onto foreign women over too many drinks at the bar. I had also heard Wilson staff talking about 'ploughing' women and speculating about which Salvo women would be 'up for it'. And yet the thoughtless actions of a few men had once again raised the suspicion that the asylum seekers could commit a sexual offence at any moment. The men were judged as one group despite the mix of ethnicities, religions and personalities. Just as the Iranians' riot would affect all of them in the public eye, disrespectful wolf-whistles from a few Iraqis were to the detriment of all asylum seekers in Nauruan eyes.

The wolf-whistling also highlighted an important point. Not every asylum seeker in Nauru was a nice person. There were men who stole, men who lied, men who played organisations off against each other. There were men who complained bitterly against every rule, and men who berated staff. There were men who I didn't get along with. There were men who had questionable pasts. Every man within the camp had bad days; some had considerably more than others. How much of their behaviour was a reflection of their characters or a side effect of conditions in the camp was difficult to determine, but it must be accepted that when you have four hundred men detained in such conditions there will be unpleasant people among them. But that didn't mean they deserved Nauru.

The United Nations Refugee Convention was not based on personality tests or character assessments. Countries should not prioritise asylum for those people who will assimilate best. These men were to be assessed on their stories. Rather than treat them with mistrust, would it not be better to treat them with kindness to instil a love of our nation and our people? To begin the assimilation process from the beginning, not after years of cruel detention?

The Tamils spoke of a Sinhalese asylum seeker in the camp who had committed a murder in Sri Lanka. When he voluntarily returned to Sri Lanka he was convicted. It is entirely possible that some of the men would have similar stories, highlighting the need for quick and humane screening policies minimising costs to our taxpayers and minimising mental harm to asylum seekers.

A Senate committee on Australia's immigration detention network found that in August 2011, the cost of community detention for the financial year 2010–11 was $17.3 million. Meanwhile the cost of running detention facilities in Australia in 2010–11 was $772.17 million.[1] The Secretary of DIAC assured the committee that community detention provides the department with the necessary access to 'clients in terms of status determination without them being required to be held in detention facilities, often in fairly remote locations'. Not only that, but the committee found that community detention 'produced markedly better mental health outcomes for detainees, which is critical to minimising the harm caused by prolonged detention in confined facilities.'[2]

---

1   Commonwealth of Australia, *Joint Select Committee on Australia's Immigration Detention Network.*
2   Commonwealth of Australia, *Joint Select Committee on Australia's Immigration Detention Network.*

Chapter 27

RUNNING EXCURSIONS ALL day distanced me from what was happening in the camp. Arriving back in the centre after a day on excursions felt like being submerged in dark water. Every day the hunger strike continued, more and more men had to be carried to IHMS by Wilson guards, too weak to move themselves. Many of the men had stopped eating and some of the men had stopped drinking water as well. A makeshift treatment area was set up to rehydrate patients with drips and cool them down with high-powered fans. The men were determined not to eat until a certain day in November, when apparently a petition to close down Nauru signed by a number of Australian residents would be given to Australian Parliament. None of the staff working at Nauru knew of the petition. It wasn't uncommon for the men to latch on to small pieces of news like this and follow them religiously. Any time a report was published on the asylum seeker topic, an asylum seeker would have the article uploaded to a USB and screening on one of the televisions in the Green Room for all the men to see. Whether such glimmers of hope would achieve anything was unlikely, yet it gave the men something to look forward to. I wasn't sure if ultimately this would help them. Or when nothing came of the petition, it would sink them deeper into depression.

Until that date, IHMS was inundated with sick men. It was not uncommon to see a man collapse in the middle of the camp. His legs would buckle underneath him and his body would flop to the floor. Over and over again I saw this.

My most personal touch with the strike came when I visited Pezhman. I found him lying on his stretcher in the steaming hot tent, staring blankly at the roof. I sat down next to him and he hardly moved to acknowledge me. I didn't want to talk to him about the hunger strike, but seeing him in so much trouble drew me to tears.

'Pez. What are you doing to yourself?'

He looked at me and his eyes almost rolled into his head.

'We start hunger strikes because we want our freedom,' he said. 'We want to complain in a peaceful way. They don't care about us until the hunger strike started. After that they listen to us. *What do you want? What's your problem? Why did you start hunger strike?*'

'What is it like?' I asked him.

'If you want to start hunger and thirst strike together it is very hard,' he said and tried to lick his lips. It sounded like two pieces of sandpaper scraping together. 'You wish for one drop of water, not water, a drop of water. You wish every second, not every minute or every hour, every second you wish for one drop of water. It's very hard. You feel too much pain on your kidneys, too much pain. You feel very weak. You don't have enough energy to do anything. You feel like a dead person. Even breathing is very hard for you.'

I wanted him to stop but I was immersed in his suffering.

He continued. 'After three days you just can't move anymore. It is very hard. But they don't care about us until one important part of your body stops, and then they care. You see many guys here do suicide or hurt themselves. They do this because they don't want to harm the others. They just harm themselves. They want to show their feelings.'

'So now that they are listening will you stop?' I asked.

I was searching for some inkling of hope but beneath his emaciated appearance there was steel in his gaze.

A day later, to the relief of everyone involved in the centre, the camp-wide hunger strike came to an end.

*

Once the hunger strike had ended there was an abundance of food to be eaten. Energy returned to the camp. The Tamils began to play volleyball again. The excursions began attracting full buses. Everyone was happy just to be eating again. While the strike had ended, the culture of eating within tents remained. It was more intimate this way. When asked to sit with them and share their food, I accepted graciously. Food was the one thing they could offer us. Dining with them was a pleasure I willingly accepted. It was one of the better times in the Nauru Regional Processing Centre.

Namdar was the only man who remained on hunger strike. He was determined to starve himself into Australia. Eventually he reached fifty days without eating. His skin had turned a mustard yellow and stretched tight across his skull. His legs and arms had lost all of their sinew and muscle. He was hardly strong enough to stand. Wilson guards and Salvos tried to negotiate with him.

'You must eat,' they said.

'Why?' he asked.

The Australian government had no offer for him, so he continued to starve himself. He was willing to die on that island, miles away from home, such was his determination to get to Australia. He was taken to the Nauruan hospital, almost a worse punishment than the camp. Still he refused all food and water. When he lost consciousness IHMS nurses fed him via a drip. Eventually an emergency evacuation transported him to Brisbane. It was said by Salvo management that the cost of a medevac out of Nauru was close to $80,000. The Department of Foreign Affairs and Trade quotes a medevac out of Bali to exceed $60,000.[1] He was the second asylum seeker to leave Nauru by medevac for Australian shores. There were bound to be more.

*

Before I left work every day I tried to do a round of the camp and talk to as many of the men as I could. Taking excursions meant that I didn't get to speak to my friends in the camp as often as I used to. I wandered over to the Iraqi tent and the men stood up to acknowledge my presence. It was a polite custom of theirs.

'Yaqub,' I cried out to my dear friend.

'Hey man,' he said. He took my hand in some kind of gangster shake he'd seen in a movie. 'Call me Omar.'

'Why?'

'My friends used to call me that.'

'So?'

'Two of them were killed in Iraq the other day.'

I nodded. Every day news like this slapped you in the face.

'Sit,' Mustafa said, politely offering me his chair.

Jabber was combing his thick hair back over his head and behind his ears, using way too much gel.

'So how was Nauru without me?' I asked.

'Oh you know, all the tents, and football and shit.' Omar smiled sadly. When you put it like that it was all so meaningless. Football was their life, tents were their life. It was all shit.

Mohammad sat forward earnestly and got Omar to translate for him.

'*Gile, gile,* Omar,' Mohammad said, Arabic for 'tell him, tell him'.

'He wants to know if you think it's possible to have a relationship between one of us and a Salvation Army girl,' Omar said with a half-smile, trying not to let the earnest Mohammad see. This was precarious ground.

'It's possible that feelings can develop between you,' I said. 'I mean one of you guys and a Salvo. But I don't think it's a good idea for anything to happen.'

Mohammad wanted to know why.

'Because for one, it is bad for her. She may lose her job. It is not allowed,' I said. 'And then it is bad for you, because you won't get to see her again. It is a very bad situation.'

I felt for Mohammad. He looked so disappointed.

'It is my son's birthday today,' Mustafa said. 'I want to send him a gift. Do you think it is possible?'

I sighed. 'I don't know. All I can do is fill out a request form and try.'

Mustafa leaned back in his chair with a smile. 'You don't know. Always this. *I don't know* and *I try. Maybe, no promises, sorry.*'

There was nothing else I could say to him.

'You need to learn this in Arabic. *Madre*,' he said.

'*Madre*,' I repeated. The guys all laughed. '*Walla, walla*,' I said beating my heart. Which meant 'I'm serious', and the guys laughed harder.

'What is happening with your family?' I asked Mustafa.

'Every month or two or three weeks I move my family to another house,' Mustafa said. 'I have two children and when I phone them I just ask, "Hi, how are you," and then I finish. I can't talk with them for more than one minute because I am crying. When they ask how long I will be here, I say, "I don't know. Who knows? Immigration?"'

'I want to learn Spanish,' Yaqub told me. 'Why not, huh? I have all this time, I should do something with it.'

'Yeah, that sounds good,' I agreed.

'Can you get me a Spanish dictionary?' he asked, knowing what my answer would be.

'*Madre*,' I said. 'I'll try.'

'And what about cigarettes? There are no cigarettes anywhere, man,' Omar said.

Every so often the camp had cigarette shortages and all the men suffered. I was sure a black market sprung up at these occasions. He knew I didn't have any, I never did, but he always asked me.

'You should stop smoking,' I said.

'You know I only started smoking in Nauru,' Omar said. 'All of us started here.'

'Why did you start here?'

'I don't know. Something to do. It passes the time,' he said.

Mustafa took me aside and showed me a thick wad of paper.

'I am to be taken to court,' he said, fear lurking in his eyes and his voice. I briefly looked over the papers. There was a summons to the Nauruan court and witness statements from the night of the riot.

'I was not there,' Mustafa said. 'I was not involved. I talked to Wilson guard and I ask them why me and they say, "I don't know." I say to him, "I did not do anything," and they say, "We know." They say, "You were angry but you did not break anything." So why am I here?'

Mustafa was charged with three offences under the Nauru Criminal Code, which is based on a superseded version of the Queensland Criminal Code.

1. Section 63—Riot

2. Section 469—Wilful damage

3. Section 66—Riotous injury to building, machinery, property

When I read over the witness statements there was no mention of Mustafa anywhere. I could see no evidence that he was involved. Funnily enough, Sidque was mentioned. *Good luck getting him back from Iraq,* I thought.

If I became involved in this I would be working outside of the Salvation Army's 'mission brief'. It could put my job at risk.

'I'll see what I can do,' I told him. No promises.

When I passed Pezhman's tent he called me in, his manner secretive. He pulled out a bundle of papers and asked me what I thought. It was the same summons to the Nauruan court.

'This is bad,' he said to me. 'On the night I did not do any damages. I did not break anything. I was asked to be the interpreter. The police, they ask me to come and talk. They told me that nothing would happen, that this would be a warning, our only warning, and now I go to court with these charges. I am not mentioned in any witness statement.'

He did not hide his fear like Mustafa. It was etched in the worry lines that creased his forehead and the corners of his eyes.

'Have you spoken to the police?'

'No.'

'Have you spoken to a lawyer?'

'No.'

'Have they given you one?' I asked.

'They have told us nothing. I have not talked to the police. I have not seen a lawyer. I have not talked to Wilson about this. The Salvation Army have said nothing to me. No-one. Nothing,' he replied. 'There were fifteen men on the list. Only three men were taken to the police station on the night of the riot.'

'I'll help you as much as I can,' I told him. No promises.

'No-one else will,' he said.

The rumour going around the camp was that a conviction on riot charges could mean life imprisonment. I should have known they were incorrect. A Nauruan policeman told me that riot charges needed a certain number of people involved to be considered riot charges. Once they were classified as riot charges there were incremental punishments depending on the number of people involved. Was that why they had placed as many men on the charge sheet as possible? Even then I didn't know if what the police officer had told me was right. No-one seemed to be certain of anything in Nauru.

It was yet another dubious situation where the men were rendered powerless. The men were already forced to cope with the uncertainty of their visas, their processing, their future. If they were charged they would never be resettled in Australia.

I waited to see if anything would be done to assist the men. The day before the men were due in court they still had not met with a lawyer or been given any legal advice. I made the decision to help my friends. I obtained the contact details of a Nauruan lawyer called Silv Peres, who I had been advised had a connection to the case. I called him the night before the men were due in court.

'I'm calling on behalf of the men at Topside who will be going to court tomorrow,' I said. 'Could you explain what will be happening tomorrow?'

He explained the next day's proceedings to me without any explanation from me of who I was or what I did.

'Okay. Well, tomorrow is just a mention. The judge will see the men, identify them and ask for details of their case. Have they seen a lawyer, have they given a police statement? These kind of things. They will not have to plead in any way. Do you think they will need me there?'

'Yes. Most definitely,' I said. 'They have no knowledge of what is happening. They've not seen a lawyer, not had their charges explained to them, not given any statements to police. They have no help. They need you.'

'Okay,' he said. 'Will they need an interpreter?'

I was sure DIAC would provide interpreters, but it was never a bad thing to have more. 'Yes. They don't speak English,' I answered.

'We have a Tamil man at the court,' the man replied.

'They're Iranian and Iraqi,' I replied. 'Can you explain their charges to me?'

'I don't know what they are,' the lawyer responded.

It was the best I could do at such short notice. The next day the men boarded the bus for the courthouse. When they arrived there they refused to leave the bus. They believed that by entering the court, they were accepting the authority of the Nauruan government. Furthermore, no legal representation had been provided. The discussion lasted for two hours, stewing up a range of emotions inside them. Fear and worry soon reverted back to their prevailing emotional state in Nauru of frustration and anger.

When they were eventually introduced to Silv Peres, they laughed. He was wearing thongs. They asked for evidence of his accreditation. He had none. These things didn't exist in Nauru. How could they know if he was a real lawyer or just a man off the street? In this Nauruan nightmare nothing was impossible.

When they finally decided to enter the court, Jawad curled up against the window of the bus and refused to leave. He was far away from home, in a foreign land that didn't speak his language, facing a court case that could put him in prison for a very long time. He had every right to be scared.

The men presented themselves to the magistrate and the trial was adjourned for another two weeks because the men had not been given appropriate legal representation and because the police case was not finalised. Every two weeks the men were brought out of the camp and taken to court, only for the trial to be adjourned for the same reasons. This happened repeatedly from the beginning of December to the end of February. I later discovered that if found guilty of the three charges the men could face up to thirteen years hard labour.

----

1   Australian Department of Foreign Affairs and Trade, 'Travel Insurance', *Smartraveller*, viewed Saturday 9 November 2013, <www.smartraveller.gov.au/tips/insurance.html>.

Chapter 28

JOEL TWISTED BACK the throttle with his right hand. The motor-bike roared, then kicked backwards. The three of us sitting in the three-wheeled trailer attached to it almost fell off the sides.

'Woah, ease up fella,' I shouted out.

'Hold on,' he shouted back and did it again.

Laura, Chris and I grabbed on to the edges of the trailer to stop ourselves from falling out. The four of us had hired the motorbike and trailer for the day. It was a novelty more than anything else. A trip to Capelle's, up to the bomber track with the old Japanese guns, down to the lake, and then another lap of the island. It was better than spending another day reading books and watching movies on our laptops.

'Have you heard Omar's story?' Laura asked me.

'Yeah.'

'It's all so tragic,' she said. 'This place, I feel so guilty for working here.'

My second rotation was already moving in a different direction to my first. I was an old hand now. Most of the staff I had been friends with weren't coming back to Nauru. The new staff arriving seemed to be going through the adjustment period I had already dealt with.

'Don't you feel like you're a part of the system?' Laura asked.

'I guess there are two ways of looking at it,' I said. 'You can work from within the system to do good, or you can condemn the system from the outside.'

It wasn't that I didn't feel guilty about working in Nauru anymore. It's just that I had made my decision to stay and I was going to do the most I could for the men while I was there.

'How are the swimming plans going?' Chris asked.

Swimming excursions were a dream for staff and asylum seekers alike. Everyone knew that a lot of tension within the camp could be alleviated with daily swimming.

'We're close,' I said. 'We have fifty Nauruan lifesavers trained. The contract between the Nauru Surf Club and the Salvos is almost finalised. Once that's agreed we will just need approval from DIAC.'

'Close' was a prediction based on hope rather than expectation. Waiting on approval from DIAC was like waiting for Godot.

'There aren't as many dogs on the street as before,' I said to Joel.

'They killed them all,' Joel said. 'Did a cull.'

'Is that a Naurumour?' I asked.

'Could be.'

We stopped off at the wooden pergolas opposite the Capelle's megastore and tucked in to our $5 burger and soft drink specials. The pergolas overlooked the beach and were caressed by a sea breeze. There were good reasons why IHMS held relaxation groups there for the asylum seekers.

'Where do you want to eat tonight?' I asked the group.

'The Bay,' Laura suggested.

'No,' Joel said. 'The Bay has never been good to me.'

I agreed. I didn't want butter chicken tonight.

'Zhongis, then,' said Laura.

'Nah,' I said. I didn't want lemon chicken tonight either.

'Why bother asking?' Laura said. 'The Menen it is.'

Joel and I shook our heads. 'Overpriced.'

'Fine,' she said. 'Eat two-minute noodles.'

A dog sauntered over, head bowed, looking at us out of the corner of an eye. It was a runty mutt with an injured hind leg. A fear of the wild dogs had been fostered among the foreign staff out of hyperbolised stories of attacks.

Joel held out a chip for the dog. Instead of taking it the dog shied away, mistaking the kind offer for some kind of trick.

'He's scared of humans, is all. He thinks it's a trap,' Joel said. 'Come on, fella.'

He threw the chip over to the dog, making it jump. After a minute of pacing around the chip, the dog nipped in and gobbled it up.

'That's what happens when you're cruel to them all the time. They get scared,' Joel said.

Gradually, Joel worked the dog closer to him by offering it chips until it was eating out of his hands. At that moment a Nauruan walked past and shouted at the dog. The dog scuttled away and didn't come back.

Chapter 29

Six hazara men lined up against six Iraqis at the Topside Stadium. The 15 metre by 30 metre football pitch was situated behind the Green Room at the back of the camp. The pitch was strewn with rocks that turned ankles and tore players' knees open. The back fence of the pitch and the camp looked onto the pinnacles. One sideline was bordered by green army tents. A crowd had gathered along the sand-marked sidelines for the first game of the season. The players shook hands, the crowd clapped.

The Nauru Premier League was an initiative of the Recreation team. We had registered eleven teams in its inaugural season: two Hazara teams, one Iraqi team, one Pakistani team, one Sinhalese team, five Tamil teams, and one Salvation Army team. The efficient running of the competition relied upon the men. The captains of each team organised the games, the referees and the disciplinary hearings. It was their competition.

The Hazaras were a clinical outfit, having already recorded one footballing title on Christmas Island. The Iraqis were larger men, stronger. They used their physical dominance to keep the Hazaras' skill in check. A yellow card was awarded to Habib for a bad foul; his indiscretion was recorded by the referee. Two more in the season and he would receive a one-match suspension.

The Hazaras took control of the match and began passing the ball around, making the Iraqis run. The rubbish-bin goalposts were keeping the Iraqis in the match. Fayiz was goalkeeping for the Iraqis, despite being on voluntary starvation and marked as a medically high-risk patient. He plucked out a cross with his monster hands and waved appreciatively to the crowd. His smile had returned.

Habib ran at the Hazara defence, shimmying this way and that, sticking his tongue out, performing audacious step-overs. His show-boating was a shining light of brilliance in the Iraqi juggernaut. The Hazara pressure eventually paid off. A weak back pass was pounced upon by Salar and guided past the keeper. Angry Arabic spewed out of the six Iraqis as Salar wheeled away to celebrate. One–nil.

The Iraqis fought back and came close to scoring. A volleyed shot zipped over the tops of the bins. The Iraqis celebrated the goal but the rules were clear. The bin height was the goal height. No goal. As the match wore on the crowd grew to a hundred. Men sat in clusters analysing the game. It was entertainment in a camp that lacked excitement, unexpected but welcome. The league would bring matches every afternoon for months. This scared some. *We will be here for months?* But for many the league was a daily focus.

The Hazaras countered the Iraqi pressure and scored a beautiful goal that finished with Salar rounding the keeper at pace and sliding the ball between the bins. Two–nil. The Iraqis were broken. With minutes to go the Hazaras scored a third. It should have been game over, but shooting at the Pinnacle end of Topside Stadium had its risks. A loose shot from the Hazaras sent a ball bouncing perilously close to the edge of the camp. If the ball had cleared the fence the result would have been reversed. A 3–0 forfeit to the Iraqis. The punishment for losing a ball was harsh but necessary. There was a severe shortage of footballs in Nauru.

The ball wasn't lost and the match finished 3–0 to the Hazaras. The game was over but the league had only just begun.

Chapter 30

In NOVEMBER two delegates from Amnesty International spent three days visiting the Nauru Regional Processing Centre. Amnesty was to be the first organisation outside of the service providers to be allowed into the camp. The men hoped that once Australia saw what was really going on in Nauru the government would have to close it down.

During the same three-day period, media arrived in Nauru. The Amnesty delegates were granted entry to examine the camp and interview the men; the media were detained at the gate. Despite claiming that the men were free to contact media outlets, DIAC cancelled all excursions out of the camp so the reporters could not meet the men.

Amnesty released a damning condemnation of the conditions at the camp and the treatment of the men.

> Amnesty International researchers found the facility totally inappropriate and ill-equipped, with 387 men cramped into five rows of leaking tents, suffering from physical and mental ailments—creating a climate of anguish as the repressively hot monsoon season begins.[1]

Amnesty's criticisms included the lack of psychological care; poor toilet facilities; the lack of space; the tents, the way the tents drew heat in the sun, and leaked water in the rain; but above all else, the effect the indefinite nature of the detention was having on the men's psychological wellbeing. Minister Chris Bowen dismissed these claims, saying that staff working at Topside were living under the same conditions. What he failed to mention was that the majority of staff were living in hotel rooms. Those who were on site had the freedom to leave. They were in Nauru being paid, supporting their families, progressing in life, while the asylum seekers were stuck in Nauru with no knowledge of when they could leave, with their families growing poorer still without their breadwinners.

The day Amnesty left Nauru DIAC released two papers to the asylum seekers in anticipation of an announcement by Chris Bowen. The first paper provided information regarding the refugee processing, while the second described the family reunification process. According to DIAC, claims for refugee status would be assessed under Nauruan law by Nauruan government officials. This assessment process was still being discussed and developed by the Australian and Nauruan governments. Once agreed, the Nauruan government would need to recruit qualified staff and interpreters and arrange accommodation for them. Then, the two governments had to agree on a contract for Australia to provide assistance to the Nauruan government. Only then would the Nauruan government be ready to begin the assessments.

'It is not known, at this stage, exactly how long it will take to hear and assess your refugee claim once the process has been established,' the DIAC information sheet said. 'It is not possible to say precisely how long you may need to remain on Nauru. Remember that you can decide to leave Nauru voluntarily at any time.'

As part of the No Advantage policy the family reunion visa options had been changed so that 'Irregular Maritime Arrivals' could no longer bring immediate family to Australia using refugee or humanitarian visas, even if they were granted a protection visa.

The DIAC information sheet stated that:

The right way is for your family to:
- *register with their nearest United Nations' refugee agency (UNHCR), or*
- *apply through Australia's family migration program—if you obtain a permanent visa*

On paper, as a theoretical policy, it was a deterrent. For the men in Nauru, who had already made their journeys, it was further punishment from a policy that had been created after they had left their home countries. Who knew how long it would be until they saw their families again? It was bureaucratic discrimination, the sword of the Western world for hundreds of years.

The Houston panel stated that:

The single most important priority in preventing people from risking their lives on dangerous maritime voyages is to recalibrate Australian policy settings to achieve an outcome that asylum seekers will not be advantaged if they pay people smugglers to attempt dangerous irregular entry into Australia instead of pursuing regular migration pathways and international protection arrangements as close as possible to their country of origin. [2]

The idea was that those who came on boats were cheating other refugees. That there were systems in place where people could wait under international protection. I sought out Salar, my long-haired Hazara friend. I wanted to know what he thought of this.

'Why didn't you come to Australia by the correct channels?' I asked him. He looked at me suspiciously. It was a rude question in Nauru, an accusation. But I knew Salar well enough to get an answer out of him. 'Why didn't you apply through the United Nations?' I pressed.

'Correct channels?' he asked. 'You show me the Australian embassy in Afghanistan. You see if a Hazara man can go there without being shot. If you go to the Australian embassy they ask you why you want to leave. If you say you have a problem, they say it is not enough. Many people have tried. We cannot go to our government and ask for visas. We are not even allowed to study in Afghanistan. How do I apply for a visa to Australia when my government wants to kill me? If you want to go to the United Nations office in Quetta, Pakistan, it is in a dangerous area. People recognise Hazara faces and they target them easily. If you go there, you have to stay for a long time and it is dangerous. Maybe you will be targeted. You think we would leave our homes if we didn't have to? You think I'd leave my family if I didn't have to?'

I tried asking Yaqub and Mustafa the same question, again knowing that there was potential to insult them with such words as *correct channels*. Again, I believed my friendship with them would allow me to play devil's advocate.

'That's very funny,' Mustafa said sardonically. 'It is impossible to leave Iraq by the correct channels. Where can I go to get a visa? You show me the Australian embassy and tell me that they will give me a visa. You know if you take the boat, you have two chances, life or death. If you stay in Iraq you are sure you will die, and not just you, your family as well.'

'Why did you choose Australia?' I asked. 'Of all the countries in the world, why Australia?'

'It's a freedom country,' he said. 'You can have your rights in Australia. We heard there was justice in Australia. We don't need anything, just freedom, justice, what is right for any normal human. I don't need someone to give me money. I have my job and I can work.'

Little Devkumar was a skinny Tamil. I called him Little Devkumar to differentiate him from my friend Dev. He had a wife and children in Sri Lanka who he wanted to bring to Australia. He told me that if they went to refugee camps they would have to wait years to be resettled. He said his children would go through puberty in a refugee camp. Maybe they would have to raise their children in a refugee camp. And that was if they could make it to a camp. The act of fleeing was dangerous, whether he fled for a refugee camp or fled to Australia. Either way the government could find out he had left and could punish his family. He told me this with a broad smile, a genial head wiggle and tears in his eyes. The average wait in a United Nations refugee camp was seventeen years.[3]

People talk of the proper channels of seeking asylum, of a queue of refugees waiting to be relocated to Western countries. *If asylum seekers can't understand these rules or deliberately try to circumvent the law they deserve to be treated like this.* I wondered where such a queue would start. From when people first start to be oppressed or just when they make it to a camp? Who is at the front of this queue? Who is at the end? If the system dictates that a man wanting safety for his family has to wait a lifetime in a camp to achieve it, of course he will try anything to avoid this. Who would want their family to grow up in a refugee camp? And what happens when you can't get to the queue? When these so called 'correct channels' aren't available? How does one seek safety then?

There are several ways to enter Australia as a refugee, which are categorised into two distinct groups, the Offshore Resettlement Program and Onshore Protection.

The Offshore Resettlement Program assesses and recognises refugees who reside outside Australia.[4] The majority of these applicants are identified by the United Nations High Commissioner for Refugees (UNHCR) and taken from UNHCR refugee camps and settled in Australia.

Onshore Protection applies to refugees who are already in Australia. In this instance, refugees can enter Australia with a valid visa, such as a student or tourist visa, and then apply to be recognised as a refugee. Or they could arrive in the Australian migration zone by sea or by air and then apply for asylum.

According to international law, to arrive in a country that is a signatory to the UN Refugee Convention without identification documents and apply for asylum is not illegal, regardless of the manner in which you come. The UN convention recognises the difficulties refugees face in fleeing from persecution and as such outlines that what would usually be considered to be illegal actions, such as entering a country without a visa, should not be treated as illegal if a person is seeking asylum.[5]

According to Australian law, arriving in Australian migratory zones without a visa is 'unlawful'. This term is misleading. The Australian government's own website states:

> Asylum seekers irrespective of their mode of arrival, like others that arrive in Australia without a valid visa, are classified by Australian law to be 'unlawful non-citizens'. However, the term 'unlawful' does not mean that asylum seekers have committed a criminal offence. There is no offence under Australian law that criminalises the act of arriving in Australia or the seeking of asylum without a valid visa.[6]

The government website also states that:

> If UNHCR assesses a refugee to be eligible for resettlement it does not mean that they have joined an orderly 'queue', and that they will be guaranteed resettlement to another country when their 'number comes up'.[7]

The Refugee Council of Australia reports that:

> Resettlement is intended to be a complement to, not a substitute for, providing protection to refugees who apply for asylum onshore. It is a way of providing a solution for refugees who have been unable to find effective protection elsewhere, but is certainly not the standard or only 'legitimate' way to find protection.[8]

The sheer number of refugees looking to be resettled makes a mockery of any notion of an orderly queue. There are roughly 45.2 million forcibly displaced people worldwide. Among this number are 15.4 million refugees and 937,000 asylum seekers.[9] Even in the UNHCR camps, where the queue is supposed to start, people are not processed by order of arrival; rather, they do it by order of need. The Refugee Council of Australia describes the UN resettlement system as a lottery rather than a queue.[10]

Later that day Chris Bowen made a public announcement. Asylum seekers who had arrived after 13 August 2012 were now being given bridging visas and were to be processed in communities in Australia. Christmas Island was sending asylum seekers to the mainland. Men on the same boats as those in Nauru, men who had arrived on boats after those in Nauru, were being awarded bridging visas to Australia while the likes of Raj, Dev and Yaqub wallowed in tents far, far away from their final destination. The 'queue' so often quoted by supporters of the policy had been redefined, punishing the four hundred men on Nauru.

The mood at the camp festered. Rashid sat alone, curled up against a pole. I went to sit down with him as he cried but as I lowered myself to the ground he got up and walked away from me. I walked over to Pezhman and a group of laughing Hazaras.

'Look after Rashid,' I said to Pezhman. 'I'm worried about him.'

Pezhman turned to me with angry eyes. 'Don't think because we laugh that we are happy. We are all dying inside.' Once again the divide was set between asylum seekers and Salvo. I realised that as much as I thought I understood their plight, I never could.

That night Shahab tried to hang himself in his tent.

———————

1   Amnesty International, *A Human Rights Catastrophe with No End in Sight*, 2012, viewed 1 December 2012, <www.amnesty.org.au/news/comments/30533/>.
2   Aristotle, Houston & L'Estrange, p. 11.
3   Refugee Council of Australia, *Myths about Refugees and Asylum Seekers*, 2011, viewed 23 March 2013, <www.refugeecouncil.org.au/f/myth-long.php>.
4   Australian Human Rights Commission, *2012 Face the Facts*, 2012, viewed 23 August 2013, <www.humanrights.gov.au/publications/face-facts-2012/2012-face-facts-chapter-3>.
5   UNHCR, *The 1951 Convention Relating to the Status of Refugees and its 1967 Protocol*.
6   J Phillips & H Spinks 2011, *Boat arrivals in Australia since 1976*, Parliament of Australia, viewed 25 August 2013, <www.aph.gov.au/About_Parliament/Parliamentary_Departments/Parliamentary_Library/pubs/BN/2011-2012/BoatArrivals#_Toc285178607>.
7   B Karlsen 2011, *Refugee resettlement to Australia: What are the facts?*, Parliament of Australia, viewed 25 August 2013 <www.aph.gov.au/About_Parliament/Parliamentary_Departments/Parliamentary_Library/pubs/BN/2011-2012/RefugeeResettlement>.
8   Refugee Council of Australia, *Myths about Refugees and Asylum Seekers*, February 2001, <http://www.refugeecouncil.org.au/f/myth-long.php>.
9   Williams, 'The Nauru 10: The Habeus Corpus Challenge'.
10 Refugee Council of Australia 2011, *Myths about Refugees and Asylum Seekers*.

Chapter 31

A TEMPEST SWEPT through the camp, flipping tent flaps and soaking the men's sleeping quarters. Every time Shahab attempted to commit suicide it rained. I thought of Pezhman's comment, 'God is crying for us'. Shahab's tent was flooded. The wooden pallets moved when I stepped on them. Water dripped from the ceiling. He was lying on his cot, draped from head to toe in a blue sheet. I had stepped inside a subterranean crypt. I sat down next to him and placed my arm on his chest. It was all bone. He stirred and pulled the sheet away from his face. He was pale and emaciated.

'I'm sorry,' he said.

I took his hand and held it tight.

'I'm sorry,' he repeated.

We embraced. His little ribs felt like they might break.

'I'm sorry, I'm sorry, I'm sorry, I'm sorry, I'm sorry, I'm sorry, I'm sorry, I'm sorry, I'm sorry.'

I felt each apology like a burn across my chest. One, two, nine burns. Shahab cried out in anguish, as if the very act of being alive pained him. All he wanted was to die. We cried together as the rain came down.

'I love you,' he said.

'I love you too,' I replied.

Then I left him in his floating crypt.

The rain did not stop. It came down in torrents for hours and hours, flooding the camp and exposing all the gaps and holes in the tents. The poor irrigation system meant the tracks between tents became rivers. The Iraqis used a pallet as a ferry. The water accumulated between the Green Room and the demountables, creating a large pool. The men had got their wish: they could finally swim. It was the start of the monsoon period.

Fayiz and Mustafa set up chairs in the middle of the pool. A defiant stance against the rain or against their oppressors? Iraqis joined them and Assad began the hair salon, everyone shin-deep in brown water. A crowd formed on the edges of the Green Room. Ulla and I grappled in the middle of the pool before falling in a heap, drawing cheers of delight from the crowd. We performed freestyle in the muddy water and the crowd roared. Ali, a large Pakistani, took his shirt off and began washing his hair and chest with shampoo while the rain teemed down.

'You're shivering,' I said to Omar. Goosebumps had emerged all over his bare arms, and he was shaking uncontrollably.

'Oh shit, you're right,' he said, looking at the skin on his arms in surprise and laughing. 'Shivering in Nauru, who would've thought.'

A ball emerged and a spontaneous game of water football erupted. The crowd grew and became more excited. Large Iraqis splashed in deep puddles, performers not players. Habib celebrated a scrappy goal by pulling his shirt over his head and wheeling away from the match towards the crowd. He swan-dived into the shallows, forgetting that beneath the water remained a gravelly rock surface. The onlookers buckled over with laugher.

It was an odd juxtaposition. Just five minutes earlier I had been comforting a suicidal *Dosh* Shahab, now I was entertaining the crowds. The soccer match became a rugby game. Men fell onto the hard rock but it didn't matter—all of the men in the rain were possessed by a spirit that placed them outside of normal societal conventions. A man was tackled into a concrete step and stood up without injury. Wilson guards laughed rather than stopping the game due to occupational health and safety issues. I was picked up by the Iraqis and paraded around the camp, cajoled by the men, and no-one tried to stop them. The onlookers enjoyed a vicarious buzz from the antics. Their homes were flooded, the heart of the monsoon period was imminent, but somehow they had enjoyed the rain.

*

Salar wrote this poem on a request form.

The fearful life and situation in my place
Made me pause and think for a while
Somewhere I could flee in a safe space
Somewhere my family can smile
I showed them hope, I showed them life
Ransomed everything for a peaceful night
Who would understand my pain
As I am crying in the rain
Only memories left and I am weak
Can't do this journey ever again
I left with a dream of safe haven at night
Hiding my loved ones promising no more tears
Taking the journey that nearly cost my life
I left with a dream expecting no fears
Reached a place where I felt now safe
Eager to share my loved ones this news
But am shocked to be in such a place
Without a destiny, so confused
All I ask is freedom, just freedom
Why you put me here
You caged my wings and my feet
Left me with memories that was once sweet
Who would understand my pain
As I am crying in the rain

Chapter 32

AFTER CHRIS BOWEN'S announcement that asylum seekers were being released into Australian communities the camp stalled. Kazem sat against a pole staring into space. Nothing I could do would make him smile or respond. He shook his head over and over again with tears in his eyes. He had never looked so young. He was twenty-seven. Hussein wouldn't respond either. He lay on his bed looking at the roof of his tent. His mum was sick, Salar explained. He was sick. He was twenty-one.

I could usually find welcoming faces among the Iraqis but when I arrived at their tent I was met with hostility. Omar looked at me with mustered spite. 'I am going to kill myself, I am just thinking of the best way to do it. I want it to be quick, efficient. Should I hang myself? Or cut my throat?'

He pulled his shirt up, defiant, to reveal cigarette burns along his stomach. My heart sank low. I sat among them waiting for the barrage.

Mustafa took up where Omar left off. 'We are put here to be forgotten about. Why else would they process the people that arrived on the same boat as me, but not me? Why were we brought here if not to be punished? This is where we will all die. I will not see my son again. I will die here.'

They all had a turn, as if I were a punching bag in a gym. 'Why us? Why are we stuck in this hell and the others are being processed? Where is the justice?'

'They sent four hundred people to Nauru and they released thousands into the community in Australia and they say they don't have advantage over us. It's not justice. Just being free, outside, is an advantage in itself, right?' Omar said.

I couldn't offer any condolences. Any words of advice would be hollow. I could empathise but I could not understand. I had never felt so separate from them. The power imbalance between us would always divide us. I left their tent, an unwanted guest.

Pez was lying on his bed looking weak and sick. I sat down next to him and he barely rolled over.

'I want to die,' he said without looking at me. 'There is nothing here for me. I have no more hope here. I do not want to spend one more day in this camp.'

The despair was all around me, in the people I admired most. Even the most optimistic were drooping.

'I will not eat or drink. I have made my choice. I have said good-bye to my family in my head.'

I wanted to comfort him but the divide was there. 'What do you believe will happen to you when you die?' I asked him.

'Nothing,' he replied with a shrug.

'That scares me,' I said. 'I used to think of death as the great-est mystery, but everyone dies eventually. Eventually we will all know what happens when you die. The years ahead of you are the mystery.'

'Why do you want to live?' he asked. 'Do you have dreams?'

'Yeah. I want to fall in love with a beautiful woman. I want to have children and see them grow up. I want to explore the world.' It felt cruel saying all this, knowing that these possibilities were so far from his reach. I was just talking to him as a friend would talk to a dear friend. 'I have been lucky to have the opportunities I have. I want to give back to this world, I want to do good things, to stop places like this from existing,' I said. Would that help him?

'What would you say if you had a twin and one day your father had a sum of money that would make one of you comfortable and successful for the rest of your life? What would you say if your father gave your twin the money and not you? So while he achieved all his greatest desires, you were left behind with no opportunities.'

He was right, there was no fairness in our system. That inequality was unbearable for men with no ability to help themselves. In Nauru the injustices of life were all that occupied their minds.

Pez continued. 'When I was a child I was taught what was good and bad. When I asked why all these bad things kept happening to me, my teachers would tell me that I should be patient. If I waited, then good things would come. Now I am aged thirty and nothing has come and I am still waiting. Must I wait for five more years? In this hell? I have waited too long.'

'Well, I'll go with you then,' I said with a sad smile.

He smiled back. 'You need a reason to die. Do you have a reason?'

'To stop you,' I replied.

He smiled again. 'Thank you. But I have a reason. I am willing to die for all these men, to shut this place down.'

He saw my pained expression and said, 'Don't worry. I'll be like a leaf falling from a tree. It will pass and you will forget about it.'

He lay back down. I had no idea what to say. Was there anything I could say that would help? I thought not. The despair was rife throughout the camp—Pezhman was simply the most poetic at expressing his pain.

I placed my hand on his chest. 'I don't want you to die.' And I left.

A few days later the cycle of violence had turned full circle.

*

For me, the day of the second riot started innocuously enough. I rounded up the Iraqis and put them on a bus. It was the first excursion they'd been on since the wolf-whistling incident.

I had a surprise for Omar. He had been asking about basketball since the first day he'd arrived. We had finally arranged permission to take the men to a public basketball court on the island.

Omar was a wizard with the ball, shimmying his body this way and that, flicking the ball between his legs and catching it on the other side without watching it, then sinking a three-point shot with ease. While playing with Omar I was watching Fayiz out of the corner of my eye. Fayiz was angry. He paced up and down the tennis court with pent-up frustration. He picked up a tennis ball and whacked it over the fence, over the road and into the next field. Then he decided to walk away from the group towards two Nauruan men who were sitting on the steps of the church next to the courts, just outside the confines of the excursion area.

As Fayiz walked away, a Nauruan Sterling guard shouted at him to stop. It was unclear whether he ignored the guard, did not hear the guard, or did not understand. Fayiz did not speak English very well. Either way, Fayiz continued to walk towards the men, with the guard following close behind. Seeing this from the basketball court I made my way over as quickly as I could, hoping I wouldn't have to mediate an argument. When Fayiz was within 2 metres of the men the guard caught up to him. He faced up to Fayiz, nose to nose. Fayiz was a tall man but the Nauruan guard was bigger still.

The guard pointed over Fayiz's shoulder and said, 'You are an asylum seeker. You do not speak to Nauruans. You come here for excursions.'

Fayiz did not back down; his eyes flashed dangerously. I got between the men and put my hands on Fayiz's chest, pushing him back gently.

'Come on, bro,' I said softly.

The guard raised his voice and repeated his insult. 'You are an asylum seeker. You do not speak to Nauruans.'

'Come on,' I pleaded with Fayiz.

'I only go because of you,' Fayiz said and allowed me to push him away.

'I am sorry,' he said.

'No. I am sorry,' I responded.

'Freedom. Freedom,' Fayiz said, wringing his hands.

'I know.'

In their incident reports the Nauruan guard and the Wilson staff on duty claimed that Fayiz had acted in an antagonising manner and touched the local Nauruan men.

*

When I arrived back at the camp the pressure cooker was on again. I returned to find a crowd around the television. There was an article on the screen with a photo of the Hazaras playing football on one of the excursions. Their faces were clearly identifiable. As I approached the group I was confronted by angry gestures, dark looks.

'You organised this,' Sher accused me. 'You set us up.'

'Always photos of us having fun, never of us protesting,' Hussein shouted at me, arms raised.

'You are only here for the money,' Nasir Ali said. 'We cannot trust the Salvation Army.'

One man picked the soccer ball out of my hand and kicked it as far as he could. I didn't know what to say. The betrayal seemed so obvious to them. That photograph meant little to the Australian papers or to the photographer who took it, but its repercussions would be devastating in here. It condemned those men who were trying to make the most of their time in Nauru, and legitimised the extremist view of the few who refused to cooperate. You could not enjoy one second of Nauru or the Australian people would exploit you.

'No more soccer. No more excursions,' they shouted.

I walked away from the men and their looks of disgust.

Later that night there was trouble in the camp. It may have been planned or it may have occurred spontaneously as a result of the anger felt by most of the men. Like the previous riot in the regional processing centre, the facts of the night's events were shrouded in uncertainty, to be pieced together in the aftermath from fragments of stories from multiple sources.

It started with synchronised cuttings, four Iranians self-harming in as many minutes. Fights broke out and rocks were thrown at the Tamils to incite them. Rocks were thrown at Wilson guards when they tried to help injured men. On their way out of the camp, Wilson guards pushed men in the face to defend themselves. Joel was pushed by a Sinhalese man and a group of Tamils rushed to Joel's side.

Wilson guards took a camera into the camp to film the violence, which only served to anger the men more. Suddenly the authorities were allowing cameras in the camp. Salvation army staff were evacuated. In the mad confusion a man attempted to hang himself in the laundry. He was resuscitated by a Wilson guard. Five men were placed in isolation and would most likely face criminal charges.

*

I found out the next day that it was Pezhman who had attempted to commit suicide. Some stories said he had stopped breathing for five minutes before being resuscitated, others said thirty minutes, others said he had just lost consciousness. What I did know was that my friend had taken himself to a dark laundry during an anarchic riot, placed a noose around his neck and tried to compress his larynx to stop himself from breathing. He had tried to cease his own existence in this world to stop the pain and silence his demons. This camp had taken a beautiful human, an intelligent, eloquently spoken man, and pushed him over the edge. I felt guilt that I had not been there. Looking back through our conversations I realised the signs were all there, but the signs were there for a lot of men. Were they all going to try to commit suicide? If our government—our people—had killed this man, what remorse would any of them feel?

I went to visit him the next day. As I walked through the Iranian tents every second man I saw held bandaged wrists. One man showed me a shoulder covered in deep, ugly cigarette burns. When I got the chance to sit with Pezhman he smiled at me. A dark scar curved around his throat between his jawline and Adam's apple. His wrists bore furious puckered scars: seven, eight, nine on each wrist.

'What did it feel like?' I asked him.

'It was terrifying. My hands went automatically to my throat. I did not think. I tried to stop it.' He was speaking slowly, pausing between each sentence so he could choose each word carefully. 'No man really wants to die. Not at the end.'

'And then?' I asked, wondering if the light at the end of the tunnel had appeared.

'And then someone was pushing my chest and I was breathing. People were crying, people were shouting. It was horrible.'

For the first time since I had met him, Pezhman looked as if he would cry. Then he stared hard at his suicide-watch guard.

'Tell this guard to go away. I have changed my mind. I do not want to die.'

'What has changed?' I asked.

'Life is a beautiful gift. I know this now. It is not something to be thrown away. But this place contaminates it. This is not life. I wanted to protest this.'

We sat in silence, my eyes wandering back and forth over the ugly bruising on his neck. How close had he come to dying?

'DIAC told me that this would affect my application for asylum,' he said. 'I told them I was sorry. I told them I do not want any more trouble. I will not try again.'

I left his tent angrier than ever before. Our government was threatening suicidal men, manipulating their mental illnesses to demand obedience. Using their hope for survival, bribing them with the possibility of asylum in Australia. *If you try to hurt yourself you will not be considered good enough to be an Australian.* It was sickening.

*

After Pezhman's suicide attempt the camp calmed down again. The atmosphere of the camp had turned full circle, yet with each cycle the actions of the men became more dramatic, spiralling closer and closer towards disaster. Even though the mood had settled there was still a residual bitterness towards me and the Salvation Army because of the photo. When I tried to get the Nauru Premier League going, the men sneered at me and asked if I would be taking pictures. The football and the excursions ground to a halt. I organised a meeting with every ethnic group.

'Do you really think the Salvation Army spend all this time in Nauru organising football competitions, excursions, music concerts to get one photo of you?' I asked them. 'This is a risk you have to take if you want to go on excursions and play football. You can choose to sit around here and do nothing and go crazy, or you can choose to join us and make the most of a few hours of the day.'

For the majority of the men this was enough to earn an apology. They understood that I was angry and hurt, and that they had offended me, and that I understood their anger. The only men who questioned this were the Pakistani Pashtuns.

'We will never go on excursions then, ever. You work for the government. You betrayed us.'

The next day they were on excursions again. It was their form of apology, I supposed.

There was one relationship that I hadn't mended, though. Farid had stopped talking to me and was avoiding my chess games. He made excuses like 'I'm too tired'. One day he told me to go home to Australia and looked at the other Iranians like a kid wanting approval from the older bullies. The divide had been erected and I was shut off from him.

Then one day I found Farid sitting at the gate, red-eyed.

'*Dosh* Farid. What's wrong?' I sat down next to him.

'Shahab is gone,' Farid croaked. I seized up. Had he finally done it?

'What do you mean?' I asked, hoping he wouldn't confirm my worst fears.

'Gone. He is in Australia.' Farid hung his head. I couldn't help but feel a thrill for Shahab. The man had suffered so much and now he had had a win.

'This is good for him,' I said, hugging Farid.

'I am alone,' Farid whispered. 'I cannot spend years here.' My heart broke for him. He had lost his only friend in Nauru.

Shahab was the third man to be taken to Australia from Nauru. He was to be admitted to a hospital. Namdar's prediction that Nauru would become the biggest exporter of 'crazies' was coming true.

Chapter 33

SCOTT MORRISON, the shadow minister for immigration, visited Nauru. The shadow minister was notorious for his continual references to asylum seekers as 'illegals', even though both major parties know that it is not illegal to seek asylum. The men were becoming sick of seeing Australian officials visit Nauru. They had lost hope that such visits would move the Australian public's heart enough to enact change.

Scott Morrison spent as little time in the camp as Chris Bowen did, nodding with approval at the rudimentary conditions. When he met with the men he refused to talk to those on hunger strike. He warned the men that if the Abbott government got in to power things would only get worse for them. There weren't many people in Nauru sad to see the back of Scott Morrison.

Chapter 34

AT THE BEGINNING of December we were informed by our cultural advisors that Muharram was about to commence. We were told that the month of Muharram was a Muslim mourning period to commemorate the death of Imam Hussain and his family members. Shia Muslims would mourn for thirteen days. All Muslims would mourn Ashura, the tenth day of Muharram, the day Imam Hussain was killed.

Zulfigar, a Hazara cultural advisor, explained Muharram to me. He said that fourteen centuries ago, there was a ruler by the name of Yazid who ruled parts of Iraq. Yazid had been appointed by his father, so when he came to power he wanted to legitimise his regime. In the eyes of most Muslims he had no right to rule unless he was accepted by Imam Hussain, the grandson of the holy prophet Mohammad and the undisputed religious leader of Islam. Imam Hussain refused to accept Yazid as he was a cruel, corrupt man.

When Yazid tried to force Imam Hussain to accept his regime, Imam Hussain fled with his family members to Kofa, a city where his supporters were in the majority. On his way to Kofa, Imam Hussain and his entourage stopped at Karbala. Yazid's army lay siege to the city, not allowing any access to food or water, demanding that Imam Hussain accept the regime. Instead of giving in, the imam fought back. He was assassinated along with his family members and his loyal friends.

We were advised that during Muharram Shia Muslims don't dance or listen to music. They don't attend parties and avoid getting married. We were advised to be respectful of all Muslims during this period, not to make jokes or laugh loudly when talking to them, and to avoid scheduling big social events.

Those who walked past the mosque tent during Muharram witnessed groups of men sitting in the sweaty tent, chanting and beating their chests over and over again. The religious zeal of the exercise and the self-flagellation were confronting. Without understanding the story behind Muharram, many of the staff had the perception that the ceremony was abusive.

Within that tent the religious leaders told the stories of how Imam Hussain sacrificed his life, his family members and his loyal friends in his battle against corruption. The philosophy of Muharram is to fight and resist injustice, cruelty and evil.

Chapter 35

AT SOME POINT during the third week I realised I'd made a mistake coming back so soon. One week had not been enough respite. I could feel my enthusiasm for the job waning. When faced with the recurring battles with Wilson Security over excursion policy my patience began to falter.

The pressures of managing staff were new to me. Not only was I dealing with my own frustrations and stress, I had to be mindful of those of my team members. The Rec team was staffed by my close friends on Nauru, which made work that much more enjoyable in the good times. During the stressful periods, however, conflict became personal.

When I asked Laura to cover the afternoon excursions she turned to me and said, 'Why don't you do it?'

'I work my arse off at this job, and I don't need you to question my work ethic. Just do what I tell you,' I snapped back.

We stormed off in separate directions, but just a few hours later we were back at the hotel bar together with the rest of our colleagues. The social scene had changed from my previous rotation. Where previously we debriefed in hotel rooms, we now played pool at the bar over a few drinks. This particular evening it seemed everyone needed to break free from the pressures of the camp. We sat outside the bar, overlooking the water, drinking and laughing and not talking about the men and Nauru. It was just after midnight when an IHMS nurse interrupted our fun. She was screaming before we could see her.

'It's past midnight and people here are trying to sleep. How dare you talk at this level. It's bloody outrageous. Have some respect. How many of you are Christians?'

In response to her question only Joel put his hand up. We dispersed, feeling hard done by. One of the hotel room blocks backed onto the social area of the bar. The ten of us must have been making enough noise to wake the nurse, although we didn't know how.

The next day we were given an official warning by Salvo HR. That evening DIAC hosted a party at the same bar which ran into the early hours of the morning. The nurse who had complained about us was singing karaoke well past midnight.

This incident was the beginning of a restrictive new period for me and my friends. We became known to all service providers as the 'Young Salvos' and were deemed troublemakers. We were told that the island was a politically sensitive location and that the Salvation Army had a reputation to uphold. Not only were Salvo management conscious of what the media might report about Salvo workers' actions on Nauru, but they were also mindful of the Salvos' reputation with the other agencies. We had to represent ourselves as a professional unit at all times, inside and outside of Topside, and adhere to the strict Salvation Army code of conduct befitting a religious organisation.

We were discouraged from going near the bar at the Menen Hotel. Instead we were shunted to our rooms where staff were sleeping. Our only other options for socialising at night were beaches that were patrolled by packs of wild dogs. Even in the rooms there were complaints levelled at staff for being too loud. At least I was sleeping at the hotel; I couldn't imagine sleeping in a tent at Topside like some of the other staff. Always in view of the camp, always with that place in your head.

Young Salvo workers were accused of bad behaviour more and more frequently, to the point where it appeared that the agencies were using complaints to play power games. A Salvation Army officer coined the phrase 'Salvo sluts' when talking to the Young Salvo women about their behaviour, and accused them of sleeping with asylum seekers, and with other men on the island. They were even accused of doing drugs in the camp at an official debrief by Salvation Army officers. There was no basis to these accusations, but several female Salvo staff were sent home for suspicions and accusations of sexual misconduct. Salvo HR recommended that the girls not do anything to enhance their already tarnished reputation. I was at the centre of one these accusations.

A male HR officer asked my female colleague, 'You and Mark are pretty close, aren't you?' insinuating some kind of sexual relationship between us. The girl had a boyfriend at the time. He never raised the issue with me.

Meanwhile, after a party one evening a drunk Wilson Client Services Officer had to be restrained by his colleagues and dragged off a staff shuttle bus after making obscene and racially abusive comments to a Tamil cultural advisor. Wilson management later claimed the outburst was a result of his diabetic condition. Salvo management assured us that the guard would not work at Topside again. He returned on the next rotation and continued to work on the island long after the Tamil cultural advisor had left. After this, many of the staff began to lose faith in the Salvation Army management.

I avoided drinking excessively on Nauru for the simple reason that it wasn't worth the trouble. Drinking only lead to arbitrary accusations that were dealt with as truth by Salvo management. More than that, I was so tired from the work that drinking was not going to make me feel better.

The social restrictions on workers made for a suffocating atmosphere. It was difficult to find space to let off steam. Returning to the packed living quarters allowed no reflection time. Instead I suppressed what I was feeling; I distanced myself. It was easier that way. Cold heart, cold mind.

After three weeks on the island it felt like I should've been finishing my rotation. Instead I was only halfway home.

Chapter 36

I STARTED PREPARING FOR the day at 7 am. I walked over to the staff kitchens and picked up a box of apples and pears the Nauruan Transfield staff had organised for me. I then grabbed a few bags of ice and a crate of water bottles. I stored all this in two big eskies. Chairs, a table, a scorebook, balls, bats, sunscreen.

By the time I was ready it was 8 am and OGN Team were already lining up. Somehow they had scouted out white shirts for everybody in their team. They had sunscreen painted across their noses, lips and cheeks. One Pakistani Hazara was standing by himself. He looked nervous yet defiant. He had joined the Kiss Team, a group of Tamils, because no other Hazaras wanted to play cricket. His teammates, the Kiss boys, were nowhere to be seen. Neither was the bus. I called David, the Nauruan bus driver.

'Where are you, man?'

'Just coming.' I'd woken him up again.

I walked down the main avenue of the camp between the rows of tents until I found the Kiss team's tent. They were all sleeping.

'Come on, boys.' I slapped the tent. 'Time to wake up. You've got a cricket match today.'

I shoved Tharsan's stretcher. 'Come on, Tharsan. Get your arse out of bed.'

He pulled himself up groggily, nodding. 'Cricket?'

'Yes. Come on. The longer it takes, the less time you have.' I pointed at my watchless wrist to indicate they were late. They wouldn't understand my English.

'Laura dance!' I heard one of the men shout. All the men stared at me, eager for me to dance. I swayed my hips like a belly dancer and the tent started laughing. They were awake but it took them another fifteen minutes to get ready. By that time the OGN boys had gone to get breakfast. Forty minutes later the bus left Topside.

It was the second match of the Topside Twenty20 Cricket Tournament, another Rec team initiative. There were six teams in the league: four Tamil teams, one Sinhalese team and one Pakistani team. The matches were three and a half hours long and played in the morning before it got too hot. If we were delayed for any reason the overs were reduced so we could get back to camp on time. Once the men returned to camp the normal excursion schedule resumed.

The matches were played at Nauru's major Aussie Rules oval, a grassless dust bowl littered with rubbish, with resident drunks sitting under nearby trees shouting in Nauruan. The phosphate refinery loomed beside the ground, pumping suspicious fumes into the atmosphere. Last match there had been seven guards on duty to watch thirty men. This match the men were supervised by three Wilson guards who fell asleep in deckchairs within five minutes of arriving.

The men set up the boundary markers using rubbish, leaves from the surrounding palm trees, whatever they could find. The men swept the pitch with leaves, and used crushed cans to mark the edges of the pitch. Water containers were used as stumps. Tennis balls were wrapped in sky-blue electrical tape to give them extra weight. The disaster of a blue ball was foreseeable but there was nothing we could do—it was that or use a light tennis ball. The scorers set up a table in the shade alongside our alcoholic spectators.

'Alright, guys—can the two teams line up,' I called out, motioning to the teams to line up in front of me and face each other.

Raj and I were the umpires for the day. I explained the rules while Raj translated, and then I asked for a fair match that valued sportsmanship and equality of men above all else. We performed the toss and the OGN Team batted first. The men shook hands and grinned at each other, then the match began.

The openers batted well and set up the team for a strong total. Dev hit forty runs before he played a loose shot and was caught on the boundary. Then Krishna got a break when he whacked the ball high into the air, and it got lost in the azure backdrop, infuriating the Kiss fielders.

'Both teams have to put up with the same problems,' I reasoned. It was never easy being a cricket umpire.

The first innings finished without incident. The OGN Team were bowled out before the end of their overs for a total of 140. This followed the trend of none of the teams actually batting for their allocated twenty overs. There was time for a quick tea and then we went back out to the middle.

The Kiss innings proved a lot more controversial. The OGN Team were a good bowling side—the wickets fell quickly, and so did the Kiss tempers. A few LBW decisions were followed by thrown bats and verbal abuse. Raj and I were accused of being cheats. These displays of poor sportsmanship made me question why I bothered organising the tournaments, and then I thought about how passionate the men were about the competition and I realised it replaced their more significant worries, for a small time at least. When we argued about cricket we weren't talking about their families, their traumas, their grievances.

The Pakistani Hazara opened the batting for Kiss and watched his team fall apart around him. He was obviously a classy player and he took to the bowling attack, in one over hitting five sixes. Unfortunately he couldn't do enough to snatch a win, and Kiss were bowled out for ninety runs, well short of their target.

There weren't enough seats on the bus to take everyone back in one go, so the losing team went home first while the winning team was rewarded with an extra twenty minutes outside of the camp.

'You played really well,' I told Dev.

'Yes,' Dev said happily. 'I got a big score.'

I said, 'Kiss team weren't very good though,' and Dev laughed.

'MAC lost to PEP?' he asked.

'Yes. PEP got bonus points so they are first,' I said.

Dev translated to the boys. 'When do we play PEP?' Dev asked.

'Next week,' I said, and Dev translated into Tamil again. I didn't need to understand Tamil to see that they were excited.

The OGN boys' bus trip home was filled with drumming and singing. Not even the return to Topside dampened their spirits.

I sat with the Hazaras for lunch while the other Recreation staff went on excursions. We ate a hot curry of vegetables and meat, with rice and some kind of naan bread to mop up the juices, and a side platter of fruit.

Sher asked me, '*Luchak*, what are these little trophies you give us for the football? No more little trophies.'

'It was all they had at the shop,' I protested. 'There aren't big trophies in Nauru.'

'This is not a trophy. This is, this is—'

'Shit?' I suggested.

'*Luchak*,' he replied. 'Go back to Australia and bring a big trophy next time. Okay?'

'Righto.'

'What's the prize when we win the league?' Hussein asked.

'When you win?' I asked.

'Yes. Of course.' He motioned for my folder. He wanted to see the league table. I put it on the table so everyone could see. Everyone at the table stood up, ignoring their food, and crowded around the piece of paper. The two Hazara teams were first and second. One of the teams had won every game, the other had drawn one game and won the rest. The next closest team was five points behind.

'See, we are the best,' Hussein said, 'so what's the prize?'

'Visas to Australia,' I replied. The boys laughed, Ratak howled. He had my favourite laugh of all the men. Slow, drawn out, loud. HAR. HAR. HAR. I imitated it and everyone laughed harder.

Mansoor tapped me on the shoulder and pointed at the Golden Boot tally. According to me he had scored six goals. He tapped his name and showed me seven fingers. He was probably right, so rather than argue I gave him the thumbs up to acknowledge my mistake.

Jan was next to take my attention. He was a small man with a smooth, unlined face. He looked so young he could've been seventeen, but his eyes were too old for a seventeen-year-old. He was probably in his thirties.

'Do we play today?' he asked.

'Maybe. We'll see who turns up to play, but probably not. You have played more games than any other team.'

The camp had returned to a peaceful type of order for the first time since Pezhman's suicide attempt and the photograph. Men had started getting involved in excursions again and the football competition was back attracting big crowds. At five that afternoon I entered the compound, football in hand, whistle around my neck. One of the Salvo employees handed me a card: yellow on one side, red on the other. As I walked through the camp a couple of the players followed me, asking for the ball so they could practise.

There was no schedule of matches because I had too many variables to contend with. English classes, medical appointments, excursions, injuries, general apathy. Instead teams were expected to turn up on the day. Some days no-one came, other days too many teams came.

Ali, an enormous Pakistani, approached me with five of his friends.

'We play?' he asked. They didn't have a team in the league so I assumed they wanted to join the competition.

'Names,' I said motioning to write them on paper. He nodded so I assumed he understood.

'Today?' he asked.

'No,' I shook my head. 'Names. You have to register.' I looked around for someone to help me translate, but there was no-one near. I showed him the league table, and showed him he didn't have a team in it. He nodded and walked away, but I wasn't convinced he'd understood.

As the league had become more reliable, it had also become more popular. Once the men saw that games took place every day more teams had started joining. The league had grown to thirteen teams: two Hazara teams, one Sinhalese, one Iraqi, three Pakistani, and six Tamil.

Another Pakistani, Nasir Ali, came up to me. He was from the New Stars. The previous day they had told me they were never playing football again because they didn't like one of my decisions.

'New Star play?' he asked. Unbelievable, as if his tantrum yesterday had never happened. I smiled at him and showed him a league table. I had taken the New Stars out of the league. He looked angrily at me, unsure what to say. I wasn't sure how far I could push him so I quickly showed him the real table which included New Stars. He half-smiled at me and walked away.

There were teams like the Hazaras, who turned up every day to play. There were other teams that rarely came. It was a juggling act to decide who would play. The first game I picked Love Team, a Tamil team, and Negombo Youth, Sinhalese. The Love Team captain was called Newman. Thevan was the Sinhalese team captain.

'Newman,' I said, imitating Jerry Seinfield, and was rewarded with a toothy grin—he loved it when I did that. The Sinhalese team shook hands with the Tamils and the game got underway. Just before I blew the whistle I saw Tharsan in the crowd. He shouted out, 'LAURA DANCE', and imitated a woman dancing sexily. But his friend put his hands up in the air, motioning for me to stop.

'NO. This is sport. No Laura dance. We are men.' He looked very serious, and then he burst out a hiccuping laugh that sounded more like a hyena than a man. And that was the new rule for the Laura dance.

It was a scrappy game with passion overriding skill. The Negombo Youth dominated the first half. It was rare to see a lot of goals in these games but the Sinhalese were three goals up after ten minutes. The crowd were laughing by the third goal. The Love Team looked demoralised by the embarrassing scoreline.

The second half started with a Love Team goal. The crowd clapped politely. It was a consolation goal, nothing more. But the Love Team suddenly had hope. The tackles became more physical, kicking up gravel and dust. The Negombo Youth keeper with his frizzy boofed hair slid along the rocks to stop a shot, cutting his knee open badly. He refused to go to IHMS, the game was too important. A corner to Love Team. The ball bounced in off a Negombo Youth leg. Three–two. Could the Love Team actually do this? The crowd drew in closer to the sidelines. The Negombo Youth's play became panicky. They started kicking the ball out every time they got possession. The Love Team tried passing but the gravelly ground and the rough tackling by Negombo Youth made it difficult. There was one minute left on the clock. The ball bounced up perfectly for Newman and he volleyed the ball between the two rubbish bins. Three–three. The crowd roared. The Love Team took their shirts off, ran down the sidelines and high-fived outstretched hands from the crowd. The Negombo Youth graciously offered their congratulations. Tamils and Sinhalese shook hands and hugged each other.

The benefits of competitive sport were undeniable. It gave the men something to talk about, something to focus their minds on. Hundreds of men turned up to watch the daily premier league matches within the camp. Iraqis were learning the names of Pakistanis. Sinhalese were thanking Tamils for a great game. A community was growing within the camp and for me personally it made working in Topside bearable. It was one success surrounded by so much failure. Moments of happiness embedded in so much sadness. Without these wins, I wouldn't have been able to stay in Nauru.

Chapter 37

IN NOVEMBER 2012 Manus Island was reopened as the second off-shore processing centre in the Pacific Solution. A good friend of mine, who asked to remain anonymous, worked on Manus Island after a stint in Nauru. She provided me with an informed comparison of the two camps.

Manus Island is situated off the north coast of Papua New Guinea, an isolated location as far from the Australian public's view as possible. My friend told me that like Nauru, the Manus Island Regional Processing Centre was unprepared to meet the needs of the asylum seekers housed within. Manus is hotter than Nauru, its wet season heavier. The camp had been reclaimed from the jungle and was infested with malaria-riddled mosquitos. The local island community protested against its existence, saying that local landowners had not given permission to use their land, creating an uncomfortable atmosphere from day one.

There were two camps within the one centre: one for single adult males (SAMs) and one for families and unaccompanied minors (UAMs). The families slept on beds in shipping containers cooled by fans; the SAMs slept in tents. The families had TVs, ping-pong, games and a children's play area; sometimes the SAMs got a stereo working if a staff member could find the cables. There was nowhere for the SAMs to relax other than an overcrowded breezeway. The two camps were separated by a fence and a walkway, the inequalities between the two camps unavoidable. According to my friend, the Salvos had a meeting with DIAC about the inadequacy of the SAMs area and the response was, 'Well, they're not supposed to be comfortable.'

Nights and days were punctuated by the screams of men in pain.

'You do nothing for us! Fuck you! Fuck God! Fuck Salvation Army! I want to die!'

Whenever there was a commotion in the SAMs area, the families ran to the fence to watch and to listen. Salvos tried to protect the children from seeing or hearing violence, but there was little anyone could do to protect them from the realities of life in the regional processing centre.

The camp itself was set up on the Manus Island naval base, bordered by a main road on one side and a beach on the other. A fence was all that separated the asylum seekers from a white-sand beach surrounded by coconut palms and rainforest. There were no excursions out of the camp, and they were not allowed to swim in the ocean.

My friend told me about the children who hung off the fenced perimeters of the processing centre, staring blankly at the water. She told me of their drawings of life in the camp. Pictures of men hanging themselves, others self-harming with blood dripping down their wrists, saying, 'I want to die'. She told me how the kids started to wilt. They smiled less and spent more time in bed. They missed school, and became insolent. She told me of children shaking the fences, kicking the gates, shouting 'we want freedom'. I had witnessed the horrors of men breaking down in Nauru, yet children were being placed in worse conditions than anything I had experienced.

The 1994 United Nations Convention of the Rights of the Child—to which Australia is a signatory—states that children who are asylum seekers should be treated no differently from accepted refugees.[1] Having children detained on Manus Island contravenes this convention. While Australian children played in parks and on beaches, our country was imprisoning asylum seeker children.

---

1   UNICEF, *A Simplified Version of the United Nations Convention on the Rights of the Child*, 1996, viewed 24 August 2013, <www.unicef.org.au/Discover/What-we-do/Convention-on-the-Rights-of-the-Child/childfriendlycrc.aspx>

Chapter 38

ONE DAY DEV approached me in the camp, looking worried.

'I have big problem. I am in trouble. They say I cause trouble, but you know me, I always help. I am always good. I don't know why they do this. What do I do?' He spoke quickly, and nervously. I'd never seen Dev like this.

'Who said you are causing trouble? What did they say?'

'Immigration, Wilson. They just tell me I'm in trouble.'

'I'll check it out,' I said.

I went to my manager with Dev's concerns.

'It is alleged that Dev's family in Sri Lanka were involved in a people-smuggling ring and that he and his cronies have been bullying men and their families in Sri Lanka for payments.' She said *people smuggling* as if it were a swear word or a racial slur. *People smuggler.* The term felt wrong in my mouth. My instant reaction was one of disgust. Cheaters, liars, traders in misery. Forcing people onto rickety boats, making them risk their lives. Conning them into paying a heavy fee. Who were these people smugglers, anyway? Indonesians? Fishermen? I realised I didn't know.

Was Dev a monster? Did he con people into making dangerous boat journeys? And was he now bullying them and their families? I couldn't see it. Dev was in Nauru, he had shared their journey. These men had wanted to leave Sri Lanka—maybe Dev had helped them. Maybe he had put his life on the line to get them out. What if he'd paid the people smugglers and now the others wouldn't pay him? What if his family had been put out of pocket?

I saw Dev as the charismatic leader of men. The good-looking, smiling man who was always willing to help. The optimist who made the most of his situation. I also saw him as the man who had pushed around young Danil, teasing him in front of a large group. Placing his hands on Danil's leg in a way that made me uncomfortable for him. I could see the bully in Dev, just as easily as I could see my friend.

What kind of man was he? A leader or a bully? A man intimidating others for money? Or a man trying to help his family? A man who took advantage of desperate people? Or a saviour, rescuing others from a horrible situation? Was he a people smuggler? And if so, what did that term really mean?

My instant contempt for the words felt like political indoctrination. *We have to stop the people smugglers' business model.* This was the first time I'd ever faced a humanised example of a people smuggler and I had no idea what it meant.

I went back to Dev.

'How did you organise the boat to come to Australia?' I asked.

He knew instantly what I was talking about.

'I helped organise my family and men from my area,' he said. 'I contacted a people smuggler. I collected money from the families. It was difficult because the smugglers kept asking for money and one man did not pay so they threatened his family.'

I didn't know what to say. Where did that leave these allegations of him bullying men? Did that mean these men owed him money? I didn't know.

'You know, I was a tobacco salesman in Sri Lanka,' he said. 'I travelled around to sell and made a lot of money. The government accused me of helping the Tamil Tigers. I was in jail twice for two years. I got married, and then I got kidnapped. When I was kidnapped my wife left me. I had to leave Sri Lanka. Too much trouble, this is why I organised the boat.'

It was all too confusing for me.

Chapter 39

IN THE WEEKS leading up to Christmas the camp boundaries were extended. The tents that had backed onto the pinnacles at the far end of the camp were moved into the new area. The area had formerly been a garden that the men could look at from behind the confines of their fence. The old garden had been demolished and flattened out, however, the trees from the garden were planted between the rows of tents. In among the gravel and the army tents the men cultivated flowers and pawpaws, adding a little beauty to their surroundings. We called the new section of the camp Paradise Gardens. Tamils helped the Salvos set up the new area. Every time I tried to pick up a plant a Tamil man would rush in and refuse to let me labour in the sun. Meanwhile the other ethnicities ignored us. We gave the Tamils priority tent allocation for Paradise Gardens and I'm sure they appreciated the gesture.

'It's like moving to the city,' Francis told me.

In the now vacant area at the back of the camp, construction of accommodation buildings was due to start more than three months after the camp had opened. Work was intended to start early every day to make the most of the light. On top of all their other sleeping difficulties, the men were going to have to endure noise pollution. The football field was closed and relocated to the cramped area between the Green Room and the classroom.

It was a bittersweet moment for the men. On one hand they were happy to know that soon they would no longer have to sleep in tents. On the other, it was confirmation that their presence here was not temporary. The government intended for them to be in Nauru for a long time and there was nothing they could do about it.

The camp's second Christmas present was much less welcome. The week before I left the island, Namdar returned to Nauru and no-one believed it.

'He can't have,' Pezhman said. 'It is impossible.'

It was a desperate statement rather than anything of real conviction. Namdar had been on hunger strike in Nauru for almost two months. If Namdar had returned, that meant hunger strikes were futile and that there was no way of getting to Australia except to wait for processing—and nobody knew when that would start, let alone when it would finish. Pezhman rushed out of his tent and sure enough Namdar was there, looking as skinny as ever. His return marked a loss of resistance. The decision stunned the men into obedience. The hunger strikes stopped, the camp wallowed yet again.

I visited Namdar in his tent.

'What happened in Brisbane?' I asked. He looked at me intently. Despite all he had been through it was obvious that his mind was still sharp.

'They took me to a hospital,' he said speaking in careful English. 'When I was good enough to move, they moved me. They promised me that I would be taken to a detention centre in Brisbane. Instead they brought me back here. They lied to me again.'

There was bitter resignation in his voice. The government had tricked him again. He was starting to see just how insignificant he was in the government's games. He was a pawn in the embarrassment of the government's offshore detention policy.

'Can you get me more time in the gym?' he asked me.

'I can try.'

'Twenty-three hours a day I am dead. One hour in the gym I am alive.'

One benefit arose from Namdar's return. The day before I returned to Australia a small group of Iranians joined the Nauru Premier League. Farid and Pez were among them. They ran around against the Pakistani team from Parachinar, enjoying themselves. They were the entertainers. One of the men hopped over the ball, this way and that, until when he finally attempted to kick the ball he missed it completely. Instead of playing he stopped and laughed while the Pakistanis ran away with the ball. Pezhman was by no means an athlete but Farid proved to be quite skilful. Indeed, it was he who scored the winner for the Iranians. I ran on to hug him when the goal went in. It gave me some hope that he could survive without Shahab.

Chapter 40

THERE WAS A limit to how long a worker could stay in Nauru before they started to break down.

My first rotation in Nauru had lasted four weeks. By the fourth week I was tired, I was drained, I was numb. I needed a rest. Returning to Sydney hadn't helped me; I'd felt disconnected, and I'd felt guilty about leaving the men. I'd had a one-week break and then returned to the fray without recuperating sufficiently. By the fourth week of my second rotation I still had another two weeks to go. It seemed like a lifetime. By the fifth week I felt robotic: wake up, work, go to bed, wake up, work, go to bed. I thought about the men constantly; I dreamt of the men. There was no escape. It left me physically and emotionally drained, and I wasn't the only one. The Hazara cultural advisor Zulfigar confessed a dream to me.

'I was climbing a mountain with my brother. He fell down the mountain and he died.'

We looked sadly at each other. It seemed morbidly prophetic.

By the sixth week it felt inevitable that the constant frustrations of camp life would boil over.

There were the trivial issues: the daily battles, the weekly arguments, the little piranhas that tore bits of flesh away from you, arguments over excursion policies with each Wilson team, the lack of communication between agencies that never improved, stalling bureaucracy, having to implement idiotic policies that seemed to restrict men only for the sake of restricting them, the living conditions for staff, sleeping on the floor of hotel rooms, the merry-go-round of Chinese restaurants, over and over again. You missed your friends, your family, your significant other. The list was endless.

Then there were the overarching frustrations: the men's constant desire for answers we couldn't give; the knowledge that slowly but surely the men's mental health was gradually and unavoidably deteriorating; the lack of improvement in conditions at the camp. The men were still living in tents, the camp was still not open despite monthly promises that it would be soon. The swimming program had been delayed due to issues with insurance and liability, and nobody knew when it would be resolved. No-one had any idea when the processing of refugee settlement claims would begin.

And then there were the suicide attempts. The self-harm. The mass hunger strikes.

By the final week I was voicing my displeasure publicly to the Salvation Army and to other agencies.

Not long after I'd traded angry words with a Wilson guard I felt a tap on my shoulder and the psychologist asked me.

'Do you need a chat?'

Our psychologists rotated in every few weeks. This psychologist had been in Nauru for two days. Each psych asked the same questions when they arrived: *What happens in Nauru? What have you seen?* After the fifth psychologist I got tired of telling my story. It felt as if they were on a conveyor belt full of faceless professionals getting paid to hear us whinge. I'm sure that was how some of the asylum seekers thought of the Salvation Army. How many times would they have to justify their stories to people? Tell and retell them to people judging whether they were true refugees or not.

I sighed and said, 'Yes. Let's have a chat,' unsure if this would be beneficial or if it would signify the breaking of the dam.

'You look frustrated. Why don't you tell me about your frustrations?' he said.

I looked him in the eye. The dam broke.

Chapter 41

I GAVE MYSELF A few weeks' holiday over Christmas and New Year's to be with friends and family. While in Nauru my manager had verbally offered me a six-month full-time contract, so I could enjoy my holidays safe in the knowledge that I would be going back soon. I used the opportunity to go road-tripping with friends. From Sydney to Avalon, to the Hunter Valley, to Byron Bay, to Melbourne, to Lorne, to Melbourne, back to Sydney. The boundless freedom of Australia was a stark contrast to the suffocating lifestyle of Nauru. My feelings oscillated between trying to appreciate the opportunities I had in Australia, and feeling guilty that the men couldn't be there to share it with me.

Despite being on the road, I couldn't drag myself away from the asylum seeker issue. On the Australian side of the iron curtain I talked legal jargon with refugee groups, journalists, lawyers, politicians and ex-government employees. The fate of these men lay in political manoeuvring, court battles, arguing definitions of laws, finding loopholes in the system. A migration agent, a lawyer who represents asylum seekers and refugees, told me of the government's attempts to screen all Sri Lankan Tamil asylum seekers and deport them without following the proper refugee processing protocol, and the subsequent scrambling by human-rights advocates to defend the Tamils' rights. I realised it was a game. The Australian government would try to get away with as much as it could until someone found out and then it would fold its cards and start again.

I requested a face-to-face meeting with Tanya Plibersek, the federal health minister. Tanya Plibersek listened for thirty minutes to what I had to say. Her face showed compassion for the men's stories, and disappointment at the awful conditions of the camp. I appealed to her, as the health minister, to investigate the inadequate health services. I finished by asking her to address the issues she might be able to affect: the promised 'open camp' policy, speeding up of the processing of the men's refugee claims, and better living conditions.

'Nobody in the government wants this policy,' she told me before I left.

'There are policies, and then there are cruel policies,' I replied.

I left not believing that anything would be achieved from that meeting.

*

Returning home and socialising was easier the second time round. I recognised that social advocacy was a necessary part of my role as a Salvo.

I was met with a range of responses. The first was admiration. The admiring were not necessarily interested in asylum seeker issues. Some just liked the idea of humanitarianism; others were keen to talk in depth about my experiences. They mused that the work must have been rewarding and marvelled at what an experience it must have been. I understood where they were coming from, and agreed that Nauru was like nothing else I'd ever experienced, but to call it rewarding was too much. Working in Nauru was heartbreaking. I didn't feel rewarded by helping these men through their grief and their helplessness. I was appreciative of the opportunity I'd had, to be employed to help others, but it was difficult to see the bitter reality of the men's lives as a personal advantage.

The second response was self-confessed ignorance, to which I did my utmost to present my views in an unbiased manner: to tell the person what I'd seen at the camp, and what I thought the situation was.

The third response was *I don't agree with the policy, but ...* These were the people who talked around the issue. They never actually stated that Australia had to secure its borders but every argument they presented was in favour of deterrence. They presented economic reasons, migratory reasons, queues, *We can't take them all*—everything that avoided the humanity of the situation.

The fourth response was from those who were opposed to the arrival of the boats. They proffered a variety of reasons why asylum seekers shouldn't be allowed in the country. They said that coming to Australia by boat was illegal; that those people were jumping a queue, taking the places of real refugees who had waited in camps for years. They said that we needed to protect our borders and stop the boats, that we couldn't take all asylum seekers, and that if we had an open-door policy we would be swamped.

I didn't know how our nation had decided that the No Advantage policy was the right thing to do. I had seen men breaking down and crying at the sight of Nauru and I'd felt ashamed. I'd held men who had attempted suicide and I'd felt guilty. I had listened to their stories and wondered why we were punishing them. Up until now, my reactions to what I had seen in Nauru were exactly that: reactions. But none of the arguments I'd heard in favour of deterrence justified the cruelty I had witnessed.

PART 3

ROTATION 3

7 February 2013 to 14 March 2013

Chapter 42

HAVING FULLY RESTED myself over the Christmas and New Year holidays, I was ready to return to Nauru on a full-time contract. What I didn't realise was just how hard it would be to get back. I was sitting in a cafe in Byron Bay when I received the email telling me I would not be returning to Nauru.

'There has been no offer of a contract and there is no vacancy at this stage within the recreation program.'

This email had come three weeks after my first request to HR to confirm my contract offer. Until that email Human Resources in both Sydney and Nauru had gone silent. My managers on Nauru weren't replying to my emails either. When my friends in Nauru confronted them about the lack of communication, they said it was out of their hands. No-one involved deemed it necessary to talk to me about my exclusion from the island. I wasn't even given the dignity of being told why. I was on the wrong side of the iron curtain with no way of getting back. I had been shut out.

I had just spent ten weeks working in terrible conditions, supporting the Salvation Army and its mission; ten weeks establishing a recreations program when before there was nothing; ten weeks working overtime every day so the Nauru Premier League could run extra games while the light lasted; ten weeks fighting to maintain the dignity and humanity of these men while others treated them as clients, patients, criminals, and numbers; ten weeks developing friendships that I would never be able to forget.

That part of my life had been cut away from me like an amputation. Pez, Omar, Dev, Raj, Salar, all of my brothers would be in Nauru for five years and I could not return to see them. I did not get to say goodbye to them. They had pleaded for me not to leave, told me that I wouldn't return and I had smiled and said, 'I'll be back. I just don't know when.' It would look as if I had betrayed them. I still had Jabber's watch. I had promised him I would fix his strap and return it to him. *This is why you don't promise anything,* I chastised myself furiously over and over again.

Suddenly I had an inkling of the men's situation, except in reverse. All I wanted to do was return to Nauru and there was nothing I could do to get that opportunity back. I soon found out that I was not the only worker to be blacklisted. Paul, the young Salvo who had established the English school—the same school the service providers championed as a symbol of the great work they were doing in Nauru—was refused any more contracts as he 'caused conflict' among staff. We suspected this meant the Salvo officers hadn't liked him. The asylum seekers still asked for him months after he left. There were many more ex-staff members who had similar complaints to ours.

For the four months of operations, the pre-deployment preparations had been a shambles. Staff only found out what they were supposed to sign, which meetings to attend or when to attend medicals by talking among themselves. Staff never knew their flight details until the day before their flight was supposed to leave, then they were expected to drop everything for the sake of the mission. You weren't told information, you had to seek it out, fight for every inch.

There was no cultural awareness training. Staff were deployed to Nauru with no understanding of the different ethnicities or religions of the people they would be working with. There was no explanation of why these men had come to Australia, what their circumstances were, and what the current immigration system was.

Underqualified staff were employed to work in a traumatic environment and were given little guidance on how to cope.

I fought to get my contract back, calling and emailing anyone I could think of. Everyone seemed to be passing the buck; no-one would explain why I was fired, and no-one would admit to firing me. And then a week later I received a call from Sydney HR, offering me a six-month full-time contract. On this contract I would be paid a salary. I would complete four-week rotations on the island, and for every four weeks I finished in Nauru I would be entitled to two weeks' paid leave in Australia. I didn't know why HR had changed their mind.

Sydney HR assured me they would get me over to Nauru as soon as possible. We set a date two weeks away for me to leave, 31 January. I completed the paperwork, I went to the travel doctor for the second time, I waited for the flight confirmations until the day before I was supposed to fly out of Sydney, then I called the Sydney office.

'We'll have the flights confirmed by the end of the day,' HR assured me.

At the end of the day no flights had been confirmed, but I had received confirmation of my accommodation in Brisbane and my compulsory attendance at training the following day. My friend Amanda received her flight itinerary at 3 pm. I called at 4 pm and was told my flight confirmation should come in any moment. At 5 pm when I called I was berated by a HR officer for calling too often. When I explained that I was supposed to be leaving the next day for Nauru I was told I was supposed to receive my flight details a week in advance, and if I hadn't received them yet I wouldn't be going. I disagreed, telling her Amanda had received hers an hour prior. HR denied that had ever occurred, even though I had Amanda's email in front of me. HR then threatened to withdraw my contract. We left the conversation there. The flight departed without me the next day.

Once again, my future was in limbo and I faced my seventh consecutive week without pay. The next day I visited Sydney HR's head office.

'Do you have an appointment?' the receptionist asked.

'Yes.'

She picked up the phone and had a hushed conversation with someone I assumed was from HR.

'I'm afraid they're not discussing new contracts at this stage,' the receptionist told me.

'I already have a contract,' I replied. Another hushed phone conversation and I was allowed up. When I arrived at the right floor I was shown to a room and asked to wait. Two HR officers entered and sat at the other end of the large table from me.

'There have been questions about your contract already and your actions in the past few weeks have reinforced our belief that you're not suitable for a role with the Salvation Army. We told you we'd call and you continued to contact us,' the HR officer said.

'I apologise for calling you so much recently but I was under the impression that I would be leaving on the thirty-first of January,' I said. 'That was what I was told. I was even booked into the meeting and accommodation in Brisbane. In my previous two trips I've had to press HR for flight confirmations, so I assumed that was the protocol. All this frustration was compounded by six weeks of unemployment waiting for a contract that I thought was going to arrive. What do you mean there were questions about my contract?'

'There were complaints levelled at you,' the HR officer said.

'What were the complaints? This is the first I've heard of any of this.'

'They were from other service providers. That's all I can tell you at this point,' she said.

'I have no knowledge of these complaints and would've expected them to have been resolved at the time, especially if they were going to jeopardise my contract,' I said. 'Having said that, I wouldn't be surprised if there were complaints made after I spent ten weeks working in Nauru with just one week's break in between. I was exhausted.'

The HR officer looked uncomfortable. 'Well, we've changed that policy so no-one can stay for longer than four weeks. It was recognised that people start to become frustrated after four weeks,' she said.

'It's hard to defend myself when I have no idea what the complaints are,' I said. 'All I know is that I fought for the asylum seekers' rights. I always believed the Salvation Army supported me in this.'

'The Rec team has expanded since you were last there. We have a football competition and a cricket competition there now,' she said.

I tried not to laugh. The person deciding my fate had no idea what I had done on Nauru, no idea how long I'd spent there. 'I set them up,' I told her. She looked surprised. 'How are the swimming negotiations going?' I asked.

'Ah. Well, still nothing confirmed. If you go back again you're expected to toe the line and not act out. We have a Salvo brand we are trying to uphold and this includes outside of work hours. Parties and drinking will not be accepted. We are looking for people that represent the Salvation Army just as much as people who can do a good job.'

'Of course,' I said. 'I understand completely.'

'I'll endeavour to get you there in the next two weeks,' the HR officer said. 'Don't call us. We'll call you.'

I knew they could do it quicker—last rotation I had been returned within a week. This time they were going to make me sweat. I had offered myself up to the HR gods and all I could do was wait.

My experience was not an isolated one. If you were to talk to Salvation Army staff working at Nauru they would tell you that 'the mission' was run by an HR department in Sydney that had no knowledge of what was happening in Nauru and what was needed out there. Too often we found that the head in Sydney didn't know what the body in Nauru was doing.

I received an email the next week with my flight details confirmed. I was flying out two days later. Despite being told I would work four-week rotations I had been booked for five weeks. I didn't care, the struggle was over. I was going back.

Chapter 43

'HAVE YOU GOT your ID card?' Amanda asked.

'Yeah, why?'

'Everyone needs to have their ID cards on them at all times now.'

'High-level security,' I said.

It was my first day back at Topside. Pulling on my Salvation Army shirt that morning I'd felt apprehensive and defiant at the same time.

'You okay?' Amanda asked.

'One hundred per cent,' I replied, projecting confidence.

We walked together across the loose gravel of Topside to the Salvo office. I felt imaginary eyes on my back from those unknown service providers who had wanted me off the island. I held my head up with pride, but it was a stiff, unnatural position. I was back but I was by no means sure of myself.

The team meeting was surprisingly normal. Each team was given their duties for the day: I was allocated computer room duty as part of the general team. I was no longer part of the Rec team. No-one came to talk to me about what had happened in the past seven weeks. Instead I was approached by a female Salvo I had never met before.

'Hi, Mark,' she said, introducing herself. 'Let's have a chat. In private.'

I followed her out of the office, wondering if this would be the chat I had been expecting. When we were alone the Salvo talked to me in a low voice.

'I just wanted to let you know that there is an intel file on you. We are aware of your writing for Oxfam and you should be careful from now on about what you write on Facebook.'

She was talking about the same Oxfam writing I had listed on my résumé. Did this have something to do with how hard it had been for me to get back? Or had the Salvos finally read my résumé?

'Thanks,' I said. 'Is there anything else?'

We parted ways. Looking for an explanation, I tracked down the HR officer on the island.

'It was about a problem with a spray can, nothing more,' she said.

'That was Chris who brought the spray can into the compound, not me,' I said.

'Oh, I can't remember then. Don't worry about it.' She gave me a less than genuine pat on the back. When I was in Australia, Salvos HR had said it was the Nauruan HR that had asked for me not to come back.

When I explained this to Amanda she just shook her head angrily.

'You're not the only one who has had trouble. People are trying to sign contracts before they leave the island because they fear if they don't they may never get back.'

'So what do I do as part of the general team?' I asked.

'Whatever you want, really,' Amanda said with a smile.

'Let's go talk to the men then.'

*

In the seven weeks I'd been away the appearance of the camp had changed dramatically. There was a two-storey structure at the back of the camp, construction had overtaken the old football field, and there was a Hindu temple and a new mosque tent.

'About one hundred men from Iraq and Iran have arrived at Topside since you were last here. There have been three suicide attempts in the past two weeks. All from the new Iranian group,' Amanda said.

With all the construction taking place the camp was at capacity with just over four hundred men. But every time you thought the camp was at capacity, they somehow squeezed more men in.

'Anyone return home?' I asked.

'Half the PEP cricket team have gone back to Sri Lanka.'

It was rare that we knew why the men left, or what happened to them once they returned.

'How's my Rec program going?'

'The painting classes have stopped. The Nauru Premier League is pretty much dead. Cricket has been postponed for a month and a half because of monsoonal rain. Still no word on swimming excursions.'

We passed a tent with four men sitting inside it. One man was crying.

'Ebrahim lost a brother this week. The men have been in his tent for several days,' Amanda said.

'What's this new building?' I asked, pointing at a two-storey structure at the back of the camp.

Amanda explained to me that it was the new accommodation block. Rumours around the camp said that the estimated cost of this building was $6 million. DIAC had stipulated that each accommodation block must house a mix of at least three different ethnicities. Maintaining these guidelines, a selection of the first arrivals to the Nauru Processing Centre were placed in the new rooms. This had caused great displeasure to the Tamil men who had arrived before any of the other men but remained in tents.

Old friends, including Farid, Pez, Rashid, Omar, Mustafa, Raj and Dev, were among the few who had moved into the 'White House'. The men slept two to a room on bunk beds. Each room had a fan in the corner, a flyscreen door and a flyscreen window, designed to allow air to cool the rooms.

'You're in luxury,' I said to Omar and Mustafa.

'Nauru first class,' they joked back.

The rooms were fresh compared to the sauna tents, but they offered no privacy. Men, guards and construction workers could look in on them at any time. Inside the rooms there was a constant sense of being watched—Bentham's panopticon in action. Construction was underway on either side of the accommodation block. The jackhammers began their chorus of concrete breaking at eight in the morning and played until the sun went down. When it rained, the flyscreen windows did little to prevent the men's rooms being soaked. Above all, the new accommodation block was a sign of permanence.

It wasn't the only one. The Menen Hotel had new demountable accommodation blocks to house the expected influx of new staff. Meanwhile the Nauruan government was in turmoil: two ministers had resigned following disputes over the processing centre and the government had still not come to an agreement over the camp's evolution into an open centre.

A week later Nauru's community leaders met and voted unanimously that they did not want an open camp. They said there had been a lack of community consultation over the establishment of the camp and as a result they could not agree with releasing hundreds of foreign men into the community.

Many of the men were approaching their five-month anniversary in Nauru and it looked as if they were accepting their fate. Imran, a Pashtun Pakistani, was realistic about their situation.

'There is nothing we can do now—it is better that we try to live. We cannot stay in here protesting, hurting ourselves, fighting against everybody. Better we stay healthy in body and in mind.'

The men sat around placidly waiting, waiting, every day waiting for a bureaucrat in Canberra to decide when they could come to Australia.

Despite the physical changes in the camp, the inefficiencies that had been present from day one remained. The frustrations of bureaucracy still existed: the complaint forms, the IHMS request forms, the petty rules. The design of the windows in the new rooms could have easily been rectified with lower awnings or blinds, but instead the men were forced to endure damp living quarters yet again. No restrictions had been placed on the new accommodation block's showers, leading the men to use an unprecedented amount of water which led to water restrictions being placed on the whole camp for a period of time. One shower a day, three minutes maximum, or else Transfield would turn the water off for certain hours of the day.

There were still complaints about the health services. One man suffered from numbness in his hands and IHMS diagnosed it as psychological until the man had a major stroke which left him paralysed down one side. The man decided to voluntarily return to Iraq so he could then go to Kuwait to receive proper treatment. A Pakistani man had injured his leg playing football in the Nauru Premier League two months earlier. He was taken to the hospital but he wasn't given stitches. Two months later his leg was still infected. Krishna broke his collarbone playing cricket. He was given Panadol and water to treat it. Sher told me he had broken a bone in his foot playing football. He too was treated with Panadol and water. Men stopped engaging in physical exercise for fear that they would not receive proper medical treatment for their injuries.

The media still influenced the camp dramatically.

'No Chris Bowen. New man,' they said with hope in their eyes, after Chris Bowen was replaced as immigration minister by Brendan O'Connor.

'New man, same policy,' I replied, feeling cruel for crushing their hope so swiftly.

Even the old Iranian group appeared to have given up fighting. Parshan looked shrivelled up and old and withdrawn. His resistance had been eroded by the inevitability of indefinite detention. Then I found out that he had been banned from excursions because he had jumped in the ocean and stayed in there despite the Wilson guards' commands to get out. When I heard of this I laughed out loud. An unexpected sensation of pride surged through me. He still had his fight, he still had his identity. He wasn't going to let them wear him down. Parshan and his friends' next antics involved taking fruits from the food mess to ferment and make into alcohol.

Their resistance also manifested on a much more serious scale. An argument between Yashar and a Wilson guard ended with Yashar slashing his head open. His bald head bore horrible wounds that would eventually heal. That night, however, he cried himself to sleep. He cried until he couldn't cry any more, like a baby running out of breath. He cried that he wanted to kill himself, that there was no escape. These were actions that no Wilson guard or Salvo was present to witness. His actions questioned the simplified belief that he was just a troublemaker. For Pezhman, Yashar's night-time weeping brought back memories of similar thoughts he had once had.

'It made me think of the hardest times I had suffered here,' Pezhman said. 'I was living the trauma again.'

'Why do you think the Iranians are the only ones to have attempted to commit suicide so far?' I asked Pezhman.

He thought about it for a moment. 'They are the only ones that see how bad this situation is.'

'Really? Do you really think that?' I asked. 'I think that everyone understands how awful this place is. I just think that the Iranians are the most passionate and vocal about their displeasure. They want to show it in the most extravagant way they can.'

'Maybe you're right,' Pezhman said. 'I think the Iranians come from richer backgrounds. They are more educated. So there is a greater contrast from their previous lives when they arrive here. The Sri Lankans come from poorer places, they seem okay with this treatment. This is what I meant when I said Iranians see how bad the situation is.'

'No-one is okay with this place,' I said to him.

*

Within days of returning to Nauru I was having nightmares again. In one nightmare I was murdering men in the camp. My head swam with graphic images of amputated legs and bloodied bodies. In another I was imprisoned in the camp and the Tamils were my captors.

Chapter 44

MY NEW ROLE in the general team was a welcome change from the frantic working conditions of the Rec team. Where before my days had been filled with excursions, sporting games and paperwork, now I was left to my own devices. I filled the occasional computer room shift, but other than that no-one told me what to do. I spent my days wandering around the camp talking to who I pleased. I reacquainted myself with old friends and met new men. I explored areas of the camp I had ignored on previous rotations due to my other responsibilities.

The English classes had improved dramatically since the early days. In October there hadn't been enough pens or paper, and the classes had been held outside in the heat. Now there was a classroom with books, computers, a whiteboard, work sheets, workbooks, and actual teachers with actual qualifications.

I visited the classroom on a Saturday during an optional reading session, and the classroom was full of attentive men. English classes usually ran from Monday to Friday and they were always full. If a man couldn't make a class he made sure the teacher was aware that he wouldn't be there and why. Learning English gave the men something to work towards so their time in Nauru wasn't completely lost. It was a dim light in the gloom. The teachers told me they had tried to introduce vocational classes but DIAC had rejected their proposal as it would contravene the No Advantage policy.

I sat on a couch at the back of the class with Sher and helped him with his reading. Sher was a small Hazara man with thinning hair, a lined face, but a boyish smile and eyes.

'You have girlfriend?' he asked me.

'No.'

He looked concerned for me, as if this were a grave problem.

'Working here in Nauru makes it difficult to keep a relationship going,' I explained, but this didn't help. Now he looked guilty. 'But it's okay, I am young, and in Australia it's normal to get married at an older age.'

'How old are you?' he asked.

'Twenty-five.'

'Me also.'

Our similarity in age made us examine each other's face and consider our different upbringings. I had thought he was much older than twenty-five. I wondered how I appeared to him, if I looked older or younger than how I imagined myself.

'You have children?' I asked.

'No.'

'You have a wife?'

'Yes.'

'How old is she?'

'Nineteen.'

'What's she like?' I asked.

'She laugh a lot, very beautiful,' he said. 'I call her but she cry. My life is very bad, she say, and she cry for one week after I call. Very sad. So now I call just one time one month. I don't want to make her sad.'

I changed the topic. 'Your English has improved a lot. When did you start learning?'

'Thank you,' he said with a head bow. 'When I arrive to Christmas Island I start. Five months ago.'

'You speak very well.'

'Thank you.'

'What does Hazaragi look like?' I asked.

He looked embarrassed and leaned in confidentially and whispered, 'I don't know, I cannot read Hazaragi, just English.' He leaned back and looked at me closely. I felt as if he'd just told me a big secret.

'Why didn't you learn Hazaragi?'

'I have big problem, very bad problem,' he said slowly, and then his story rushed forward as if he was worried that if he stopped he wouldn't be able to start again. 'When I was eight years old, my father died—ah, I cannot speak of this but very big problem, very bad. I have just my mother, my brother younger and me. I went to work as a mechanica, I have just eight years. I walk one hour to garage, there and back. My mother walk me and it snow and it very cold, too much cold. One hour there, one hour back, I was child when I work mechanica for my family so I cannot study. All my life I work, I am very good as mechanica. I make my motorbike, I have car, I make some money, not many. I met my wife, life was very good, but then Taliban come. They say me, make me motorbike, free. I say I cannot, I have family, I cannot work free. If I work free I cannot eat. I have mother, wife, brother younger, he is fifteen, in school. I say no. Taliban come to my house, they shoot at me, I put my hands up like this.' He put his hands up to protect his face. 'They hit me here.'

He showed me his hand. There was a scar running down the outside of his right hand. 'I cannot use this finger now, but I am lucky, I am alive. I say then I must go, it is not safe, and I never return to Afghanistan.'

In his English book he had written over and over again, *I want to live in Sydney, Australia if I get out of here alive.*

Chapter 45

'COME ON.' Sibilraj took my hand. 'Birthday party.' Sibilraj was a dark-skinned Tamil who liked to talk about girls. He led me to Tent 3A where fifteen men were squashed inside, standing around a table. A humble arrangement of food was displayed with delicate precision. Eight apples stacked on top of each other, three packets of chips, four bottles of Coke, five chocolate bars.

The two birthday boys stood at the head of the table and the men sang 'Happy Birthday', finishing with a cheer. A tray of plastic cups of Coke moved among the men. Another tray of potato chips went in the opposite direction.

A Tamil man jumped up shouting, 'PHOTO!' He pulled out an origami paper camera—'Smile, please,'—and then he pulled at the edges and paper shot outwards, imitating a flash.

'Look, polaroid,' he said.

Inside the origami camera there was a piece of paper. Three men were drawn on the paper. Everyone began lining up for photos with the birthday boys. 'The flash is too bright,' the Tamil man muttered and then the camera was out of film. 'So sorry,' he apologised.

'Security,' someone shouted. 'Hide the camera.'

If they could do this with so little, imagine the party they would have when they got out, when they could buy whatever they wanted, whenever they wanted.

*

Valentine's Day was going to pass unnoticed in Nauru. Most of the men didn't celebrate the day like Australians would; it was foreign to them. Even if they had understood its significance this would only have served to sadden them. Unwilling to allow Valentine's Day to flop, Salar and I began writing Valentine's Day cards. The cards were illustrated with roses, love hearts and cupids. On the inside we wrote heartfelt poems such as:

> *Roses are red*
> *Violets are blue*
> *There are no women on Nauru*
> *So I choose you*

And all were signed, *Love, your secret admirer.*

Fifteen cards were distributed at random on stretcher beds throughout the tents. As far as I knew nothing was heard of the cards, and then one day I found a case note in a Tamil file I was reading. The man had reported to his case manager that he was happy that day because he had received a Valentine's Day card.

Chapter 46

I TOOK THE opportunity offered by the general team timetable to get to know the Pakistani and Sinhalese men. Many men in the camp were from Pakistan, some were Hazara immigrants from Afghanistan, and a large group were Pashtun men, Shia Muslims, from Parachinar in Pakistan. They drew a map of the Parachinar area with signposts to significant landmarks such as the Afghanistan border and Karachi. On the majority of the roads out of Parachinar they marked *Taliban here*.

According to the Australian Refugee Review Tribunal, the Pakistani Taliban is separate from the Afghan Taliban, and is made up of a number of different militant Sunni groups that were driven into Pakistan during the NATO invasion of Afghanistan in 2001. These terrorist groups positioned themselves on the border of Pakistan and Afghanistan, in an area known as the Federally Administered Tribal Areas (FATA).[1] Parachinar is located in the heart of the FATA.

Every so often news would filter through that a family member of one of the Pakistani men had been executed by the Taliban. I wondered how one summons the resilience amid the turmoil of such a camp to deal with the immeasurable grief of losing one's loved ones.

Imran was one of these men. My friendship with Imran developed slowly over a mutual love of words and philosophy. We referred to each other as kindred spirits, Siamese twins separated at birth. He enjoyed the company of the female Salvos, even if he confessed to me that his libido had disappeared in Nauru. He boasted of his ability to woo a woman with his words, so I began calling him the Silver Tongue.

'Why do you call me that?' he asked.

'Because you have a way with words. It's a compliment in our culture.'

'Ah, good. Then please call me Silver Tongue.'

Imran never went on excursions so we did not get to know each other until my third rotation in the camp.

'The excursions remind me of all that I have not,' he told me.

Imran liked to make bold statements and see how I reacted to them.

'People act like children here,' he said to me.

'Go on,' I said.

'They are constantly confused by new rules in the computer room, in the canteen, at IHMS. Everything is rules here and they are constantly changing. It is impossible to keep up. And they are in English, which is difficult for men to understand. I have seen grown men crying here, really crying, because they are helpless. They cannot help themselves with very small problems. They become like children.'

He had a talent for turning initially provocative statements into insightful observations.

'Working in Nauru is draining,' I confided in him, in a rare moment of weakness I reserved for the men I knew best. 'I spend four weeks here each rotation and by the end of the month I'm exhausted.'

He smiled wryly at me, as if to say, *Oh really? Four weeks is hard, is it?*

I rushed to make up for my gaffe. 'I know it's easy for me in comparison to you,' I said. 'I don't know how you guys live here. You've shown how strong you are.'

'It is not strength,' he said. 'If you put a bird in a cage, you don't remark on how strong it is. At first it will attack the bars and beat its wings and be very angry, and then it realises that there is nothing it can do, and it will remain in the cage very placidly.'

'Maybe I would change my opinion of the bird if I knew the pain it was going through.'

'You know what I have just realised?' he said. 'I have realised that to seek asylum is a crime.'

'No it's not,' I replied and he smiled—he had caught me out. 'Why do you say that it's a crime?' I asked.

'Well, look at us,' he said. 'Is this not a prison? Are we not prisoners? So therefore we must have committed a crime.'

*

The Sinhalese appeared to be a close-knit group, united by their ethnicity, although each of their stories was unique. I got to know the men on excursions and through cricket tournaments. After hearing the Tamil men speak of the discrimination they'd suffered from Sinhalese officials, I was interested to hear the Sinhalese asylum seekers tell their stories.

I was closest with Sanji, a skinny kid who couldn't have been more than nineteen years old. He looked happiest when he was playing cricket or football. He spoke in a whisper that forced you to lean in to catch everything he said. He told me he was nervous about meeting girls, but he wanted to marry an Australian girl. He was a good-looking kid, and I was sure he would be able to get a girlfriend in Sydney if he could muster the courage to speak to her.

'Sri Lanka very dangerous for me,' he whispered. 'I was very afraid to go anywhere. There were bombs, and guns, and it was very dangerous for anyone. There were no jobs so I went to Dubai to get work, but I could not find any jobs. I did not eat there and I come back with no money. I never have money, in all my life. I was only happy when I played football for my village. I played forward and I scored many goals and many men come to watch me play.'

Thevan was at a wedding when he received a call from his uncle telling him to get on a boat and leave Sri Lanka that day. Thevan had been a fisherman. All his life he had suffered at the hands of the Sri Lankan navy, who regularly stole his fish and physically assaulted him. It was a form of prejudice but would it be deemed as appropriate enough to earn him protection from the Australian government? A month after he arrived in Nauru, his father was kidnapped and tortured by the Sri Lankan government, which was trying to find him. His family were threatened and were forced to move homes.

AJ was a good-looking, muscular man. He always dressed well and was immaculately groomed, with glistening curly locks. He played drums and guitar and sang, often improvising songs on the spot in Sinhalese and in English. His most popular song request for Salvos to sing was 'Hotel California'. On one excursion AJ performed six flips in front of the bus like an Olympic gymnast. His girlfriend had been raped and murdered in Sri Lanka. He assured me there was a long story that followed this incident, which drove him to flee for Australian shores by boat.

Arjun liked to make people laugh. He danced like a snake at the music concerts, making silly faces that had everyone in stitches. He had been a boat captain and talked of his expertise in navigating fishing expeditions. Despite his talent as a fisherman he'd struggled with poverty throughout his life. He was the captain of a boat that had arrived at Christmas Island. He was the only Sinhalese man on the boat, and the only man from his boat to be deported to Nauru. He had a family and children in Sri Lanka. Again I was faced with a real-life people smuggler. He didn't look evil, he looked like a man who needed money to support his family.

Many of the men confessed that when they'd left their home countries they had no knowledge of a refugee convention and no understanding of Australian immigration policy. Many of the Sinhalese men were worried they did not fit within the United Nations definition of a refugee. The knowledge that they might be denied entry to Australia was compounded by the fact that for a lot of them returning to Sri Lanka could result in jail time, physical violence or harm to their families; some even feared for their lives. For whatever reason they had left Sri Lanka, there was no doubt that they feared returning, yet they joked and laughed. They welcomed Salvos to their dinner tables, offered them food and seats. They were polite to staff, respectful to the women. I got the impression that they were the only men in the Nauru Regional Processing Centre who didn't want processing to start.

*

I was in Nauru a week before my former manager returned to the island. She was recognised by Salvo staff as the only manager who truly supported the workers. Her unfailing optimism inspired the workers around her and instilled a faith in her that no other manager I worked under in Nauru could replicate. Before her arrival in Nauru no-one had approached me about the circumstances of my contract or explained to me what I was supposed to be doing in Nauru now that I wasn't involved in the Rec team.

To make it more confusing, I was constantly placed in Rec team roles. Most of the Salvo staff weren't aware of the struggles I had endured to get back, and didn't know I wasn't working in the team anymore.

'Mark, you're running the excursions, aren't you? Can you just—'

'Ah, sorry, Mick. No, I'm not. You'll have to ask Ellie about that.'

'Oh, that's odd. What happened?'

I made a conscious decision to ignore the politics and suppressed any desire to follow up the complaints levelled against me. The struggle to renew my contract had made me grateful just to be in Nauru. I didn't want to draw any more attention to myself, I just wanted to continue working there. And then finally my manager gave me the story straight.

'You really pissed off Wilsons,' she said laughing. 'They said you were unprofessional, you were too social with the men and didn't take charge of the excursions properly, and that you were unmanageable. Apparently you didn't listen to them. They didn't want you back here.'

'Unmanageable? Lucky you're my manager and not them,' I said.

I gathered from other colleagues that it had been my manager who had fought to keep me on the island. The saga left me feeling betrayed by the Salvation Army. At the time these complaints were levelled, I had done everything the Salvation Army asked. Management never discussed the complaints with me, nor told me the job I was doing was incorrect. I believed I had the support of the Salvation Army, when really I only had one manager to thank. Any allegiance I had for the Salvation Army began to deteriorate from this point onwards. Despite all the confusion and uncertainty of my position, I still felt like I'd won. And so I went back to doing what I did best even though I wasn't officially a part of the Recreations team. The newest Rec program was the running group, a program I had helped set up with another Salvo at the end of my last rotation. I made that my new baby.

*

Ten men lined up at the gate of the compound, wearing high-vis vests and an assortment of footwear and clothing that could be loosely described as sportswear. The Wilson escort almost outnumbered them. There was a lead car in front of the group and a chase car behind, as well as two Salvo runners, one at the front, one at the back. The running group commenced at six o'clock in the evening, giving the men one hour to run before darkness set in.

The group ran past the boom gate and onto a potholed road. The intimidating pinnacles dropped away to the right, the sun setting on the ocean horizon. The sky was limitless. There were no fences. The men ran in the midst of an orange glow. Once the running began the guards disappeared. Breathe in, breathe out, one foot in front of the other. No fences, just the horizon. The group followed the road 2 kilometres to the edge of an incline that led to the rest of the island and then returned to the camp. At the end of each run the men heaved in the steamy night air, they high-fived and hugged each other and clapped runners in to the finish, no matter how slow their time. When one of the Tamil men finished his run he started to smack his head over and over again with both hands.

'What are you doing?' I asked, worried the Tamil man would hurt himself.

'I have running mind now, I need Topside mind now.'

The running group quickly became popular with a group of about thirty men. In the thirty there were men who wanted to run the 4 kilometres in under ten minutes and there were men who couldn't run 4 kilometres in one stint. Saeed, a rotund Iranian man, joined every day, a thin jumper stretched across his large gut, Dunlop Volleys tight around his large feet. He confessed he hadn't run in four years.

One day Saeed managed to leave the camp on his own. The men lined up at the gate for running group, their IDs were collected, and the group moved to the front boom gate, but Saeed was already there. Somehow he had managed to walk straight through the front gate of the men's camp, past the guard's checkpoint, past the Transfield, DIAC and Salvo offices, all the way to the last exit without anyone noticing. The Wilson guards were furious—his jaunt would make their managers question their professionalism.

'How did you do it?' I asked him.

'I walk,' he said. 'I wave. "Hello, friendly guard. Hello." And they wave back, and I walk to here.'

---

1 Refugee Review Tribunal (Australia), *The Pakistani Taliban*, Issues Paper, January 2013, viewed 11 November 2013, <www.refworld.org/docid/514313f12.html>.

Chapter 47

WITH CONSTRUCTION TAKING place at Topside the staff mess was always full. One day I sat next to a long-haired Canstruct worker with a scruffy, unkempt beard.

'How ya going, mate?' I asked him.

'Alright, ay.' He spoke with a lazy drawl.

'How's the work for Canstruct?'

'Well, it's not the hammock holiday I was dreaming of.' He laughed. 'It's hard work, ya know? It's not like work conditions in Australia. Twelve-hour days, no days off, in this heat too. My first trip in February, I worked thirty days straight. I was exhausted afterwards,' he said. 'I spent my time off recovering.'

'How are your rotations structured?' I asked.

'Four weeks on, two weeks off, but it's more like ten days off when you take into account all the travel time,' he said.

'Same with the Salvos.'

'What do you guys do in Nauru?'

'We do the support work with the men,' I said. 'The case management, education, sport, lifestyle. We pretty much try to get them through the experience of living in Nauru.'

'How do you cope with the politics of it all?' he asked.

In the previous rotation I had begun to reserve my opinion around other organisations, but with Ian I immediately got the sense that he was of the same opinion as me by the way he phrased the question.

'It isn't easy.'

Ian told me he was a painter, a carpenter, a jack-of-all-trades, from a construction family. He was separated, with four kids. He had originally been interested in the work to try something different. His friend had asked him to join the Canstruct team, but after two rotations he had realised the work was most definitely not what he wanted and he was reconsidering. He wanted to see his kids again, but he also wanted to set himself up financially. For the first time in his life he was working purely for the money and no other reason.

'Do you think the construction has been rushed?' I asked him.

'It definitely has, hasn't it?' he said. 'I mean, they went from constructing the first two accommodation blocks to importing prefab rooms. That kind of construction is expensive, ya know? And it's not good craftsmanship. They're using steel and nuts and bolts, instead of wood. It's not sustainable. They'll need to be refurbished every ten years, most likely. It could've been done a lot cheaper, I reckon, but they wanted it done quickly. So they spend more money and get worse quality. That's not how I like to work, but I don't have to like it. As I said, I'm here for the money.'

Chapter 48

GREG LAKE SAT opposite me at the table in his hotel room. He was staying in one of the new accommodation blocks at the Menen. He had an air-conditioned room to himself; there was an en suite and a double bed and a stove. Of course, DIAC officials were well looked after with their own rooms and business-class flights to and from the island.

Greg was the new director of DIAC on Nauru. He had been my school captain when I was aged thirteen at Normanhurst Boys High. He had been a likeable adolescent with a kind face and a genuine desire to help us younger kids. From the little I had seen of him in Nauru it didn't appear that too much had changed. He took his time meeting the men and the staff, and to both he was open with his role in the camp.

'Whether you agree with this policy or not, we are in Nauru to perform a job and we have the opportunity to make life as good as possible for these men,' he'd said in an address to the Salvation Army.

The last time I had seen Greg, he was singing a song by The Whitlams at a high school function. Now we found ourselves in the midst of the asylum seeker debate.

'There is a view that the Department of Immigration is an evil organisation,' he said, 'and that the workers in it are bad people. That we agree with the policy; worse, we enjoy our work. Admittedly there are some people who probably do agree with the policy, but that's not to say we all do. When all is said and done, we are public servants, we represent the people of Australia. We do what the democratically elected government of Australia tell us to do. It's not important if we agree with the policy or not.'

'But to absolve yourself of all responsibility by saying "It's my job to do what people tell me to do" implies you have no autonomy,' I said. 'That's how people have justified atrocities in the past. There has to be a point where you say, "I have exceeded my ethical limits and I can no longer continue with this".'

'Well, you have a choice, don't you?' he said. 'You can take on the role and try to do the best work you can from within the system, or you can withdraw and allow someone else to take your position and then you've got to ask yourself, how will this person treat these men?'

'So where do you draw the line?' I asked. 'Where do you say enough is enough? When someone goes crazy? When someone kills themselves? When we are told to kill them?'

'I think we can safely say it won't get to the point of us killing them,' Greg laughed. 'But that line in the sand is up to each individual. As bad as it is here, the Gillard government did not want this policy; ministers have resigned from cabinet over the policy. Having the Salvos contracted in Nauru and Manus rather than SERCO is evidence of their goodwill.'

'It's a bandaid on a bullet wound,' I said. 'I'll send you to a prison and ask you how you feel about it. It's a move to placate the lefties.'

'So you're saying the Salvos aren't worthwhile in Nauru?' he asked.

'Not at all,' I said. 'In fact, without the Salvos I think things would be infinitely worse. I just think it's hypocritical to suggest that the government has the men's welfare at heart when they send them to offshore centres and place them in indefinite detention.'

'I agree, but they could make it worse if they wanted to. Ultimately, this is a policy that the Australian people want. It has become an election issue of protecting our borders. If the Australian people wanted a fairer system then the government would implement it, but the Australian people don't want that. They want to protect our borders.'

'But if the Australian people knew just how bad it was here, do you think they'd agree with the policy?' I asked. 'There's a reason there's a complete media ban on the camp. People think that if the Salvation Army are in Nauru it can't be that bad. I think if the Salvation Army were serious about protecting the rights of the men they would have fought harder, they should have been threatening DIAC with dropping the contract to ensure certain rights were upheld. Instead they are pandering to the government's wishes, too worried about losing their contract.'

'That may be true, but maybe they should never have taken the contract in the first place. I think the majority of the Australian people don't want asylum seekers in the country and if it means the Pacific Solution then so be it, as harsh as that is.'

'Then why does the government have to implement such a cruel policy? They go above and beyond the call of duty.'

Greg shrugged his shoulders. 'It's a deterrence policy, it wouldn't work if it wasn't harsh.'

When I left Greg I felt more confused than ever. It was easier to hate DIAC when they made themselves the enemy. Greg provided an alternative perception of DIAC, demonstrating that it was possible to work within the system, even one such as DIAC, to make a difference. Despite all his logical arguments our conversation made me think of Charlie Chaplin's words: 'We think too much and feel too little.'

Chapter 49

I WALKED UP the stairs of the plane, Omar directly behind me wearing headphones that dented his afro. We sat next to each other, me in the middle, him by the window. The plane pushed us back into our seats as it took off from Nauru. Omar waved goodbye to his island prison, waved goodbye to fences, the pinnacles, the guards and restrictions. The four-and-a-half-hour plane ride would be the longest Omar had spent in an air-conditioned space for five years.

The plane food came out, plastic and uninviting.

'The food in the camp was better,' Omar said with a smile.

'I told you you shouldn't have complained about it,' I said.

We arrived in Brisbane and caught our transfer to Sydney.

'Mum, Dad, this is Omar.' My dad shook his hand warmly, my mum hugged him.

'It's a pleasure to meet you,' Omar said.

My dad drove us from the airport to the northern suburbs, talking about the football results. We took the Cahill Expressway over the Harbour Bridge. Sydney Harbour splayed out before Omar's misty eyes: the Sydney Opera House splendidly white, yachts, skyscrapers, jacarandas.

'You don't mind if we head over to Tom's, do you?' I asked.

'Of course not,' my dad said, but I could tell he wanted us to stay and talk to him.

We walked around the side of a two-storey house, past a big white gum tree. There was a small crowd sitting in garden chairs round the back. Omar shook hands with my friends, who were unsure how to start a conversation with a real-life refugee, a man who had just spent five years in jail thanks to their country's immigration policy.

'You want a beer?' Tom asked.

'Sure,' Omar said.

'Of course he does,' I said. 'How long has it been since you had a beer?'

'Too long, man,' Omar replied.

He was given a Little Creatures and he joined the men standing around the barbecue cooking up a feed.

'Do you guys have The Roots?' Omar asked them. They stared at him, stunned that an asylum seeker liked hip-hop, then everyone laughed.

'Sure, let's chuck it on.'

I woke up and remembered Omar and I were still in Nauru. He had been in Nauru for five months, and if what DIAC said was correct he still had years to go.

Chapter 50

ATASH WAS A well-known figure. He was vocal in his denunciations of the camp and had been suspected of being a ringleader in the first riot. It was hard to have a conversation with Atash because his mind always reverted back to how bad the camp was. I judged that he was in his mid-forties. He was an engineer, single with no children. He had been taken from Nauru to Australia with a medical condition after a sustained hunger strike.

One day Atash returned from Australia. He was taken from Brisbane Immigration Transit Accommodation at three in the morning and deported to Nauru. Mission workers witnessed him lying on the floor of the Brisbane international airport crying uncontrollably, totally devastated. After spending three months in Australia, believing he would be processed in the Australian system, he was suddenly facing incarceration on the island all over again. When he arrived in Nauru he did not acknowledge anybody. He lay on his stretcher, in his tent, motionless. His eyes were open but he did not look at anything. He refused all food, refused any kind of communication.

His story was revealed to me by a Salvation Army worker who had worked closely with him. While in Brisbane Atash had been diagnosed with gallstones, a condition that would need surgery to rectify. He was taken to the Royal Brisbane Hospital, where he gave written consent to allow the doctors to perform the surgery.

He was placed on a waiting list. While he waited for his operation, another opportunity came up for the surgery to be performed at the Toowong Private Hospital. Atash was given the choice to go to Toowong Private Hospital or remain on the waiting list at the Royal Brisbane Hospital. He said he was unsure what would happen to him if he signed two different sets of consent forms, likening it to committing your hand to two women. By refusing the second opportunity for surgery Atash gave himself more time in Australia, a much more desirable option than being returned to Nauru. After he verbally refused the second offer he was returned to Nauru without undergoing an operation, even though it was expected he would need it in the future.

Soon after Atash returned the camp atmosphere began to heat up again, as if it were coming out of hibernation. In the early hours of Sunday 17 February, three of the new Iranian arrivals escaped from the camp. It wasn't a terribly difficult thing to do. They jumped the fence at the back of the camp and ran into the pinnacles. At first the Wilsons radios were alive with chatter.

'Charlie Three to Romeo One. We have a breach. I repeat, we have a code green.'

'Whisky One to Charlie Three. There are three men in the pinnacles.'

'Romeo One to Whisky One. We will need a ladder.'

After the initial excitement of their escape it became clear that the men had nowhere to run. One of the men had climbed a tree; the other two were stuck in the harsh and uninviting pinnacles. They had no way of getting food or water, they were easily recognisable as asylum seekers and they had no way of getting off the island. The Wilson guards told them that if they didn't return to the camp the police would be called and they would face criminal charges. The men returned to the camp. It was the start of a new period of resistance.

The new Iranian group staged a protest on Tuesday 19 February. The group marched through the camp chanting, 'Close the Nauru'. A code blue was called, a medical emergency, a man had cut himself.

Another Iranian jumped the fence and escaped into the pinnacles. Some of the men sewed their lips together using blunt paper clips. In among all this a Hazara man suffered a psychotic episode. One man jumped a fence into the construction yard, climbed the scaffolding and threatened to jump. He may have succeeded if it wasn't for the Wilson security guards who held him back from the edge. In the late afternoon, Ebrahim, a bull-necked Iranian with curly hair, jumped into the phone room, ripped a fluorescent light tube from the roof and smashed it against himself. As he jumped through the phone room window ten Tamils jumped out of the bunker, like something out of the Three Stooges. Ebrahim walked into the crowded Green Room, cutting himself with the broken light in violent slashes across the chest, neck, head and arms. He was 5 metres from me. I saw the red lines on his body slowly begin to ooze blood. He didn't flinch once, but his invincibility to physical pain contrasted with the anguish of incarceration etched so visibly across his face.

The old Iranian group was disappointed in the new group's actions. It seemed they had forgotten that this was them two months earlier. It felt odd to be watching it all over again. A new group of men using extreme displays to show their displeasure. At times it looked like a performance, then it became more serious than anything I'd ever seen before. They began hunger-striking, despite Namdar's past experience demonstrating the Australian government's determination to keep this camp open. Soon enough they would learn that their efforts were futile, that they were only making their situation worse and that the more they protested, the more they disrupted life in the camp for everyone else. Soon enough the monotony of life in Topside would overcome them and subdue them, just like Imran's bird in a cage, and then we would watch a new group arrive and go through the same process.

Each new arrival of men brought more tension to the camp, and with no foreseeable end to processing the mood grew closer and closer to disaster.

Chapter 51

ALI WAS A MULLAH. I had often seen him holding a Koran, deep in discussion with men of all ethnicities. He was softly spoken yet his voice commanded your attention, even if you couldn't understand his language. His beard was neatly trimmed and his fingers were stubby. Fifteen years ago the Taliban had started attacking his family. They killed four of his brothers. Ali lost many family members when a large boat capsized off the coast of Indonesia, drowning a group of Hazaras. While in the camp Ali had tried to transfer $250 back to his family in Afghanistan. Due to clerical errors the transfer had not been successful, which meant his child had not received the proper medical treatment and died. Despite all the sadness, Ali remained a dignified man using his faith as a platform to carry on. Life for him was not a pleasure, it was a struggle. He was a battered piece of driftwood in a high storm, just waiting for the calm.

During the protests Ali suffered a psychotic episode that lasted for three days before he was forcibly removed from the camp. According to the Hazara men taking care of him, he spent the first twenty-four hours within his tent, unwell. The second day he was taken out of the camp on a stretcher to IHMS, who returned him to the camp that same day. He spent the next twenty-four hours swearing, running around the camp with his shirt off, crawling in the dirt, barking like a dog. He had lost touch with reality; he had lost his mind. That night he slept at the gate to the camp. IHMS waited for consent to remove him but after several days it became clear Ali was not going to recover soon. Watching Ali lose grasp of his sanity was an unnerving experience. His world had become a nightmare; his eyes were glazed yet panicky. He saw a different reality to what the rest of us were seeing. For the Hazara men this was particularly upsetting. Their religious leader, their mullah, the man they revered and looked to for spiritual enlightenment had crumbled from within. This came just days after the bombings in Quetta on Saturday 16 February that killed hundreds of Hazaras.

The men told me all of this while sitting at the front gate of the camp waiting for sleeping pills that didn't work. They took them, but the relief from insomnia was temporary at best. Most of them hadn't achieved a full night's rest in Nauru. Every evening Sher waited two hours for one sleeping pill. I wondered how much a packet of sleeping pills would cost, and how many hours I could buy him back with that packet. Twenty dollars for a packet of ten pills? One pill would cost me $2 and give him back two hours. Would it matter? The purpose of those pills was to kill hours. Then I wondered how much the Australian government was paying to make him wait in this centre.

'My mother was killed in the bombings in Pakistan,' Sher said. 'My auntie, my cousin too. Dead.'

I sat numbly with him in the dark. He didn't cry, I didn't cry.

Muhammad was a Hazara who looked like Chief Bromden from *One Flew Over the Cuckoo's Nest*. He had been trying to call his family to see if they were okay. Their phone connection was cut, and he had no other way of contacting them. They didn't use the internet and he couldn't get hold of any friends to find them. He didn't know if they were dead or alive and he didn't know how he could find out. He was having trouble thinking, he couldn't retain memory, he couldn't enjoy his time with friends. He spent his days fake smiling.

Salar sat with us on the stony floor of the camp. He had deep shadows under his eyes. The usual mischievousness that crept around the corners of his face had faded.

'In Afghanistan, Pakistan, they kill us with pistols and bombs. Here you destroy our minds,' Salar said. 'I lost many friends in the bomb in Quetta, many family. One friend asked me if he should come to Australia. I told him I could not say yes or no, there is too much change in policy. How could I advise him? He has gone missing since the bomb. If I had told him to come he would be alive.'

We sat in silence, picking rocks out of the gravel and throwing them at a pole. The aim was to hit the pole, but when one of us hit the pole the game did not end. It was a popular game in Topside.

'Another friend, they found just his hand,' Salar continued. 'There was too much explosion, you know. One of my friends told me he had lost seven of his friends. Most of the Hazara people in Nauru have lost at least one friend or family in that bombing. We have always been oppressed, we always stay quiet. Keep it here.' He touched his heart. 'This is why we go crazy in here.'

While the Iranians protested and cut themselves and tried to jump off scaffolding, the Hazaras sat in groups, quiet and sorrowful. In the previous week I had begun to question whether the camp was so bad. Maybe we did need screening policies to prevent criminals coming to Australia. The men had to be kept somewhere, didn't they? The food wasn't so bad. It was a tough system, but it was a system. Think of all the people waiting in awful refugee camps in Africa. My approval of the camp was fleeting. I rationalised it in my own head as an acclimation to the traumas of the centre. I couldn't keep being shocked by suicide attempts and self-harm. The mullah's psychotic episode scratched away the calm facade of the previous weeks to reveal the hell that this place was. Men's sanity teetered on the edge of a bureaucratic precipice. How could I ever have doubted the horror of this place?

'For me Nauru is the end of the life, the end of the hope, the end of the world,' Salar said. 'I have lost my hope. I am dizzy here. What will happen to us? Someone should answer us. This is our right to know our future. Everybody started smoking in Nauru. One packet, two packets a day. It is bad for our health, we should stop, but we don't care. When people stop caring about us, we stop caring about ourselves.'

We sat for a while in silence. I wanted him to get it all out. When I felt he had finished I changed the subject.

'What does *luchak* really mean?' I asked Salar. The men assured me that their title for me meant 'loafer' and 'junkie', but neither of these explanations fit the laughter that accompanied the name.

'You really want to know?'

'Yes.'

'It is a guy who does nothing but try to meet girls. He spends all his money on parties. He has no responsibility.'

'Oh, okay. Well, call me *luchak* then,' I said with a wry smile and Salar laughed.

'In Afghanistan this is a very bad term, but we know with you this is a joke.' He added that last part almost as a disclaimer to make sure I wasn't offended.

'It's okay, I get it. If I was a real *luchak* I wouldn't be working in a camp with four hundred men,' I said.

'But in Australia you have a girlfriend?'

'No, I was seeing a girl, but she had a boyfriend in France so it was complicated.'

'What do you say about all this cheating and lots of girlfriends?' he asked.

'Well, I guess it's not uncommon,' I said. 'Especially at my age. Most people don't get married until their late twenties, and before then you have different girlfriends and boyfriends. It's about living your life and not missing out on opportunities, and sometimes relationships can prevent you from doing what you want. What about in Afghanistan?'

'In Afghanistan you do not have girlfriends and boyfriends,' he said. 'Not publicly anyway. If you have a girlfriend, it is in secret. You don't want people to know. And you do not cheat. This is very bad. This is a very Western thing, I think.'

'Have you had girlfriends?' I asked.

'Of course,' he said with a cheeky grin and we both laughed.

'Do you drink?' I asked. 'And go to parties?'

'As a culture we do not drink,' he said. 'I drink, but I know my limits, and I only drink a few. It is very bad to drink too much, it is an embarrassment to you and your family, you know?'

'I guess,' I said. 'In Australia it is very different. People drink a lot, too much, all the time, and often they embarrass themselves and their family. I guess it is a cultural thing.'

In the next few days a medevac was organised for Ali. He did not receive the medical attention he needed until it was too late, once he had already been broken. Another $80,000 spent treating his mental illness on the mainland.

*

This is an edited letter written by the Hazaras to DIAC in response to the mullah's psychotic episode.

> *Honourable Greg Lake Director of DIAC,*
> *Nauru Regional Processing Centre*
>
> *In the Name of God the Most High*
> *'Every single human being is a limb to the whole and one human body called "humanity". As they are from the same essence and origin. If a part of the body is in pain the rest of the body can not be in ease, for sure will be suffering.'*
>
> *(Poem of Saadi, the famous Persian/Dari Poet of 7th century, these verses are currently mounted as a precious tablet of human values, on the wall in the Security Council building)*
>
> *Hereby we would like to pay our due respect and complaisance and say; peace be with you. We would like you to kindly consider the piteous and baleful situation of us; the Hazara people and amiably pass it to the higher authorities of the Australian Government; such as Parliament, Minister of Immigration and the Chief Committee of Human Rights.*

We expect that the authorities who have the full capacity of decision making, to scrutinise our situation with respect to the definition of refugee; according to the Convention of United Nation for refugees.

The following items would briefly unfold the bitters of our life, and hopefully leads to more amiable and fairer ordinance:

When we were in Afghanistan and in Pakistan, we could see the perishing of our family members in the worst possible way, by the hands of oppressors before our eyes. The image of their torn bodies and bloody coffins are still in our memories. Our life was always full of fear and horror and we could not think of being alive for the next day. We did not have any other option but to leave our homeland, and with ultimate perplexity and astonishment we started to seek refuge wherever we could.

The majority of Hazaras who immigrated to Pakistan, during the last two decades begun to face the most terrible fate. The outburst of filthiest beings called Taliban and Al Qaeda, the two notorious terrorist groups. These cancerous groups started reproducing and forming more and more under different names like, Lashkar-e-Jhangvi and Sipah-e-Sahaba in their native pest hole 'Pakistan'. These groups were produced to commit any possible crime and to impose atrocities against the defenceless people of Hazara to the level of mass killings. Our Hazaras, like distressed haw trying to run away from the wolf pack, entered the den named Pakistan.

Why is this all against this innocent nationality? Just because of being Hazara and being Shia. The Leader of Lashkar-e-Jhangvi during a phone interview said to the BBC reporter that his main objective is to eradicate the Hazara and Shia generation from Afghanistan and Pakistan.

We the Hazaras in Pakistan and in Afghanistan are like wounded birds getting stuck in the ditch, worried of being hunted by the cat. We have no means of flying and no hope for survival.

In Alamdar Road in Quetta, Pakistan in January 2013 as a result of a suicide attack, 250 innocent Hazaras were killed which was broadcast by world's media. A short time after this genocide another suicide attack took place on the 16th of February 2013 and left larger number of dead and injured people behind much more than the number of previous suicide attack.

During the latter suicide attack which was severe and numerous, people were unable to collect the bodies of their relatives and family members. At this shocking moment for the Hazaras, just next to them the merciless enemy of Lashkar-e-Jhangvi started firing out of joy and rejoicing the massacre with the loudest music. There was no-one from any services like ambulance or police to rescue these people. We can't tell how painful this is and would be for those who were present at the scene and those who suffered the loss of their beloved ones.

Those of us who live in Iran are restrained from work by the government, and they can't walk in the community freely. When they get caught by the authorities, are deported without giving a chance to see their family or take their family with them. This deportation takes place with torture and lots of humiliation. Their children are deprived from school and any kind of education.

We, the Hazara asylum seekers in Nauru, have lost our primary or secondary members of our family during the last catastrophic incident in Pakistan. We held the funeral for consoling one another and mourning here in detention centre for the loss of our beloved ones. Being in detention centre is multiplying the grief and sadness for us. Imagine the situation of our remaining family members in Pakistan with the fall of this calamity on them.

We heard about Australia and its values which would not allow any discrimination of any form against its residents and we noticed that being Hazara and being Shia is not considered as a sin here in Australia. Justice and real democracy does exist in Australia and human rights are seriously respected here. By knowing these facts about Australia and our desperateness for having a shelter above ourselves led us to Australia.

We were not sure if we would be able to make it, because of the extreme danger along this horrifying journey. We thought of becoming the meal for the fishes along this inevitable danger which was obvious for us and for all, but we had no choice. Miraculously we made it and were lucky enough to get to here, the humanitarian country of Australia. Then due to the order of Australian authorities we were transferred to Nauru.

We, the sorrow stricken Hazara Wilders, spent more or less one year to get here with huge risk. It is the fifth month after spending already one year on the way that we are confined in Nauru detention centre.

As you witnessed, one of our friends, who was always trying to mentally support others, is so distressed and because of the seriousness of his health condition, was transferred to Australia for further treatment. He was teaching us and encouraged us to learn English and try to make the most of our time while here. As a result of pressure and loss of a few of his family members he couldn't resist. This is an example of our situation which is extremely hard to cope when our families at the other end of the world are suffering the same if not more.

We, the Hazara refugees, are worried so much about our families as well as ourselves due to uncertainty and long wait for our refugee process which is unbearable. Therefore we kindly request from the Department of Immigration and Australian humanitarian government to consider our sorrowful condition and for the sake of helping us to put an end to our long lasting agony.

Once again we need your kind attention and fair decision to save our and our families' lives.

Sincerely yours,

Hazara asylum seekers, Nauru Regional Processing Centre, Nauru

20th of February, 2013

Chapter 52

THE FIVE O'CLOCK news announcements originally started by the Salvos were replaced by five o'clock protests by the new Iranian groups. Dotted among them were a few from the old Iranian groups, a few Hazaras, a few Iraqis, a few Pakistanis. The Tamils and Sinhalese did not join them. The men wrote slogans on their shirts.

We are not criminals

We are refugees

We want freedom

They made banners out of bedsheets. Every day until the Iranian New Year they marched through the camp chanting.

Close the Nauru. Protection not detention. Nauru is Guantanamo. We are refugees, not criminals.

Larger men were stationed on the sides of the marches, looking suspiciously like intimidators. It didn't take long for stories of harassment and intimidation to filter through. Some men from the old Iranian group were scared. They didn't want to get involved as it could risk their applications for asylum. It was said that one of the men who had jumped the fence had only done so because he was threatened. An Iranian reported being punched in the face because he refused to join in the protests.

Julia Gillard addressed the media, saying that any attempts to protest or self-harm would not help the men.

The men who had been in Nauru for five months found the protests disruptive. They knew that such actions got them nowhere, that the Australian public frowned upon dissent and expected the men to wait quietly and calmly out of sight, and if they did that, maybe then they would be accepted into the country. The protests and the consequential intimidation made life in the camp more difficult than it already was.

It was unclear whether Atash was involved in these protests, or whether it was coincidence that the marches and protests had started up just days after his return to Nauru. Every day he stood at the front gate of the camp by himself, head pressed against the wire, looking through the gaps in the fence. Each day he stood there for a long time. No-one ever approached him. One day I stood beside him.

'What are you thinking about, Atash?' I asked.

He looked at me resentfully. 'I am in a very bad place,' he said. Then he turned back to the gaps in the fence. Our conversation was over.

Then one day Atash was no longer at Topside. A rumour spread through the camp that he had been arrested and was in Nauruan jail. It filtered through that he had hit an Afghan. Sher.

I went to Sher to ask what happened.

'He was crazy,' Sher said. 'He hit me in the head.' Sher motioned a fist to his temple. 'He knock me down. He say, "You are a dog. You are a donkey."' I knew that these were racial slurs Iranian men used against Hazaras. 'He said many bad things. I said, "Why do you do this?" He said he has a very bad situation. I say, "So do I." He kicked me like this.' Sher threw a boot into an imaginary person on the floor. 'He was crazy. It make me too much angry. I have bad situation, we all have a bad situation here, but I treat all people with respect. This man is a very bad man. He also hit Yousef to the ground. You know Yousef?'

I nodded. Yousuf was a frail, elderly Hazara with glasses.

'Yousuf is a quiet man,' Sher said. 'He walk from his tent for food and then back to his tent. Nothing more. Why hit him?'

Atash returned to the camp after just a few days in lock-up.

This incident hinted at some of the racial tension that simmered in the camp. The Hazara and the Iranians shared a complicated relationship. Reza, one of the Hazara cultural advisors, explained it to me. Many Hazaras fled the Taliban and became illegal immigrants in Iran. They were uneducated and worked the poorest jobs. According to Reza the Iranians looked down on them, treated them like dirt, made them aware that they were the lowest level of society. Now that they were in Nauru, the two races were treated equally. In fact, the Hazara were represented by more cultural advisors and the Iranians were insulted by this. They claimed that the Hazara cultural advisors were racist towards the Iranians and were using this moment of power to reverse the racial oppression they had suffered at the hands of Iranians. There were levels of complexity within this camp that I was only just starting to discover.

*

At some point in the past few weeks the men's lawyer, Silv Peres, had disappeared. It turned out his wife had suffered a heart attack in Fiji and he had left Nauru to visit her. No-one had told the asylum seekers on trial. Two Australian barristers, Jay Williams and David Burwood, had volunteered to assist in the trial. They were sent over as part of the NSW Bar Association's Pro Bono Scheme. They only had a short amount of time to prepare for the plea. They performed interviews with the accused using interpreters, read through all the witness statements, and met with the public prosecutor—all within the context of an unfamiliar foreign legal system. Despite all the obstacles the barristers faced, they made a big impact. Five of the accused were let off without having to make a plea, including Mustafa and Pez. For the remaining ten men, the last of the three charges was dropped, leaving the wilful damage of property and riot charges. Under current Queensland law there must be twelve accused to constitute riot charges. This law had been amended since Nauru had based its laws on the Queensland

Criminal Code; in Nauru a prosecutor only needed three men to constitute riot charges. It was an unexpected blow for the barristers. All ten of the accused pleaded not guilty. It was now up to the Australian government to prove their guilt. The case was adjourned to 24 April for the hearing.

The Nauruan government was determined to convict the men. The precedent needed to be set. In the eyes of the police commissioner, leniency would open the island up for further problems. Harsh measures would discourage future revolts.

Chapter 53

DURING MY THIRD rotation I avoided the politics at the centre and spent time with the men. I felt less invested in the camp and more invested in the people. It was as if I'd had a bad break up with Topside and I didn't want to get attached like I had on previous trips. I didn't want to get hurt again. The knowledge that I would be coming back until the end of June also made the experience less of an emotional roller-coaster. I felt myself slowly step away a little and start to take on less, mentally and emotionally. I could feel myself being less affected by the camp.

Outside of Topside conditions had improved dramatically. The Salvation Army had finally achieved some kind of stability since signing staff on full-time contracts. The quality of its employees had risen significantly, as though the first few months had been a trial-and-error period. Tent accommodation was a thing of the past. Rooms 161 and 163 at the Menen were the only two rooms that were overcrowded now, usually reserved for Young Salvos. The inequality of the policy wasn't lost on us, but we embraced the rooms and enjoyed the company of our colleagues. We were now allowed to go to the bar, and there was a new nightclub in town called Jules. We had a social life again.

Goodbyes were difficult to avoid during my first two rotations. The men counted down to when you would leave and confronted you on your last day. With so few staff and a low return rate, good-byes were felt strongly. The men believed Salvos wouldn't return; Salvos weren't sure that they would be offered new contracts. Missing personalities had a huge impact on staff and asylum seekers alike. As the camp settled into a groove and staff started to sign full-time contracts, goodbyes became less tumultuous. We felt less responsibility and fewer expectations because we knew we would be returning and we knew that someone good would replace us when we had our holidays.

When I left Nauru for the third time tension inside the camp was as high as it had ever been. Men were jumping fences, there were regular suicide attempts, and a large number of men had been taken to the Australian mainland with medical or psychological conditions. Twenty-two incidents were recorded in one day. Every day there were protests and with the protests came the associated pressures and bullying within the camp. The riot court case was still taking place. Atash was soon to be charged with assault.

One of the hardest parts about working in Nauru was the lack of progress. Worse than that, the men seemed to be going backwards. While the processing of their refugee claims was non-existent, their mental and physical health was slowly deteriorating. If they weren't being processed, what were they doing there? The men, the camp, they stood outside of time. Meanwhile I felt separated from my home life, and as much as I wanted to help the men there was only so much I could do from within the Regional Processing Centre. More and more I felt the need to tell people what was really going on in Nauru.

*

During my time off in Sydney I heard a rumour that Massoud and Ali, the mullah, had been sent to Villawood Detention Centre. There was no way of contacting them to let them know we wanted to visit, so on Thursday 28 March 2013 Amanda and I drove out to western Sydney on the hunch that they would be curious enough to see visitors, even if they weren't prepared to see us or didn't remember us.

I remember the date well because on the front page of the *Sydney Morning Herald* there were two stories. In one, former Labor chief whip Joel Fitzgibbon declared that families living in western Sydney earning $250,000 a year were 'struggling'. Mr Fitzgibbon said he was concerned about taxing the superannuation earnings of the wealthy. The other story reported that the government was exploring the possibility of extending community visas to asylum-seeker families. It stated that asylum seekers released on bridging visas were prohibited from taking paid employment as part of the overall No Advantage policy and received 89 per cent of the dole as financial assistance, the lowest payment in Australia's social security system. That amounted to $30 per day to pay for food, clothes, rent, bills, transport. The men housed in Nauru dreamed of such good fortune.

It was almost a year ago to the day that I'd first visited Villawood. I had been horrified by my initial experience of a detention centre: the barbed wire, the catatonic men, the pervasive atmosphere of hopelessness. Returning to Villawood brought back the visceral displeasure that I had grown accustomed to stomaching in Nauru.

'You booked?' the SERCO guard asked. Since I had last come to Villawood with Fabia SERCO had changed visitation rules so that you had to book a day in advance by either fax or post, a purposefully backwards system to make it difficult to see the men. We told the guard we had. We placed all our items in a locker excluding the nuts, Tim Tams and baklava that we had brought as presents for the men. We passed through the metal detectors and then waited for the final door to be unlocked.

The guard spoke into a microphone. 'Massoud, Ali, you have visitors.' She then looked at Amanda and said, 'If you stopped playing with your hair, Little Missy, and pushed the door you could go in.' The door clicked open.

We stepped inside the barbed-wire compound and into the vaguely familiar visiting area: first a small grass area with picnic tables and kids' play equipment, and then a building with couches, a television, toilets and a kitchen. Lots of Chinese families sat around talking. The Chinese inmates had most likely overstayed their visitor's visas and were waiting to be deported. We sat for thirty minutes in the building waiting for either of the men to come out. Maybe they had a medical, or maybe they were at a meeting with DIAC, or maybe they didn't want to see us. Either way it didn't look like they were coming out. We struck up a conversation with Sonni, an Indian man.

'Why are you in here?' I asked.

'I overstayed my visa,' he said.

'How did they catch you?'

'Well, I was playing poker at a casino and they told me all bets were off, but I accidentally took a chip away and so they accused me of stealing. I had a thousand dollars and they accused me of stealing twenty-five dollars, so the police came and took me and caught me, and now I am here. I tell you, the guards are very bad here. They are lazy. They don't like to work. They will only do the smallest amount. Never help you.'

At that point a guard came over. 'You two are not here to see Sonni. You are here for Ali and Massoud. Sonni, you must go.' It was now a rule in Villawood that you could only talk to the men you had booked to visit.

Sonni left, saying, 'I don't want to make trouble.'

Not much later both Massoud and Ali came out. We hugged and smiled and looked at each other. Ali looked healthy—his eyes were soft but intent, and not mad. Massoud couldn't stop laughing. 'Amanda. From Nauru. Here. Thank you.'

The men brought tea and we sat and ate the nuts and biscuits.

'Are you the only two from Nauru here?' I asked.

'No,' Mahmoud said. 'Ebrahim is here also.' Ebrahim, the bull-necked Iranian who I had seen viciously attack himself with a fluorescent light tube.

'How is it here?' Amanda asked.

'Better than Nauru,' Massoud said. 'Anything is better than Nauru, but I still cannot sleep. Do you think they will send us back to Nauru?'

'I don't know,' I said.

'Tell Joe I said hello,' Massoud said. 'Tell her I love her. Like a mother,' he said. 'She is my mother in Nauru.'

We assured him we would pass on his message to the IHMS nurse.

'Thank you to come,' Ali said. 'I'm sorry. My English very bad.'

As far as I could tell from the few words he spoke to us, he seemed to be doing okay. I couldn't really know without speaking to him in his own language. At least he wasn't scrabbling around in the dirt like an animal. He talked with a group of Hazara men who sat behind us. I recognised one of them. It was Ishmael, a flat-faced Hazara. He had been in Villawood on my first visit a year ago. We embraced but it was not a joyous reunion.

'I am here three years now in Villawood,' he said with more than a hint of bitterness. 'Waiting, waiting, waiting. No word. All of us are,' he said, pointing to three other Hazara men. 'We are residents of Villawood.'

No matter how nice it was to see Massoud and Ali, the thought of Ishmael being in Villawood for three years played on my mind. How much longer would he stay in detention?

*

I was not the only member of my family to become entangled in the asylum seeker octopus.

My father runs a refugee clinic at the Children's Hospital at Westmead, Sydney. He attempted to foster a seventeen-year-old Hazara orphan who had attended the clinic. I believe the political terminology would refer to the boy as an Unaccompanied Humanitarian Minor who is a ward of the Minister. He attended a school near my parent's home. His application for asylum was processed within months of his arrival in Australia and he was granted refugee status. No longer an asylum seeker, he was ineligible to live in the unaccompanied minors' home. He was told by an official from DIAC that he would be moved interstate within weeks unless he had someone over the age of twenty-one who would look after him for the nine months until he turned eighteen.

My parents arranged to meet the boy to discuss the possibility of fostering him. Before they got the chance my parent's application was rejected by DIAC. My parents were not contacted. Instead, a DIAC official rang the boy to say my parents were not suitable. Why? DIAC was his guardian and did not have to explain. When pushed, the official told the boy there was 'no prior relationship' and my parents were 'culturally inappropriate'.

An email from DIAC to a contact of my father said:

> DIAC is only placing clients in NSW with close family relatives. This decision is made on a case by case basis in conjunction with consideration of the client's age, the length of the relationship and regular contact with the nominated carer and other support available to Unaccompanied Humanitarian Minors in that state. In relation to the decision concerning the specific case you have raised, this is not a reflection on the abilities of Professor and Mrs Isaacs, but rather consideration of the full picture of the client's needs and available services.

So the boy was moved interstate, destination unknown. Natural justice dictated that my father could appeal the decision but the official declined to provide contact details and my father was unable to find any avenue of appeal.

It was expected that the government would start deporting unaccompanied minors to Nauru in the near future.

And with that, the excitement of having a Hazara in the family was swept aside. It was a sombre way to send me off. For the first time since I had started going to Nauru, I felt like I was going back to work. It was starting to become routine. I contemplated whether this would be my last rotation.

PART 4

ROTATION 4

31 March 2013 to 25 April 2013

Chapter 54

WHEN I ARRIVED back for my fourth stint in Nauru I had been returned to the Rec team, now called the Lifestyle team. The team had doubled in number but the workload was the same, promising easier days. I was asked to restart the football and cricket tournaments, and to work on the excursions again. The swimming program was still waiting on DIAC for approval.

The Salvos once again had a new operations manager. I was beginning to feel that it didn't matter who was in charge, our work more or less stayed the same. The Salvos had more staff than ever before, local people were being employed, and a group of social workers from the Multicultural Development Association (MDA) had been recruited on short-term contracts to assist with the Salvation Army workload. MDA was responsible for settlement services for the asylum seekers in Brisbane who had been offered bridging visas.

'Men from the same boats as these guys are in Brisbane, free to walk about the city and do whatever they wish,' said Garth, one of the MDA employees. 'I have been settling half of Rashid's boat in Australia. There are just four hundred men here, right? We could have them settled in twelve weeks. And yet they're stuck here.' He added, 'The settlement work is rewarding. You can see the men progress. Here, it's hell. When I first came here I was shocked. I hated the first four days. The conditions are appalling, and the amount of self-harm is confronting. I felt like I was a part of the immigration department's system, like I was legitimising the camp's existence. I questioned every second of my work here, I couldn't not. And then I started to become accustomed to it all, started to feel numb to the pain.'

'It's nice to see people outraged again,' I said. 'It's too easy to get settled into this place and treat it as a job. You forget that what happens in this place isn't normal, and it isn't okay. It's refreshing to have you damn the place.'

Garth's remarks about the inequity of the system were echoed by a former worker at Curtin Detention Centre in Western Australia, who had physically handed over bridging visas to men at Curtin who had been on the same boats as many of the men in Nauru.

'Curtin is worse than Nauru,' he said. 'There's a lot more leniency in the organisations in Nauru. In Curtin, SERCO run everything and there is an attitude that the men will attack at any moment. I worked there six months and never had a real problem with the men, but we were trained to fear them.'

I had been in Nauru for six months now and returning to the centre gave me an odd feeling of familiarity. The joyful reunions of previous return trips were replaced by warm hugs from old friends. I sat with the Iraqis and Omar embraced me.

'Good to have you back, man,' he said.

'Good to be back,' I replied.

'I had a dream about you,' Khazem said.

'Yeah,' I said with a smile. 'What about?'

'I dreamt you were at the Philippines airport,' he said.

My mind did a backflip. 'I had a dream last night that I was at the Philippines airport.'

Jabber hugged me and said something to me in Arabic. '*Gile, gile,* Omar,' he said.

'What did he say?' I asked Omar.

Omar gave me a surly look. 'I don't want to say it.'

'*Gile,*' Jabber insisted.

'Yeah, go on,' I said, pushing Omar. 'What did he say?'

'Some gay shit,' Omar spat. He really didn't want to say it.

'*Gile*,' Jabber said again, and smiled at me.

It looked as if we were dragging the words out of Omar's lungs with a hook but finally he spoke. 'He said that he is really sad in Nauru but when you come he is happy again.'

Jabber smiled broadly at me and nodded furiously.

'The President *Luchak*,' Salar announced to the Hazaras. The corner of his mouth twitched upwards into a smile, the way I had come to expect from him.

'My loyal *luchak* subjects,' I proclaimed.

Ulla imitated me garbling in a version of English I did not know. I used to look at him, a man the same age as me, and think how much his face had aged. Now I saw the youth in his spirit. He smiled and laughed like a young man, entertained the men like a young man, got angry and resentful like a young man and swallowed his resentment as quickly as a young man would.

It was strange to say but the mood in the camp appeared jovial. Men had been settled into a second accommodation block. The camp, now officially referred to as a centre, was heavily under construction, but all the men, now called transferees, were expected to be moved into housing accommodation within two weeks. That wasn't the source of their good humour, though. Something else was afoot.

The five o'clock protests had ceased as a gesture of good will for Iranian New Year. Not long after, on 15 March 2013, Nauruan parliament passed the *Asylum Seekers (Regional Processing Centre) Act 2012*. The asylum seekers were to begin processing six months after their initial deportation to Nauru. The process model was based on the Australian immigration system. The Australian government was to assist with the processing by initially providing immigration staff and legal personnel to conduct interviews.

Teams of Australian lawyers began arriving in Nauru for two-week stints to take interviews and hear stories. The men had hope again—they could see a process, progress. First they would tell their story to a lawyer, then they would be expected to tell it to an immigration officer. That officer would decide if the man was a refugee or not. After all that stress it seemed so simple.

Men sat around the camp reviewing the documents needed for their interviews. Asylum seekers have been accused of throwing their identity documents into the ocean to help them claim asylum in Australia. In my experience, many of the men had passports, or birth certificates, or identity cards, or some kind of documentation that would back up their claims for refugee status. The men who did not have documentation had not necessarily 'thrown it away'. Many of the Hazaras from Afghanistan and Pakistan did not have birth certificates and their countries would not issue them with passports. Those men who were stateless, like the Kurds, had no country to assist them with such things.

The men who were preparing for interviews refused to participate in activities, sports or excursions. They needed time to analyse their stories, to prepare themselves mentally. They were studying for the most important examination of their lives. Once the men had spoken to the lawyers their relief was momentary. Anxiety settled in just hours afterwards. There was still a final interview with the immigration officer to go. 'Final interview' became an explanation for erratic behaviour. It was only ever said in a whisper. The term carried a reverence that was usually reserved for solemn prayer. Men would hear 'final interview' and give the man who uttered the phrase a knowing look, a look that both wished the man well and acknowledged the gravity of his situation. In this matter the ethnicities were united.

After the final interview the men were forced to wait again. Nobody knew how long the interviews would take or when they would learn the outcome, but at least they had taken another step closer to freedom. The predicted five-year wait didn't look possible now. It couldn't take that long, surely? Processing had started but it only led to more questions and more waiting. Had they said enough? Had they suffered sufficient oppression to get a visa? Could they prove it? How long would they have to wait now? What would happen when people failed the exam of life?

It was said that there would be a tribunal in Nauru, based on Australia's Refugee Review Tribunal, to review negative decisions but it was unclear how this tribunal would function. DIAC officials suggested that any criminal or antisocial behaviour would affect the asylum seekers' applications. Nauru's antiquated legal system still upheld that self-harm and suicide attempts were against the law. It was even suggested that association with such behaviour could also affect cases.

The DIAC officials who had recorded the first interviews were expected to provide a response within a few months. If the men were confirmed to be 'genuine refugees' by DIAC they would then have to pass an ASIO assessment. There were no time limits on the ASIO checks. If the men failed the ASIO assessment they would either be deported or held in detention indefinitely without right to appeal. In May 2012 Ranjini, a pregnant Tamil mother who had arrived in Australia with her two sons, had been given a negative ASIO security assessment despite having already been found to be a legitimate refugee. She faced indefinite incarceration without ever knowing why ASIO had found her a threat to Australian communities. In August 2013, the United Nations Human Rights Committee found Australia to be in breach of its obligations under international law, committing 143 human rights violations by indefinitely detaining 46 refugees for four years, on the basis of ASIO's 'adverse security assessments'.[1] It hardly seemed a fair and equitable system.

DIAC officials held a Q & A with Salvo case managers and cultural advisors. In it they confirmed that asylum seekers who were approved as refugees would not necessarily end up in Australia but could be resettled in any of the countries that were signatories to the United Nations Refugee Convention. I wondered how the rest of the world would view this passing of the buck. *We don't want these asylum seekers—you take them.*

---

1   Amnesty International, 'Australia guilty of 143 human rights violations, says UN body', 22 August 2013, viewed 22 August 2013, <www.amnesty.org.au/news/comments/32569/>.

Chapter 55

I ARRIVED AT work on the Transfield bus, my ID number was recorded by the Wilson guard at the front gate, I signed my time sheet and checked in at the Psycare computer kiosk, a daily self-monitored wellbeing exam that we completed for the psychologists. *What percentage of okay are you?* the questionnaire asked me. *100 per cent.* I had a full day preparing programs for the Lifestyle team ahead of me.

'You might be able to help.' A Salvation Army case manager pointed at me. 'Have you got a good relationship with Yashar?'

The question dragged me out of my pre-shift daze. I looked at the case manager and the Wilson guard next to her and nodded. To say Yashar and I had a good relationship was a stretch—the majority of our interactions consisted of throwing Persian insults at each other across the Green Room, but even sharing these seemingly insignificant moments meant that I had a better relationship with Yashar than most of the other Salvo mission workers. To most he was intimidating and confrontational; at least he talked to me.

Yashar was an Iraqi Kurd who had moved to Iran with his family when he was a child. He had been stateless his whole life, a second-class citizen. When he arrived in Nauru his significant other had left him. Yashar was the first man to attempt suicide in the camp.

He had tried many more times. He had scars across his stomach and his head from self-harm; he verbally insulted everyone; he broke up sporting games, kicked balls away, knocked chess games over. He was branded the troublemaker of the camp and every day there was something new with Yashar. One day he decided to parade around the camp naked. The Emperor. When he was forcibly removed by two Wilson staff he resisted, twisted and turned. After the incident Yashar came out of IHMS sporting a knee brace, complaining of ligament damage and broken ribs. The police were called to the scene and there were rumours he would be charged with indecent exposure. It wouldn't stop his protests. Too many of his antics had already gone on his record—the chances of him being granted a visa to Australia were diminishing, and maybe he knew this. I had often thought that we were watching his mental state slowly deteriorate, watching him ruin his life. Or were we watching Nauru ruin his life?

'Good,' the Wilson guard said. 'We've got ten minutes to move Yashar out of the camp. He's going to Australia.'

'Yashar's going? Why?'

'We don't know,' the case manager said. 'We haven't been told anything except that he's moving. Now.'

'Does he know that he's moving?' I asked, wondering if I was to break the news to him.

'He's just been told,' the Wilson guard said.

And then the magnitude of what was happening to Yashar hit me. After six months of self-harm in Nauru, Yashar was being moved to Australia and he had ten minutes to pack his bags and say his goodbyes. It seemed cruel. He had been robbed of any kind of anticipation. Instead it would be a mad rush of action and emotion with no time to fathom it all.

'We need you to talk to him,' the Wilson guard told me. 'Make sure he doesn't pack mountains of the welfare clothing. He can only have one of each welfare item. One bottle of shampoo, one cake of soap, one T-shirt. You get the idea. He can have as much underwear as he likes, though. And he's got to be gone as soon as possible. He can't miss the plane.'

When I arrived at Yashar's room his roommate Mohammed Reza was packing his bags for him. I recognised Mohammed Reza as the old man from a swimming excursion who had held a Nauruan child to him and cried. Today his eyes were dry. Yashar stood in the middle of the room looking dazed, chewing on his fingernails. Behind the confused expression I could see deep concern in his eyes. I looked closely at Yashar. He was just twenty-three years of age but his face had taken on a yellow tone that made him look middle-aged.

'You're leaving Nauru,' I said, trying to channel enthusiasm and hope.

'I don't want to leave my friends,' he said. 'They send me to a hospital for crazy people.' I thought he would be overjoyed to leave Nauru but he looked like a scared little boy.

Mohammed Reza stuffed Yashar's minimal belongings into a bag emblazoned with cheesy slogans that were intended to be encouraging. *Love yourself. You'll turn out okay.* Two tracksuits, a pair of pyjamas, three T-shirts, headphones, cigarettes, four pairs of underwear. The majority of the belongings were provided by the camp, except for one childish doll with orange hair.

'Do you want to get changed?' I asked Yashar, thinking that pants that constantly fell below his waistline were not the best option for him to take to Australia. He agreed, and changed into a nice pair of shorts and a fresh T-shirt. He didn't have time to shower or clean his teeth.

The bag was taken by Wilson guards, while the Iranians in the room hugged and kissed him. Words were said, Persian well wishes. It was a sombre affair. Yashar knelt down to tie his shoelaces and tucked the loose ends into the side of his shoe.

'Can you take care of my friend for me?' Yashar asked me, pointing at a cup. Confused, I looked inside. There was a crab in it. I nodded, not sure what taking care of a crab would entail.

Then Yashar, Mohammed Reza and I walked through the camp with an escort of Wilson guards. Yashar walked with his head bowed, not looking around him. Not many people noticed the significance of the moment. One Iranian cottoned on, and approached us.

The men conversed in Farsi and shook hands. Yashar didn't look him in the face, as if he was ashamed to be leaving.

We walked out the gates and they closed behind Yashar. I wondered if he would ever come back to this prison. Yashar and his bag were sat at a table in the processing area of the camp usually reserved for new arrivals. The Wilson guards wrote out an inventory of his possessions while I acted as a witness.

'I waited for this day for six months and now I don't want to go,' Yashar said.

'You'll be in Australia, though,' I said.

'No. I will be in a hospital in Australia,' Yashar said. 'Same, same, Nauru.'

'Anything is better than Nauru,' I replied, drawing on Mahmoud's Villawood conclusions.

'I go to the repair shop and when I am fixed they send me back. A general service.'

'How many kilometres do you have?' I asked.

'Maximum. They will reset me,' he said. 'I'm a 23-year-old in a hundred-year-old body. I don't want to go to a crazy house.'

It dawned on me that he was going to a mental health ward, and that he was going alone. It was not the entrance to Australia he had expected when first leaving his home country.

'We will leave for the airport in thirty minutes,' the Wilson guard said.

After all that rushing the tempo lulled. Yashar finally had a chance to sit and think on what was about to happen to him. He refused food and water. His complexion faded from yellow to grey and then it all became too much for him and he excused himself, overcome with emotion.

And then it was time to go. A Wilson guard shook his hand, smiled kindly at him, wished him good luck. Yashar apologised for being so difficult. An IHMS nurse wished him well, brought him a fresh jumper, 'Because the plane will be very cold.' She had always seemed so cold and professional and yet here she was displaying kindness at the most important hour.

'Come with me,' Yashar said to her.

'No,' she said. 'I have to stay here. You'll be fine, Yashar.'

Then it was my turn. We embraced.

'I'm sorry for making trouble,' he said.

'It's not your fault,' I said. 'It's this place.'

He nodded. Then he got in the car and the door closed. He looked out the window at me and waved goodbye and the car left Topside.

Chapter 56

THREE WEEKS INTO my fourth rotation I felt my passion fading. I was doing the same programs I had started in November, six months earlier. Nothing had progressed. I had made suggestions to the Lifestyle team, none of which had been acted upon. The camp still wasn't open, the swimming still hadn't been confirmed. The energy that had existed in the camp at the beginning of this rotation had evaporated, replaced by gloom. At every step I was met by depression.

I visited Yashar's friend Parshan after Yashar had departed. In previous months they had been accomplices, partners in crime. I didn't know how good their relationship was now, but I knew the two were linked in an odd way. Parshan lay on his bed with his feet resting on the ladder of his bunk bed, listening to music. He didn't talk to me, just shrugged in answer to my questions. The next day I visited him again and he had not moved. He didn't move for another day after this. Every time Yashar was mentioned he withdrew further. His personal Wilson guard told me it was the first anniversary of Parshan's father's death.

'He has lost his hope,' said Farid, the BFG.

Parshan had graffitied a gravestone on the wall next to his bed. His name was written on it, 'seven months ago dead'.

While I was visiting Parshan a few of the Iranians showed me a letter they had received from the Australian Human Rights Commission. When the men had first arrived in Nauru in October they made complaints against the Commonwealth of Australia to the Commission under Articles 2, 9(1), and 10(1) of the International Covenant on Civil and Political Rights.

Article 9
1. Everyone has the right to liberty and security of person.
No-one shall be subjected to arbitrary arrest or detention.
No-one shall be deprived of his liberty except on such grounds and in accordance with such procedure as are established by law.

Article 10
1. All persons deprived of their liberty shall be treated with humanity and with respect for the inherent dignity of the human person.

The letter said that it would investigate their complaints where possible. This was made that much harder by the fact that Gillian Triggs, the president of the commission, was denied access to the camp by DIAC.[1]

A few days after Yashar's departure, thick-bearded, long-haired Mahdi overdosed on pills he had been hoarding from IHMS appointments. He was carried limp and lifeless from his room and had to be resuscitated.

I walked past Mohammad's tent.

'*Ghanari*,' he shouted. I stopped and ducked my head inside his tent. The Iranian man was lying on his cot, looking sickly. 'Come here, *ghanari*.'

I stepped inside and knelt beside him. 'What's up? Are you sick?'

He motioned a rope around his neck. 'Last night,' he said. He smiled sadly. Mohammad always acted so cheerful. He could be seen walking down the Green Room with a bounce in his step and a smile that made his eyes crinkle. He always pinched my cheeks and told me how beautiful I was. He was still smiling even now but it didn't have his usual effervescence.

'What? Why?' I said without thinking. I was shocked; I didn't expect such an act from him.

'I am a sad man.'

'Oh no.'

'What?' he asked, and he looked worried that he had upset me.

'I am sad. For you,' I said quickly. 'You are a dear friend and I don't want you to be unhappy.'

I held his hand and he gripped it back. 'Thank you, *jigar*,' he said. *Jigar* meant 'liver' in Persian. Slang for a person who is your life, someone you cannot live without, usually reserved for a lover.

'I wish I could do more for you,' I said. 'You are too beautiful to die like that.' We shared a giggle.

The unexpected breakdowns were the worst. Habib the football player was always a talkative man, but when he opened up about his home troubles it brought me to tears.

'I don't have any more money. I can't even pay for my family's food. My family cannot eat. My little boy cries on the telephone because he isn't eating. He asks me why I don't love him. If I loved him I'd be there with him. What can I do? What can I do? Please tell me. I don't know what to do. My wife said she will leave me if I do not provide for her. And if she does, then what? What do I have to live for?'

A Hazara man told me of his weekly conversation with his four-year-old daughter.

'"What time do you come home?" she asks me. "Tomorrow," I say. "You always say tomorrow. Where are you?" she asks. I say, "Australia." "Where is Australia?" she asks me. "Very far," I say. "Why don't you come home?" she always finishes.'

When the man finished I asked him, 'Can you write to her?'

'No post, no internet. Just phone one time one week.'

Haider was reported as being upset and I was asked to speak to him. The large Iraqi man could be intimidating when he towered over Salvo mission workers with his dark frown, but that day he opened up to me straightaway.

'I'm not good,' he said.

'Why?'

'It's the same, always the same. I am bored of all this.'

Despite all the changes to the camp—new buildings, new Salvo management, new terminology, new programs, new classes, new teachers, new sports, new competitions, new rules—deep down none of it really mattered. It was the same situation, just wrapped with a prettier bow. The men were still in a prison far from their families. The start of processing had been a momentary buzz, a novelty of progress that moved them from one waiting room to another. Their futures were just as uncertain as they had been the week before, and they were still living in a camp whose days were punctuated by medical emergencies.

This was what worried Dev. He looked thinner than usual, his skin was pale, he had stopped smiling and stopped caring about cricket.

'I'm feeling sick,' he told me. 'I have not eaten in two days. I am not hungry, I think too much about my interview. I have spoken to the lawyer, so now I must wait for my result. How long do you think it will take?'

'I don't know.'

'What will happen to me if I am not successful?'

That thought was not pleasant to entertain. If ASIO did not approve his security clearance he could be held in Nauru indefinitely, or he might be deported back to Sri Lanka. Signatories to the UN Refugee Convention were not supposed to deport people if there was risk of torture, cruel or inhumane treatment, or punishment, but that hadn't stopped Australia in the past. Either way, Australia would never accept Dev past our borders as a refugee and all this would have been for nothing.

*

On Friday 19 April, it was confirmed that there was a minor being held in the camp. The Iranian boy was immediately removed from Topside and relocated to temporary quarters 20 metres beyond the fence. The process was so swift he wasn't even allowed to move his own belongings, despite having lived in the camp since January.

That duty was left up to Salvation Army mission workers and Wilson guards, who struggled to identify which belongings were his. He was not the first asylum seeker in the camp to claim that he was a minor; this was just the first known claim to be confirmed. The boy alleged that his family had emailed his birth certificate to DIAC a month before he was moved from the camp. The boy would not be allowed back in the men's camp of the Nauru Regional Processing Centre again. A week later he was flown to Australia.

---

1   B Hall, 'Human rights chief warned off islands visit', *Sydney Morning Herald*, 5 March 2013, <www.smh.com.au/federal-politics/political-news/human-rights-chief-warned-off-islands-visit-20130304-2fgy9.html>.

Chapter 57

ON TUESDAY 23 April 2013, the consortium of Julian Burnside, Geoffrey Robertson and Jay Williams filed a constitutional challenge to the existence of the Nauru Regional Processing Centre and the detention of asylum seekers in Nauru, serving a writ of *habeas corpus*. The principle of *habeas corpus* gives every person the right to challenge arbitrary detention by a government and to make their case against such detention in a court. This writ provides integral protection against a government's ability to imprison people without trial.

The following day this challenge was acknowledged by the court and the date was set to hear this challenge on 10 June 2013. All trials concerning the asylum seekers' criminal charges were adjourned until 17 June 2013. Jay Williams petitioned the court to order greater access to men for legal representation based on article 5.2 of the Nauruan constitution, which mandates access to legal representation in the place in which a person is detained. Jay Williams said that he had been repeatedly denied access to his clients in the camp by DIAC and indicated that numerous complaints had been made to him by the men facing criminal charges and other men being detained within the Nauru Regional Processing Centre, who claimed that their requests to access legal representation had been denied. The judge declined to make an order immediately because DIAC was not a party to proceedings, but acknowledged the complaint and said that he would write a letter to the Nauruan Minister for Justice and Border Control, to be forwarded to DIAC.

If the consortium could successfully convince a judge that detaining asylum seekers in Nauru was unconstitutional, it would be a significant step closer to shutting down the Nauru Regional Processing Centre.

*

By the end of my fourth rotation all the men had been moved to housing blocks. After seven months in temporary accommodation the asylum seekers must have felt some satisfaction when the final tent was removed from the camp; an empty expanse was all that remained. Construction on the final three accommodation blocks started and finished within a week. Another accommodation block was on the way, signalling the government's intent to house more asylum seekers in the centre. New kitchens were being built; a large recreation block was almost finished.

The Lifestyle team reinstated old competitions and finally came up with new programs. Yoga classes, running groups, marathons, the second season of the Nauru Premier League, the second season of the Mr Nauru Cricket Cup. The kitchens continued to cook reasonable food, even if it was the exact same food the men had been eating for seven months. The camp was a noisy construction yard and it would be for many more months. Dramatic improvements had been made to the camp since its opening in October—Topside would be shown off as a top-class facility—and yet self-harm, suicide attempts and mental illness prevailed. The more dramatic displays of displeasure were fading. For many this meant a subdued acceptance of their fate, out of a need for self-preservation and to withstand their mental degradation. Some couldn't stand it, their resistance deteriorating into mental illness and catatonic depression. It was less confrontational, less tabloid. The condition of men like Parshan who hid under the covers for weeks on end would not be reported to the Australian public.

What made this more frightening was that by all accounts conditions in Manus were not improving. Staff and asylum seekers alike experienced food shortages, water shortages, malaria-spreading mosquitoes, intense heat (even worse than Nauru), and a camp that flooded in the rain. In an email my friend working in Manus told me that at one point all they had for food was cabbage. The ABC reported on Tuesday 16 April 2013 that DIAC delivered a scathing assessment of its own temporary accommodation on Manus, saying the asylum seekers' living arrangements were cramped and presented 'key risks in terms of safety and health'.[1] Women and children were being detained in Manus despite countless medical reviews condemning the Australian government for placing children in detention. The risk of infection and illness meant that small children were restricted from being sent to Manus. Women who became pregnant there were sent to Australia because children could not be born into such conditions. My friend told me that when the asylum seekers became aware of this, the fornication rate escalated dramatically.

Meanwhile there were plans afoot to build another offshore-processing centre on Nauru.

*

No matter how long I stayed at Topside I knew I would never be there as long as the men. The thought of spending five years on the island sent me mad—and I had the freedom to leave the camp, go for a swim, have a beer, contact my family. I loved these men and each opportunity I had to leave Nauru I had returned for them, and yet I knew eventually there would be a day when I would say goodbye to them.

In the final days of this rotation I told my managers that I might not return. I didn't tell the men anything but some of them sensed it straight away.

'You aren't coming back, are you?' Omar asked.

'Maybe,' I said, but my heart wasn't in it. I had almost made it out without saying a proper goodbye to any of the men. He looked deep into me. Was he hurt?

'Oh man,' he said and he pulled me into a strong hug. It was an uncharacteristic display of emotion from Omar and it brought me close to tears.

'Why? Why now?'

'I don't know, it just feels like it's time.'

'What are you going to do?'

'Go to Japan for a holiday and sort my head out. Then I'll see,' I said. 'Who knows? Maybe I will come back.'

He shook his head. 'I'm going to miss you, man.'

'Me too.'

It was hard to walk away from him, the one man to whom I had confessed my true feelings. I didn't want to tell the men I wasn't going to come back because I didn't know if I would or not. I didn't want to put them through the turmoil of saying a final goodbye, only to arrive two weeks later and say 'Surprise, I'm back!' Instead I crept out of there, hiding my guilt inside me like a bad secret.

*

I gave myself a holiday to Japan, a country completely removed from the asylum seeker debate. I hadn't made a conscious decision to avoid Nauru so effectively but I appreciated the distance. In Japan, no-one I talked to knew about the asylum seeker issue in Australia. I could avoid debates in social situations or questions surrounding my job. When I did tell some Japanese friends about my work they clapped and called me a hero. It was the perfect place to forget about the camp.

I took three weeks off, and told my manager to expect an email confirming whether or not I would be coming back.

While I was in Japan the ABC broadcast an episode of *Four Corners* called 'No Advantage', which examined the offshore processing centres.[2] The report contained secret footage from both Manus and Nauru, including interviews with asylum seekers detained there, as well as interviews with former Salvo staff, an IHMS doctor, and a range of people associated with the centres. The Major, my former boss and the former operations manager of Manus Island Centre, broke his deed of confidentiality and spoke out against the injustices of the centres. Finally, someone from the Salvation Army had publicly voiced support for the men, despite the threats of contractual termination and retribution the government laid at the feet of the organisation and the Salvation Army laid at the feet of the workers. It gave those of us working in the centres the confidence to speak out.

Four Corners also outlined the extraordinary cost of the policy. Australian government contracts for Nauru alone totalled over $400 million. That included a $200 million contract with Transfield for running the centre, a $75 million contract with the Salvation Army, and a $70 million contract with Australian construction firm Canstruct.[3]

The public reaction to this report was lukewarm. There was an outcry against detaining children on Manus, but there was little compassion for the men in Nauru. A friend at Amnesty International told me that the government had announced that it wouldn't give in to media pressure and refused to stop women and children being sent to Manus. Meanwhile, the government had placed a ban on cattle exports after Four Corners showed that cows exported from Australia were being mistreated in foreign abattoirs. The 'No Advantage' report faded away with no real changes taking place.

The reaction in Nauru was the complete opposite. Friends on the island told me that every man in the centre had a copy of the program on his USB stick. The episode was replayed on a loop on all the Green Room televisions for days after the broadcast. Although no-one knew for certain who had been involved in the interviews, the men who were suspected of assisting the ABC were respected and congratulated by fellow asylum seekers and certain Salvos for being brave enough to speak out on behalf of the other detainees. These men had their rooms raided by the Nauruan police. The police did not have warrants and were not given permission by the men, although it was unclear whether they needed either of these things. The police found nothing, and no-one could prove that any of the men were involved.

After the *Four Corners* episode all staff were to be 'wanded' with metal detectors as they entered the camp. Days after the program aired the Salvo operations manager resigned. It was the third time the Salvos had changed management in seven months.

On 16 May 2013 the federal government excised the mainland of Australia from Australia's migration zone for all unlawful boat arrivals. Under the *Migration Act* such 'unlawful non-citizens' no longer had a right to apply for a Protection Visa. The Minister for Immigration and Citizenship would have to waive this restriction to enable an applicant to apply but was not obligated to do so. Accordingly, no asylum seekers arriving by boat since August 2012 have had their visa applications processed, aside from the minor who was removed from Topside. Australia signed the United Nations Refugee Convention in the aftermath of the Holocaust. Fifty-two years later it discarded the global goodwill on which this convention was founded.

The significance of the changes to the *Migration Act* faded out of the public consciousness days after the news was broadcast. For those who supported asylum seekers it was just another disappointing policy amid years of disappointing political decisions.

*

While in Japan I quit the Salvation Army. I was tired. Tired of everything to do with Nauru.

I needed a new challenge. I didn't know what I was going to do next, but I felt like I had done all I could in Nauru. I didn't want to go back.

As my mind worked through the notion of quitting, one insidious motive crept into my head. Completing one more rotation would earn me a significant amount of money. It was the first time the work had become about the income and not about the men. It was this thought that pushed me to quit.

Days after resigning, on a complete reversal of fortunes from two rotations ago, I received an email from my manager asking me to come back. The swimming program had finally been approved. She thought that I deserved to see it, considering how hard I had worked to make it happen. It was a lovely gesture of goodwill that pulled the right heart strings. She knew I wouldn't be able to resist.

I said yes without considering all the other positives that a return to the island would bring. I knew I wanted to see the program. I knew that I didn't want to disappoint my manager, who had shown so much faith in me. I also wanted to say a proper goodbye to the men. One last rotation would give me the right kind of closure. I wanted to see all the staff again, too. This last rotation would see out my contract and finalise my agreement with the Salvation Army. As it happened, this would be the most tumultuous rotation of all.

*

Shortly before my departure for Nauru I woke up to an email from human rights lawyer and refugee advocate Julian Burnside, AO QC. He was asking me to make an affidavit in the constitutional challenge. He attached two statements regarding conditions in the camp, one from Wilson management and the other from the Secretary for Justice and Border Control of Nauru. The statements claimed that the fencing around the camp was there to protect the men from construction and the pinnacles. They said that the men were free to roam the Regional Processing Centre at their will; that the men were not physically restricted from leaving any area of the camp; that the very structures put in place to hold the men within the centre against their will were actually put in place for their safety. They asserted that the only restrictions placed upon the men were consequences of their visa restrictions. They wanted to give the impression that the men were not housed in a detention centre, that their civil liberties were not being restricted.

For me, there was an even more personal element to the case. The two statements cited the excursion program as an example of the men's freedom. A program I had established to give the men more freedom was now being used to restrict their freedom.

I didn't know much about the case, what the ramifications of making a statement would be, or whether my statement could influence the outcome of the case, but I knew what I was reading were lies, and if I didn't speak up these lies would be recorded as truths in a court of law. I only had a few days to make my decision before I left for Nauru. I told Julian Burnside I would make a statement. For the past eight months I had been making decisions based on gut instinct. Everything was happening so fast I didn't have time to reflect, so I did what I felt was right. I was sick of the constant lies this place generated and defended as truth.

It wasn't until I was sitting alone in the office of Shine Lawyers overlooking Hyde Park in Sydney that I noticed the frantic beating of my heart. In the ten minutes I spent waiting in silence for the lawyers, my mind achieved unnerving clarity. The full extent of my decision hit me. I was about to give evidence in court against my own government. My mouth went dry. I took a gulp of water. All I was doing was telling the truth, I reassured myself.

Two other Salvos, Jack and Amanda, joined me in making affidavits. Amanda and I had been through a lot together in Nauru. We had been there since the camp opened. She would still have been there had it not been for Salvos HR. They had grudgingly offered her temporary contracts for months, telling her she needed to 'behave' but not explaining in what way she had misbehaved. Eventually they didn't offer her a new contract. Amanda took an internship with an organisation fighting for women's rights in India. It wasn't until after she'd booked her flights to India that the Salvation Army contacted her again.

'Amanda, we are ready to redeploy you,' the HR officer said.

When Amanda explained what had happened, the HR officer responded, 'Your contract terminates in October 2013. You have to fulfil your contractual obligations.'

Amanda's first temporary contract had been four weeks long, running from September 2012 to October 2012. A typo had set the date of termination to October 2013 and now Salvation Army HR were trying to enforce that error as a contractual agreement.

When Amanda confirmed that she was going to make an affidavit, I warned her that the Salvation Army would most likely not hire her again.

'I don't care,' she said. 'I'm sick of being bullied and made to feel like shit.'

---

1   E Griffiths, 'Immigration criticises own Manus asylum centre', ABC Online, 16 April 2013, viewed 2 May 2013, <www.abc.net.au/news/2013-04-16/immigration-report-scathing-of-manus-island-centre/4632728>.

2   ABC Television, 'No Advantage', *4 Corners*, aired 29 April 2013, <www.abc.net.au/4corners/stories/2013/04/29/3745276.htm>.

3   ABC Television, 'No Advantage'.

PART 5

ROTATION 5

23 May 2013 to 13 June 2013

Chapter 58

I RETURNED FOR my final rotation both dreading the impending court case and jubilant to be back. There were obvious doubts in my mind about the case but they couldn't overwhelm all the other emotions coursing through me.

Touching down in Nauru was a poignant moment. I remembered Mustafa telling me that when he'd first arrived he thought they were landing in the ocean. Even when the plane did land on solid ground, you weren't certain that it would stop before the runway ended. Arriving in Nauru knowing I would never have to go back felt good. Really good. The long, long journey was coming to a climactic end.

The island was hot, but nowhere near as hot as it had been in October. Rubbish still littered every bare patch of land. When we arrived at the hotel there were accommodation issues. We had over eighty Salvo staff and rooms were being taken away from us. Hotel rooms were overflowing again. Trusty old 161 was back to having eight men in it. The new management had arrived on the same plane as me and they demanded private rooms the moment they arrived, unable to share with one other person for even a night.

I immediately noticed a pessimism among the staff that was worse than usual. There was a lack of trust in the new management, who had been recruited from SERCO. A lot of the new Salvo staff had also previously worked for SERCO. One of the former SERCO workers I had met on my previous rotation was infamous for having an aggressive attitude towards the men. Staff who had been in Nauru since September questioned why the Salvation Army was hiring people from a company that ran detention centres in Australia. The Salvation Army had been brought to Nauru to provide humanitarian support, not replicate centres such as Villawood and Curtin.

I found two new Salvos sitting outside the camp doing nothing. When asked why they weren't working, they replied that they hadn't been given any duties. To us old hands this was telling. For us, a break in responsibilities meant we got a chance to speak with the men. For many of the new Salvos this wasn't even considered. Meanwhile, Wilson Security had been taken over by Transfield. To me, it appeared that Transfield was going to push the Salvos out and take full control of the camp.

My manager had been medevaced off the island. What IHMS had originally diagnosed as an asthma attack turned out to be a serious case of pneumonia. It was suspected that the pneumonia was caused by the phosphate in the air. Staff googled *phosphate poisoning* and saw that it could do serious damage to health. Phosphate mining had also occurred on Christmas Island.

*

The Salvation Army had introduced new shirts for the work staff. Blue shirts with red sleeves for the plebs, yellow sleeves for management and team leaders. We were told the intention was to make the hierarchy of staff more obvious to the men. This didn't match our understanding of the camp. The men knew who the managers were and they couldn't care less about the shirts. All the shirts achieved in the camp was to make the men more apathetic towards management. It seemed more likely to us that the shirts were intended to remind the workers of the hierarchy.

There were more buildings in the camp, more construction. The camp felt smaller than it ever had, cramped into less than half the space it used to occupy. Fencing moved all the way to the edge of the Green Room, sectioning off the entire area where the tents had once been pitched. The Charlie 5 pergola was now right up against the entrance to the Green Room. There was no space around the edges of the camp—you walked from the Green Room to the accommodation blocks through fenced-off walkways. We were assured that the new Rec building was almost finished.

It was only once I had begun talking to the men again that I realised all my anxiety about returning to Nauru, the unease that had begun to churn my gut in the morning before each shift, was not a result of the men. It was a result of the island. Once I was with the men it did not feel like work. I was just chilling with my mates. I realised that I wasn't accepting money to work with the men, I was accepting money to put up with the atmosphere of Nauru.

Those men who had been in the camp since September were finishing both sets of processing interviews.

'We have a saying in Afghanistan,' Salar said. 'A man wants to marry the princess of the kingdom. He goes to the king and says, "I have the permission of my mother and father to marry the princess, I just need your approval." Now, all he must do is wait for the king.'

It was relaxing in one way: their fate was out of their hands, they had done all they could. At the same time, the inability to affect their own fate made it all the more infuriating.

With my manager absent, my promised role of Swimming Program Coordinator never materialised. Instead I resumed work as a staff member in the Lifestyle team. I wasn't surprised: it was the same old story of broken promises, miscommunication and lack of respect for staff.

The swimming program had been established before I returned to Nauru. Four two-hour excursions a day to the boat harbour. I went on the first excursion I could and watched the men frolicking in the salt water, Nauruan lifeguards observing from strategic positions to prevent drownings. There were the expected restrictions that everyone had to get accustomed to: a rope sectioned the men off from the rest of the boat harbour; no swimming past the rope; no diving in from the top step; no flips. The men donned life jackets and reef shoes and jumped into the water. Many of them had never learned to swim. They bellyflopped loudly and gracelessly, but rose to the surface as happy as I'd ever seen them, oblivious to the Salvo workers' cringes. Men lay on their backs; they freestyled, backstroked, dog paddled; they held onto the rope and watched others. They remained in the water until the very last possible moment. I was watching the fruit of seven months of negotiating. It was worth it to be back just for that moment.

The evening of my second day back in Nauru the affidavits were filed in court. The Salvation Army was about to learn that I had spoken out. Jack and I thought it best to approach management to explain on our own terms our reasons for making statements. Jack was still off-island so I was to speak for both of us. I suddenly realised that I was completely unprepared for the conversation. I berated myself for not having asked my lawyers how to talk with the Salvation Army about this. When management found out, surely they would fire me and send me home. And what could I say to stop them?

Walking into that office I suppressed a nervousness in my chest that was a close cousin to fear.

*

I approached a member of the management team and told him that Jack and I had decided to make statements. His facial expression didn't change but I could tell he was very annoyed.

'Well, that is a serious breach of your contract and your confidentiality deed. You will be fired,' he said abruptly. 'The government will come after you.'

I didn't know what to say. I had expected there to be a discussion of sorts.

'We felt our statements to the court were a question of conscience and we felt that we had an obligation to tell the truth. We were advised by our lawyers that making a statement in court would not breach our deeds of confidentiality and any action taken against us would constitute a contempt of court,' I replied.

'Well, you've been misled, you've received incorrect advice, and now you're going to deal with the government,' he said. Again I wasn't sure what to say. Here I had two completely opposing views of my fate. Each side was as confident in their opinion as the other.

'You should have discussed it with the Salvation Army,' he continued. 'This is not your crusade. I just can't understand why you did this. Tell me exactly what you did.'

I knew I shouldn't say too much, just tell him to speak to my lawyers, but at the same time I wanted him to understand why I'd done it. I wanted to justify my actions. I was holding on to the impossible hope that maybe the Salvos would support us.

'We were presented with an affidavit from Wilson management that was misleading and untruthful. We felt morally obliged to counter that statement. I'm not entirely sure where we stand legally, but if we have breached our contract, so has that man,' I said.

'Moral obligation?' he spat. 'What you did was morally wrong. You should have shown loyalty to your employers. The Australian government hired you to do a job.'

'I did what I thought was right,' I said. 'I wanted to support the men. I didn't lie, I told the truth. I thought this would be in line with the Salvation Army's mission.'

'Why didn't you contact us and ask for advice?'

'I would have but we didn't have time,' I replied. 'There were only a few days to make the decision and in my experience it is extremely difficult to make contact with management who are working on Nauru.'

'Don't tell me that,' he said. 'You had plenty of contact with management when you were organising your holidays. The government will go after you and your lawyers won't have a leg to stand on. The only way you could be safe is if you were subpoenaed.

If you made the statements voluntarily you've got no hope. What do you expect to achieve from this?' he asked. 'What do you think the outcome of this case will be?'

'Our lawyers are attempting to prove that the way these men have been detained in this camp is against the Nauruan constitution,' I said. 'I hope we can make steps toward closing the camp.'

'You're wrong,' he said. 'This camp will not close. This case is centred around the ten men on trial's welfare. If you win, at most it will push forward the opening of the camp to give the men more freedom and this was inevitable anyway. We are just waiting on the Nauruan government to approve it. You are sticking your neck out for a very small gain.'

I was starting to doubt myself, to doubt my knowledge of the case and the next month's proceedings. After all, what I knew was based on other people's advice rather than my own sound knowledge and experience.

'Well, if that's the case at least I'm helping those ten men get justice,' I said. 'If they're found guilty they'll never be allowed into Australia.'

He countered again. 'Justice? You think the Australian government are going to give them visas after the way they've behaved? You will have little influence on a case that will have little influence on this camp. You should contact Salvo legal to provide you with proper advice. Send me an email telling me exactly what you have done. I showed you faith—back in January I questioned whether you could stay professional, not take all this too personally, and you can't.'

I walked out of his office feeling extremely unsure of where I stood legally, in terms of my current contract and any future reprisals by the government. Was I fired? Could I go in to work the next day? He also left me doubting exactly how much effect I was going to have on the case for the amount of risk I was taking. I needed clarification of the case's realistic goals and exactly what influence my statement would have on the case. My arguments of *I did what I thought was right* and *My legal counsel told me* felt feeble against that tirade. I was deeply worried: worried for my future, worried that I had made a huge mistake, worried that I had put myself in a position where I wasn't in control. I felt like I was about to be tactically sacrificed in the opening moves to better position the knights, bishops, and queens.

I walked into the camp, my mind racing but my body numb. I approached the men I knew best among those I could see straight away. Salar, Omar, Mustafa, Imran. They were the only men I could find so quickly. I told them a brief version of what had happened.

'I may not be able to come in here ever again,' I said. 'It's been a pleasure knowing you.'

They hugged me tightly and said, 'Thank you.'

Hussein pushed himself out of his chair, angry. 'Why do the Salvation Army get rid of the good workers and keep the bad ones? Anyone who helps us is sent home. Fuck the Salvation Army.'

I hoped that wouldn't be the last time we would see each other.

That evening Reza overdosed on a mixture of antidepressants, sleeping pills, mosquito repellent and cleaning products. The men had been hoarding the antidepressants since December. Little Reza who had been taking private English lessons with me. Little Reza.

*

The day after the meeting I had a rostered day off, so I didn't get the opportunity to test my precarious position with the Salvos. Jay Williams called me and assured me that confidentiality deeds did not restrict people from speaking in a court of law. That the deed had been set up to prevent workers from speaking to the media. He said that the member of the management team had effectively been bullying me, threatening me. As Jay put it, 'protecting his $75 million contract'. Amanda's words rang in my ears: 'I'm sick of being bullied and made to feel like shit'.

Jay said that my role in the case was pivotal and that any attempts to punish me for speaking out would be held in contempt of court. If I was fired, he would personally represent me for unfair dismissal. Julian Burnside backed up Jay's comments, saying the way the member of the management team had treated me was outrageous and in contempt of court. Jay confirmed that they were trying to prove that detaining men in the Regional Processing Centre was against the Nauruan constitution and the principle of *habeus corpus*; in turn, the Nauruan government was arguing that the only restrictions placed on the men were those demanded by their visas.

A win would prove that the past nine months of detention were illegal. It would set a precedent that the detention of innocent men in such places was illegal. It would show that the Australian government had acted unlawfully. In the past few weeks I had held on to the naive view that this would mean the camp would be closed. Over the past days, and in my conversation with Jay, I gathered that even if the camp was deemed unconstitutional, the government could alter the rules to make it fit. The immediate response to a win would be simple: open up the camp and provide the civil liberties the men should have had months ago. It wouldn't close the camp but it would improve conditions for the men and it could set up potential conflict between Australia and Nauru. The complication was that up until now, the Nauruan government and the Nauruan community did not want to give the men the freedom to wander the island. The Nauruan people were opposed to an open camp. If the Nauruan government continued to resist the Australian government's push for an open camp, maybe the camp would close down. If they were forced to open the camp when the island wasn't ready, what would happen? Furthermore, it would make it very difficult for the men on trial to be charged when the very camp they were imprisoned in was proven to violate their human rights.

The conversation with Jay reassured me in some ways, but left me disappointed in others. I had to hold on to the mantra that this was one small but necessary step forward.

I went in to work two days after my conversation with the member of the management team. No-one stopped me at the gate, no-one sent me home. I went about my business as usual, except I was given the added thrill of being able to see my friends again.

'Not gone yet,' I said to Omar and winked.

The previous day seventeen Palestinian men had arrived in the camp.

'They're hard bastards, those Palestinians,' a Wilson guard told me. 'They'll make the Iranians look soft. They come from a tough area of the world. They're all crazy. We could easily have some battles in here again.'

'It feels like one big experiment, doesn't it?' I replied. 'Let's keep adding ethnicities to the mix until it all explodes.'

It was the first intake in two months. We were told it would mark a period of regular arrivals that would mirror the opening months of the camp. No-one was looking forward to it.

That day I took the Palestinians on their first excursion out of the camp. They were a very young group: eighteen, nineteen, twenty-three years old. One boy told me he was sixteen and had travelled across the world with his brother and uncle. What would be the best option for him now? As a minor he could be separated from his immediate family and sent to Australia, or he could remain in Nauru and face the hardships of the camp with them.

The bus toured the island, driving around the picturesque lake that was too polluted to swim in, past the ex-president's house which had been attacked when he sent the island bankrupt, and in among palm trees and old phosphate mines. Despite DIAC employing a multitude of interpreters, not one Arabic interpreter was available to help us. One of the Palestinian men volunteered to translate for me as I told them about Nauru and explained how the camp at Topside worked.

Some of the men responded well to the Salvation Army's gestures of goodwill. We talked of their journeys.

'I left Israel in September 2012. I went to Jordan, Egypt, Malaysia, Indonesia, Christmas Island,' one man said, nodding and smiling.

Others were not so responsive. 'Why were we taken to this hell?' one man asked. 'We were forced and handcuffed and the police abused us.'

The bitterness was heavy on his tongue. Of the hundreds of asylum seekers detained on Christmas Island, these seventeen had been chosen to be sent to Nauru. No amount of kindness we offered them could wipe away the taint of misfortune. It would take a long time for the men to silence the questioning of their fate in their own minds.

I continued to speak despite the heavy air of pessimism, and then our volunteer interpreter began to cry. He bowed his head low and pushed it against the window. With him weeping there was no-one to translate. The bus was filled with silence and his quiet sobs.

At the end of the day I was approached by a manager I trusted, who knew of my decision to make a statement in the constitutional challenge. He took me aside so we could speak alone.

'Take tomorrow off,' he said to me. 'I need to put out some fires.'

'What's happened?'

'When DIAC found out about your decision to make a statement they demanded that you be sent home from the island immediately. Management were going to do it but they've had a change of heart,' he said. 'They sought advice from Salvo legal and it looks like they're sitting on the decision for now. You see, both DIAC and the Salvos want to send you home but neither of them want to be the one to sign off on it. Neither one want to be seen as the bad guy, because whoever does it is going to cop major flak in the media. You've put them in a real shit position, mate.'

I felt very lost and alone. What was I doing in all this? Why had I put myself in the middle of this giant political battle?

'If the Salvos fire you, they'll be seen as the charity organisation that won't let their workers tell the truth. Everyone will hate them and DIAC will drop them from the contract. If they don't fire you, DIAC will be furious and will drop Salvos from the contract. I wish you'd talked to me about it first, hey?'

'Do you think I've done the right thing?'

'Morally, yes I do,' he said. 'You did what you thought was right. I would've done the same thing at your age. No-one can take that away from you. But you could've done it in a better way. Now that I have a little more experience behind me, I would say that you should've waited to be subpoenaed. That way you would have had to give evidence in court and the Salvation Army would have to support you.'

I sighed. It was difficult to know who to trust. 'So why didn't the lawyers subpoena me, rather than take my voluntary statement?'

'Because they don't give a shit about you, mate,' he said. 'I'm sorry to say it, but lawyers are in this game for one thing: to make a name for themselves and to make a lot of money.'

'But they're working pro bono on this case,' I said.

'This time, maybe. And then they'll make a name for themselves and the next case they'll make big bucks. I've seen it before—they use witnesses to get what they want, the witness will get roasted at the stake by the prosecutors, and then at the end of the day all the lawyers from both sides will go have beers together and play a round of golf. The opposition lawyers will do everything in their power to make you an unreliable witness. They'll dig up every bit of dirt on you, they will attack your character, and afterwards your statement will be worth nothing and you will have to deal with the consequences of losing your job for a valiant cause. Hell, I've been that witness.'

I felt deeply tired. All I wanted was to go to bed and wake up in Japan again, far away from Nauru and everything that I was about to face. But I had come too far now. I was being dragged along by the riptide of Australian politics, and I only had myself to blame.

Chapter 59

AZAD WAS TOO skinny, and he wore his pants around his navel. Azad and I had shared rooms for months on end in Nauru. We flew there together on our very first rotation. We had seen a lot of the more traumatic aspects of the camp together. Where there were five or six Hazara cultural advisors, there was only one Iranian. Azad had been the Iranians' only point of call for the majority of that difficult period from October to December.

Azad had found it difficult to assimilate into Australia. He had Iranian friends, but he wanted to meet Australians. He believed it was difficult to make bonds with Australians. The Australians he had met weren't interested in stepping outside their comfort zones, not for an Iranian man. Azad and I had become close friends over our time in Nauru.

On our first rotation I convinced him to jump into the ocean for the first time in his life; before then he had only ever walked in. He ran to the edge of the boat harbour, hugging his life jacket to his chest, prescription goggles strapped tightly to his face. Just as he was about to jump he changed his mind, but it was too late—the momentum of his body took him over the edge. He twisted in midair, desperately trying to claw his way back onto solid land, but his fingers groped at thin air. He landed in the water, and after a few seconds of silence the life jacket brought him back up to the surface.

'I'm a king,' he shouted, thrusting his fists triumphantly in the air.

When Azad found out I had booked my trip to Japan he'd asked me, 'Can I come?'

'Sure,' I'd said, not thinking he actually would.

Ten minutes later Azad had bought a ticket to Japan.

'Do Iranians need a visa to get to Japan?'

'I assume so,' I'd said.

After a lot of difficulty Azad had got his visa, just days before our departure date. It was the first time he had ever travelled to another country for the sake of travelling.

I spent my 'suspension' day with Azad. We wandered down to the boat harbour and had fish and chips and pineapple Fanta.

'I'm tired,' I told him.

'Is there anything I can do?'

I shook my head. There was nothing anyone could do now. I felt my resolve ebb out of me and I laid my head down on the table.

'I'm tired of being here,' I said. 'Of the all-powerful DIAC, of the petty complaints from other service providers, and the inequalities between management and staff. I'm tired of the constant bullshit that we have to put up with. The lies, the mistruths, and the expected loyalty we should have to the people who lie the most.'

'You are doing the right thing,' he said. It felt good to hear that from someone again. 'I am proud of you for telling the truth. Many people would not do this in your case. They would be selfish. But you are putting yourself at risk for what you believe. The Salvation Army are a Christian organisation. They are here to support the asylum seekers. If they acted on behalf of God like they said, they should support you.'

'Then why do I feel like I'm in over my head?' I asked.

'It's not so bad.'

I snorted. 'Just pissing off the government and the Salvation Army, all for the chance to have a lawyer tell me how bad a character I have and that I'm not suitable to make a statement in court.'

'Only the managers will hate you and who cares about them, they are just worried about money. The workers won't hate you. The men will love you.'

'It would've been easier to just stay quiet and do my job,' I said. 'I'd probably have got a promotion too.'

'When I was in Iran I joined a protest,' Azad said. 'There were lots of posters published from the protest. For the next month, I received phone calls from unknown phone numbers. There were knocks on my doors. I stayed in my house, very scared. I spent a month waiting to be taken by my government.'

I almost started crying, but instead I started laughing. Azad had given me the perspective I needed. What was I worrying about? It wasn't as if my life was being threatened.

'Ever since I started working in Nauru I have begun to gain insight into all the privileges I get as a white Australian male,' I said. 'I thought I appreciated this before Nauru. But working with these men, seeing the trouble they go through just to have an inch of what I have, I understand full well how lucky I am. And being your friend has taught me about this more than ever before. In Japan, the way you were treated compared to me, based on the colour of our skin. It's not fair,' I said.

'That is why I'm a nihilist,' Azad said. 'You don't choose your colour, your race, your nationality. Whether you are good-looking or ugly, able-bodied or disabled. It is all luck, bullshit luck. Some of us have it, some of us don't. But you have to do your best with what you have.'

*

In the days after my conversation with the member of the management team, Shine Lawyers sent a letter to the Nauru government, DIAC and Salvos Legal.

The letter stated:

> We put you on notice that if any further threats are made to our witnesses, or if any reprisals are taken, we will refer that person's action to the Supreme Court of Nauru and you should be aware that such conduct could amount to contempt of court

and perverting the course of justice. The punishment for contempt
includes imprisonment.

The following day I went back to work. Dev's cricket team was playing the Sinhalese team. Dev had recruited well this season and as a result his team was the favourite to win the competition. The Sinhalese team was last season's champion. It was billed to be a blockbuster of a match.

The match was delayed by two hours when one bus arrived at 9.30 am instead of the two buses booked to arrive at 8.30 am, thanks to a bus driver meeting organised for 9 am. Although we started the match late, we couldn't finish late as we had to abide by the timetable. Thankfully it didn't matter. Dev's team were bowled out for eighty-six runs in eight overs. It looked like the Sinhalese team couldn't lose but they capitulated for fifty runs, and we finished with half an hour to spare.

That afternoon I spent playing football with Hussein and Salar. The Premier League had fallen apart again in my absence, this time after the Iraqis and the Hazaras were involved in a punch-up that had the Salvos evacuated out of the camp. I refused to start it up again. The Palestinian who had refused to look at me the other day joined us. He was quick and skilful, and laughed when he played.

At the end of the day I received a phone call from the CEO of the Salvation Army Offshore Missions. She was in Nauru for a few days and wanted to talk to me about my decision to speak in court. I met her in the Psycare office, still sweating from the football match. It was a short conversation in which she assured me that the Salvation Army would not take action against me for making a statement in court. They would not fire me, nor would they send me home from the island. Furthermore, the member of the management team was to approach me in the future to resolve the matter.

I, in turn, apologised for placing the Salvation Army in a difficult position. I told her that it was never my intention to harm its reputation or jeopardise its contract. I explained that Jack and I were asked to provide evidence in court. We told the truth. We provided information that should be deemed equally as important and legitimate as the Wilson statement. Regardless of personal relationships and politics between agencies, should it not be considered the right thing to do to offer evidence of our experiences when asked to ensure that justice has a fair chance of being realised?

I left the office feeling like I had been vindicated.

The member of the management team never came to talk to me.

On 28 June, the Nauruan government called a state of emergency. It was declared that parliament was not functioning and not passing legislation. An early election was called for 8 June 2013. It looked like I was going to be in Nauru to see the next president.

Chapter 60

I WALKED INTO Parshan's room, ignoring the *No entry* sign on the door.

'Be careful going in there,' the Wilson suicide watch said to me. 'He has been unstable lately and we know he has a razor blade in there. We're not allowed to search their rooms anymore so we can't take it.'

The windows and door were covered with sheets so no light could enter. There was nothing in the room but a bunk bed; any personalised touches were distinctly absent. The room stank: the stifling odour of sweat, body odour and despair was instantly over-powering. It clung to me, making me feel nauseous. Parshan was curled up in a ball at the end of his bed inside a blue sheet. He lay on a white mattress cover stained with blood. Parshan had slashed his chest a few days ago and slashed his wrists the night before. Staff had come in to change the sheets earlier that day but he had told them to go away.

I sat down on his bed like I had several times in the past, and before I had a chance to say anything he writhed away from me shouting, 'GET OUT. GO AWAY.'

His reaction was so forceful I shied back away from him. There was nothing I could do for him. Seeing this room, this black hole of despair, made me think of Dev's comments about Sri Lanka. That on the surface the war was over in Sri Lanka, but if you took the time to delve into the darker regions of the country you would still find oppression. It was the same in Nauru. You could choose to see surface Topside and think, *This place isn't so bad.* Play football, talk to the men who were coping, joke with Salar and the Iraqis. Or you could wander over to A Block and find men hiding under blankets in darkened rooms. Several of the Iranian men who arrived in September, including little Reza, had been taken to Australia in the past week. Their numbers were slowly dwindling. They needed to win that court case or something bad would happen. Something worse than Parshan locking himself in a darkened room, slashing his wrists and his chest.

Meanwhile the Australian media reported that twenty-eight life jackets had washed up on the Cocos Keeling Islands.[1] They were believed to be the remnants of another asylum seeker boat. Offshore processing was a policy of deterrence. The government line was to 'save lives at sea', 'stop the people smugglers', yet Senate hearings indicated that after nine months the No Advantage policy was not having the desired result. The number of asylum seekers had risen that financial year, from an expected 5400 to at least 22,500.[2] It shouldn't come as a surprise that the UNHCR reported that global refugee numbers were rising and that an extra 7.6 million people were displaced worldwide, including 1.1 million refugees.[3] The policy wasn't stopping boats and it wasn't saving lives.

With an election imminent the Australian political parties were vying to see who could develop the most punitive policy to deter asylum seekers, the logic being that the crueller the policy, the less likely these people would be to get on the boats. The crueller the policy, the more votes you won.

There were just one hundred days left until the election. How bad could the policies get?

*

During the second week of my final rotation another eleven men from Iran and Iraq were welcomed into camp by thirty Salvo staff.

The new Salvation Army management announced to the staff that it was 'the best intake ever'. This proclamation was met with sniggers. Management had been on the island two weeks, they had missed the days when we were informed of intakes an hour before the men arrived; when intakes arrived and we didn't have beds ready for the men; when three Salvos met forty new men and we didn't have the correct cultural advisors employed to talk to them. One intake we didn't even have tents for the men. What made it all the funnier was that this intake the Salvos had been expecting thirty Vietnamese asylum seekers—the Salvos had even hired Vietnamese cultural advisors. *Best intake ever.*

Management then graciously offered a Red Shirt dinner to all those workers who were 'below' a yellow shirt. We were all equal, but some were more equal than others. The staff joked that we plebs would be offered gruel because we didn't know any better. While management tried to placate the growing resentment among the workers with free meals they began to enforce strict dress codes which included hiding all tattoos, apparently to avoid offending the men in the camp. Tattooed staff were now being told to cover up.

We continued to gain staff at the same rate we lost rooms. A DIAC officer made a speech at a Salvos staff meeting. He told us how hard he was working to find us extra rooms, and that we were doing a great job and we were really respected. He understood how difficult it was to sleep in crowded quarters, but that the DIAC officers who slept one person to a hotel room were different because they had to work three months at a time. 'And anyway,' he said, 'some people prefer to sleep on stretchers'. That comment was followed by uproarious laughter. 'You're a joke,' someone shouted. It was the same story we'd been hearing since we'd arrived on Nauru.

That same meeting we were told by management that an entire room of staff had become ill with gastro. It was a lie and everyone knew it. One girl had food poisoning and IHMS had quarantined the entire room. Four healthy staff members were locked in there, unable to leave, and served rice, bread and water. IHMS stated that anyone who visited the room had to be quarantined too. Management and DIAC visited but they weren't quarantined.

'Remember to wash your hands outside of the camp, too. This island is not sanitary,' management said.

The local Nauruan staff were not impressed.

'We have to sit in this meeting, with no relevant information for us, where we are not even addressed, and be told how dirty our island is,' Rioli said. 'You don't see us getting gastro.'

The meeting continued. 'With the imminent Nauruan election we've been asked by the Nauruan government to remain indoors over the weekend,' one of the new managers said in a singsong baby voice that everyone was beginning to hate. 'This is their day. It is culturally significant and we don't want to be seen.'

Again Rioli looked shocked. 'What does that even mean? It is not culturally significant.'

The intent was clear, though. Election day would be a day of celebration, when Nauruans would drink heavily and we were to avoid them.

The final announcement was that the Red Shirt dinner had been cancelled.

'Just don't bother,' one Salvo shouted out.

After the meeting the staff continued to mutter. Never before had there existed such inequalities between staff and management. While in previous months I could sit alongside the operations manager and have a beer and discuss our lives in Australia, now we were seg-regated by the colour of our shirts. While Red Shirts were packed into tighter sleeping quarters due to the room shortage, Yellow Shirts resided in the dongers. These dongers were spacious and airy with free wi-fi, washing machines, and ovens. Some managers were even given the privilege of reserving their rooms during their two-week respite leave. No longer was there a car for the plebs to use on rostered days off; it was decided that management needed all the cars they could get.

One team leader said that if the Salvation Army Nauru mission were a country we would be on the verge of revolution.

On my first rotations the absurdity of the situation would have annoyed me. Now I found it all sadly amusing. The unfortunate result of this staff discontent was that the asylum seekers were the ones who would suffer most. Good staff were sick to death of working in a place like Nauru.

Within the camp, Raj was one of the first men to receive an appointment slip that read *Refugee status determination*.

'Are you sure that they will tell you your refugee status?' I asked.

'I have done all my interviews. It has been two months,' he said. 'It must be this interview.'

'I wouldn't expect anything, Raj,' I said, thinking that if refugee status determination were to take place the Salvation Army would have been told.

'I looked up *determination* in the dictionary. It is the right meeting,' he said.

'Good luck then,' I said, still not believing he would find out yet. We hugged and he smiled broadly, the excitement and hope flushing his face.

He did not find out his refugee status. DIAC called him in to confirm details he had given them two months earlier. Raj's note was an 'error in paperwork'. It was then announced that the men would receive refugee status determination four to six months after their final interview.

Wilson guards began asking men what they would do if they got a negative response to their refugee status determination, creating suspicion and fear in their minds. The men started predicting negative responses. And what would happen if the men did get negative responses?

*

After the affidavits had been filed in court things started to change in the camp. Wanding of staff and asylum seekers stopped; apparently the threat of secret cameras was over. There was no longer a gate on Charlie 5, and the men could walk themselves to IHMS and back via fenced-off walkways. Limits on walking groups had been lifted, although Wilson guards still found that hard to compute and every so often insisted upon capping the numbers. Amazing what a court case can do to galvanise security into permitting the men some basic civil liberties. The swift changes to the camp were a cover-up of the injustices pressed on the men over the past nine months.

In that second week I received an email from my lawyers.

'As envisaged, the Secretary for Justice has requested your attendance in court for cross-examination next week. Our counsel, Julian and Jay, will be in contact with you in due course to prepare you for the witness stand. Thanks again for your assistance.'

My gut felt like steel in the days leading up to the trial. The men could instantly tell that something was wrong—they knew our moods better than we did. Several men approached me with a friendly hand on the shoulder, or a kind word. They thanked me for what I was doing.

It was in these days that I began to slowly divulge to the men that I would not be coming back. It was a difficult conversation. 'Why are you leaving?' they would ask in a hurt tone. Guilt laced my mumbled responses of the frustrations of working in Nauru. Eventually I came to the conclusion that I hated Nauru, I really hated it. 'What are you going to do?' they asked me. 'I don't know,' I replied, 'travel, be free of this place.' My guilt faced off against their jealousy. The conversation dripped with injustice. 'Come back,' they pleaded with me. I shook my head. Stone cold.

The day before the court case, a Wilson guard told me that all Wilson employees were secretly told to pack plain clothes to work in as the camp might become open on the day of the court case. The Salvation Army announced it was introducing educational classes about Nauru for the asylum seekers, nine months after the camp had opened, highlighting the minuscule amount of community liaison between the Australian organisations and the Nauruan community. The men had never been formally introduced to the local people.

And what would happen if they did open the camp? Would any of the men commit crimes or try to force the Nauruan community into closing the camp? It was possible. No-one was expecting a quick and seamless transition of four hundred men into a community of 10,000 people. Even if the transition went okay, would it really make a difference to the men? All they cared about was processing.

'We will have no money,' Dev said. 'We can't buy anything. We can't take water. We can't take food. Where will we go?'

'To the beach,' I said. 'Get out of here.'

'There will still be guards everywhere,' Dev said. 'We will not be free. We will still be in Nauru.'

---

1   B Hall & D Flitton, 'Asylum seeker debate marked by tragedy and discord', *Sydney Morning Herald*, 27 December 2012.

2   Editorial, 'Significant drawbacks in the no-advantage policy on boats', *Sydney Morning Herald*, 29 May 2013, viewed 31 May 2013, <www.smh.com.au/opinion/editorial/significant-drawbacks-in-the-noadvantage-policy-on-boats-20130528-2n9gm.html>.

3   United Nations Human Rights Commission 2012, *UNCHR Global Trends 2012*, viewed 1 July 2013, <unhcr.org/globaltrendsjune2013/UNHCR%20GLOBAL%20TRENDS%20 2012_V05.pdf>.

Chapter 61

I DIDN'T HEAR from my lawyers until the day of the court case. They left Brisbane on the Sunday night red-eye special, arriving on Nauru on Monday morning just hours before the case was due to be heard. Jack had missed his Thursday flight and was lucky to have his ticket rescheduled for the same flight as the lawyers. For me this meant a week in isolation, a week of not knowing what was happening or what was expected of me.

The Salvos I worked with were supportive, at least the Red Shirts were—one of them told me we were inspirational. She wanted advice on how to be more active outside of her role. It was reassuring to have their support, but I wanted to talk to Jack, to discuss how we would deal with the cross-examination.

When we did finally reunite we embraced and went for a long walk. 'We're doing the right thing,' Jack reassured me.

I wanted days to plan and mentally prepare. Instead I was given a rushed conversation in the hallway of the Menen Hotel with Jay and Julian on the day of the hearing.

Julian had white hair and round glasses. His fashion sense was charmingly eccentric: pink chinos and a loose white caftan. He shook my hand and smiled eagerly. Jay Williams was much younger, more Australian-sounding than Julian with his slightly British accent, and just as welcoming.

After we had greeted each other Julian asked, 'When would you like to give evidence?'

'As soon as possible,' I replied. 'I still have to work.'

'Well, why don't you come with us in an hour,' Julian said. 'We'll call you first to the stand.'

My eyes glazed slightly. 'Sure.'

Suddenly the previous weeks of tension had culminated in an hour of intense heart beats that did not cease until I was sitting in the witness box. Jack and I were given a two-minute briefing in the back of the car as we drove to court.

'Listen to the question, answer the question,' Julian said. 'You don't need to do any more than that. The more information you give, the more you'll play into their hands. Unless of course you can stick one to them, then go for it. But be very careful of the wording, of exactly what the lawyer is saying to you. If you need the lawyer to repeat the question, ask him to. This is not an exam. You'll be right.'

'Can you explain a little more about what will happen in court?' I asked.

'Of course,' Julian said. 'As it is a *habeas corpus* challenge, the onus is upon the Nauruan government to prove that the detention is lawful. Their legal team have relied on three primary arguments as to why the detention was lawful. Firstly, that the applicants are free to leave Nauru at any time if they ask to do so.'

I snorted loudly.

'Yes, yes. Just preposterous,' Julian said. 'Secondly, they argue that the restrictions on freedom of movement do not amount to detention, and thirdly, that the detention is authorised by the Constitution of the Republic of Nauru. We will obviously try and prove that the men cannot leave if they ask to do so, that the restrictions on their movement do amount to detention, and that the detention is against the Nauruan constitution.'

Julian had an air of confidence about him that was impossible not to soak up. He spoke in a clear and dignified manner that commanded your attention. I listened to Jay and Julian talk as I tried to project assuredness.

'I mean, it's just ridiculous that the detainees were denied access to legal representation for over six months,' Julian said.

'The Office of the Public Defender has been vacant for over ten months, hasn't it?' Jay said. 'The local pleader had carriage of the matter, who is not a qualified lawyer, and they've been off-island for three months. So finally we had the Solicitor General of Nauru move into the role as acting public defender.'

Jay Williams did not speak, he presented. 'And the prosecution brief was incomplete,' he continued. 'It was missing witness statements, some statements were unsigned, there were missing pages, misidentifications, incorrect ID numbers.'

'Quite right,' Julian said. 'To top it off, there is no independent legal officer on-site in the processing centre, no ombudsmen, no representative from the Republic of Nauru and no representative from UNHCR or the Red Cross. Who are the men supposed to go to for assistance?'

Emma Stephens, the young solicitor, was the least intimidating of the trio of lawyers. When Julian and Jay followed tangents of legal conversation, Emma explained the assumed knowledge that was lost on me. Despite arriving that morning the three of them had already been up to the camp.

'I'm worried about the men,' Emma said. 'They were very suspicious of us. They accused us of working for the government, as if we were part of some big conspiracy. After all the work we've done it was quite devastating.'

'Jack and I will talk to them,' I said.

The Nauruan Court was not an intimidating structure. Five rows of benches to the left and the right of the court room were divided by a centre aisle. We sat on the right side of the court with the lawyers and several Salvos who had come on their day off to show us their support. Abbas arrived bright-eyed and smiling. He looked enraptured with the lawyers. Parshan also attended court, much to our surprise. It was the first time he had left his room in forty days or more. He walked slowly, shuffled, with feeble steps; his beard was thick and he had dark shadows under his eyes. Each step looked to take deep concentration. He cast his gaze to the floor. He looked like a shadow. We greeted him and he managed a nod and a limp handshake.

On the left side of the court were the government lawyers, a man and a woman. When they entered they joked with Julian and Jay. I couldn't help but think of my manager's golf comment. The woman directed a cold look at me and Jack. One of the Wilson representatives, who sat on the left side of the court, kept looking at us and furiously scribbling something in his notebook. A few more Salvos arrived and sat on the left side, too. One of them approached our supporters.

'You're not supposed to be here,' she said.

'Why not?' one of them asked.

'Management has said that nobody can come to court,' she said.

'But it's a public court. It's our day off,' someone replied.

The Salvo frowned and made a call, then came back to them.

'Well, you're most definitely not allowed to speak about what is said here,' she said.

'Why not?'

'What is being said here is confidential information and to speak of it would be a breach of your contract.'

'But it's a public court. There is a BBC journalist over there.'

I was anxious. I didn't want to make a fool of myself and I didn't want to say something wrong. More importantly, I didn't want all this to be for nothing. I read through my statement again, in an effort to remind myself of what I was going to say, and it gave me confidence. Everything I was saying was the truth. I didn't need to be anxious about what I was going to say, I just had to say what I knew.

When Julian and Jay changed into their robes they became much more impressive figures.

Abbas was first to the stand. The point that made the biggest impression on me from his cross-examination was when the lawyer suggested that Abbas had always had the option to voluntarily return to his home country with IOM.

I was glad I would be one of the first to be called to the stand. It made me think of high school speeches, when I would always volunteer to go first so I wouldn't have to sit in class waiting for my turn, frantically over-thinking what I had to say.

The cross-examination was easier than I'd expected. Once I got into the witness box my heart calmed. Earlier in the week Wilson Security had issued a response to our statements, using the recent changes in the camp to argue against them—as if a week of leniency reversed the months of oppressive rules. The lawyer worked that angle into his cross-examination.

'You would agree that now there are no limitations on running group numbers?' he asked me. He started every question with 'You would agree', trying to persuade me of my own convictions.

'I would not. I've still seen Wilson Security, even in the last week, restrict numbers on excursions,' I said. Even though the rules were different, some of the Wilson security guards didn't deal with change well.

'But you would agree that every man has the opportunity to leave the camp at least once a day?'

Again I disagreed: just because there were excursions didn't mean everyone could leave each day. There were numerous restrictions on this. The lawyer had been advised by a man who had never been on an excursion, who did not understand the excursion program as well as I did—or maybe they knew that and they were trying to talk me into a false statement. The cross-examination did not attack my character or attempt to damage my credibility as I had been warned. When Jack was called the entire line of government questioning was irrelevant because he had been off-island during those imperative two weeks when the changes to the camp had been implemented.

The most significant part of the day came when Julian Burnside cross-examined Lisa Lo Piccolo. It was a long, gruelling process for the Nauruan Secretary for Justice and Border Control. She stated that the Nauruan government was in charge of resettling any asylum seekers who were given refugee status, however, no agreement had been reached with any country to take the refugees.

When asked what was being done to begin this process, she said that the Nauruan government was being assisted by the Australian government. When Julian asked her if the Nauruan government was implementing the No Advantage policy, Lisa Lo Piccolo denied his suggestion, claiming she had no knowledge of the policy. Then under cross-examination she accepted that she knew the policy but denied that the Nauruan government was implementing it. What became apparent through the cross-examination was that the first asylum seekers were expected to receive their refugee status results in the coming months yet there was no resettlement program close to being finalised.

After the court proceedings for the day were complete I felt physically lighter. I felt as if I were floating towards the sky like a helium balloon. At the boat harbour Jack and I screamed our lungs out underwater. Months earlier we had been doing that in frustration; now the relief was indescribable. All that stress and tension were over. We had made it.

*

As promised, Jack and I met with the Nauru Ten the following day—at least, we tried to. The majority of them were not interested in talking to us. We managed to get three of them in a room. Atash, Mahmoud and Reza. I could see immediately why Emma was so disappointed by her meeting with them the day before.

'This court case does nothing for us,' Atash said. 'Open the camp? This is what the government wants. Then we will be here forever. This is a plan from the government, the lawyers are working for them. We are alone in this.'

Atash looked crazy. In his eyes flared a wild fire that scared me. I hadn't seen eyes so intense in any of the men in Nauru.

Nothing we said could turn their minds to our point of view. They didn't care about the benefits of an open camp, not for them, nor for the other men in the camp. They ignored the possibility that if they won this case it might help them avoid the criminal charges they faced. They were completely paranoid about everyone. Who could blame them? After what they had been through, why would they trust any Australian?

Chapter 62

LEAVING NAURU WAS liberating and upsetting at the same time. I was about to be free of that oppressive atmosphere; free of the constantly critical organisations; free of the omnipotent government. No longer would I have to work in unreasonable conditions while being patronised by managerial staff who knew less about the camp than the workers did. I was free from getting myself in trouble for caring about the men, free from the men and their traumas—and despite all the hardships of Nauru, once again the thought of leaving those men behind almost drew me back there. At the very end, I forgot all the hardships and remembered their sad eyes. But this time I wouldn't be going back.

I knew I had made a difference in Nauru. The programs I had established in my first months had returned to the men some freedom, had entertained for some small time, and now the swimming was a legacy I could be proud of, one I knew was doing the men immeasurable good, and in return Nauru had helped me grow. Never before had I understood the privileges of being a white Australian male. Those three characteristics entitle me to a world of opportunities that 99 per cent of the world's people can never dream of. Meanwhile I witnessed our government inflict cruelty upon some of the most desperate people in the world.

We were counselled by our psychologists that saying goodbye should not be a personal matter and that we had to consider who we were saying goodbye for. Was our purpose in saying goodbye for our own peace of mind or to help the men? We should not draw it out and we should remain distant. They were our clients and we had to make way for the next worker. It was not our place to grow sentimental.

I found the cold professionalism of that perspective unsatisfying. There was no purpose in me saying goodbye other than to acknowledge that I would be leaving these men with whom I had just spent the last nine months.

I stepped inside the camp at 11 am with a heavy heart. I stepped out of the camp at 5 pm needing to sleep for a very long time. With each step I met a man, looked in his face, into his eyes, shook his hand, hugged him, said goodbye. Each time I looked at a man I knew that there was a high likelihood we would not see each other again.

'Why?' they asked, over and over again. At first I tried to explain. I tried to tell them how frustrating the work was, how our best efforts were ignored or went unrewarded. I tried to explain the constant pressure from the organisations to behave and toe the line and how we felt like the government was constantly watching over us, how difficult it was to work in such a claustrophobic environment. Even after my explanation they continued to ask why. I was leaving for many reasons and no matter how I put it, all it felt like was that I was leaving them. In the end I just said three words.

'It is time.'

I sat with the Iraqis in one small room and we told stories until we were all breathless with laughter.

'Remember the time Awas went swimming in his white shorts and no undies. He sat on the step proud as punch, not even caring that he was offending everyone around him, and the Nauruan life-savers said if he didn't wear underwear on the next excursion he'd be banned.'

'And when we played basketball and everyone could get the ball in the basket except Mustafa.'

'What about your first massage with Jabber? Where you kept screaming.'

'And when Asaad gave you the haircut in the laundry. You were sitting next to the washing machines with your shirt off, Asaad was shaving your head, and the managers of Wilson and Transfield were around the corner trying to get Parshan out of his room. Everyone kept walking into the laundry and you were telling them to shut up in little urgent whispers.'

We laughed until they began to cry. I don't know how I didn't cry in that little room. Puffy-eyed Mustafa, red-eyed Omar, sniffling Asaad, everyone hugging. It tore at my chest to go, but I had made my decision and my psych's words rang in my head. *Who is this goodbye for?* It only dawned on me days after I had left Nauru that I hadn't said goodbye to Jabber.

I found Dev looking sadder than I had ever seen him, shoulders curved in, withdrawn, face crumpled.

'Everything will finish when you are gone,' he said.

'Not true, my friend,' I said. 'The camp will be open soon and then you can play a real five-day test match.'

We hugged and said goodbye. The words felt inadequate. How could we express the overpowering emotions, the significance of this moment in words? I may never see Dev again. He will be stuck in Nauru for who knows how long, at the end of which he may end up returning to Sri Lanka. What would become of him? What would become of all these men? Goodbye was a pathetic way to end it.

Thankfully there were happier farewells.

'I will see you again,' Raj said. 'Of course we will see each other again.'

I held his four-fingered hand tightly. 'You know, Raj,' I said. 'Someone once asked me, if I could elect a president of Topside from all the men in the camp who would I choose. You were the only man I could think of who would represent all men justly and equally, no matter the race. That's probably the biggest compliment I could ever give a man.'

'Thank you,' he said.

Salar gave me his cheeky smile and said, 'Ah, *Luchak*, you leave us to chase girls.'

'Of course,' I said. 'Wouldn't you?'

We laughed. 'But thank you, *Luchak*,' he said. 'You were very good to us. You did everything for us.'

The Iranians didn't give me much of a send-off, except for Farid.

'Thank you, *Dosh*,' Farid said and gripped me to him in an immense bear hug until I had to plead with him to stop.

Abbas looked at me with hard eyes. It was a far cry from the Abbas in the court room who had been so excited I could actually see a bounce in his step.

'What did you think of the case?' I asked him.

'I think it's a game,' he said coldly.

'Of course. It's politics, it's one big game,' I said. 'And hopefully we win.'

'We are pawns. You are a pawn. We always lose.'

The last person I saw was Pez. He was asleep, curled up in the foetal position on his bed. When I came in, I woke him. He rolled over and smiled at me.

'Mark. Good to see you,' he said.

I stood in front of him, unaccountably nervous. 'I've come to say goodbye,' I announced.

'Oh no,' he said with such sadness I had to look away. I realised that in the last three weeks I hadn't been to visit him. I felt terribly guilty and ashamed.

'Mark, I'm depressed,' he said. 'I haven't left my room in days. I'm not eating again. I've stopped caring about everything. I just can't care about life.'

I was dry-mouthed with worry. We had had similar conversations in the past.

'I remember you told me once that no man really wants to die in the end,' I said.

He smiled. 'I'm not going to commit suicide,' he said. 'I don't care enough about my life to take it. I have nothing to live for, but I have nothing to die for.'

'Pez!' I cried out. 'You are one of the most beautiful men I've ever met. You inspire me. You have an incredible mind and future. Please keep the hope. There will be a day when this is all over. It may be in one year or five, but it will be over. Nothing can last forever. And when that day comes, you will think, *Well, it wasn't so bad.*'

We smiled at each other.

'You are my brother,' he said. 'I hope to see you in Australia soon.'

'You will see me in Australia,' I said, hoping that if I put enough belief into those words my wish would come true.

I left the Nauru Regional Processing Centre dry-eyed and calm. It was all over. As I stepped out of the gate, I shouted out: 'CLOSE THE NAURU.'

Chapter 63

JUDGE JOHN VON DOUSSA released his findings for the constitutional challenge on 19 June 2013.[1] Judge von Doussa agreed that the applicants had been brought to Nauru against their will for the sole purpose of processing their claims for refugee status. He agreed that the conditions of their visas effectively amounted to detention. He also agreed that the argument that the applicants are not detained because they have voluntarily chosen not to return to their country of nationality is a hollow one in the circumstances of those on Nauru who are subject to such conditions.

Judge von Doussa ruled against the claim that the asylum seekers are being unlawfully detained at Australia's processing centre on the island, stating that although the asylum seekers are being detained, this is a lawful part of their visa conditions.[2] He cited the *Immigration Act* and Nauru's constitution, stating that the men were being held for the purpose of processing their claims for refugee status and it was well recognised that this process may take a protracted time and he did not think it amounted yet to an excessive delay. After all the turmoil of the previous month, we had lost. The application was dismissed. Later that year Amnesty International would criticise Nauru, Papua New Guinea, Australia and New Zealand for their roles in the offshore processing policy, stating that 'the planned forcible removal of hundreds of asylum-seekers to detention facilities on Manus Island for the stated purpose of processing their claims offshore would amount to refoulement and thus violate Australia's and New Zealand's obligations under both international refugee and human rights law.' Furthermore, Amnesty International would state that it was concerned about 'the credibility of some of these countries' refugee status determination procedures', and about the lack of financial and institutional capacity to uphold their protection obligations effectively.[3]

*

One month later, on the evening of Friday 19 July 2013, hundreds of asylum seekers detained within the Nauru Regional Processing Centre revolted.

---

1   Williams, 'The Nauru 10: The Habeus Corpus Challenge'.
2   Radio New Zealand International, 'Nauru Court Rules Against Asylum Seekers', 19 June 2013, viewed 20 June 2013, <http://rnzi.com/pages/news.php?op=read&id=76926>
3   Amnesty International, *Pacific Island's Forum Meeting: Human Rights Briefing*, September 2013, <www.amnesty.org/en/library/asset/ASA05/001/2013/en/5e80f0f6-0fde-4478-915d-2d77758a03d7/asa050012013en.pdf>

Chapter 64

I HAVE SPOKEN with Salvation Army workers, team leaders and managers, and asylum seekers about the July riots. It appeared that the riot started in a similar manner to the two uprisings I had been present for in Nauru. Several arguments started over what should have been menial issues but were symbolic of greater frustrations. First, the government announced yet another delay in processing. Then a fight over a television became a representation of the ever-present perceived discrimination against the Tamils.

The Tamils who had so often threatened to protest on a large scale finally did so, but what started as a peaceful protest against unfair treatment within the camp was hijacked by a group of men who set fire to buildings, causing a reported $60 million worth of damage. Shouts and screams filled the night sky, madness ensued in the darkness and flickering bonfire light, and many of the asylum seekers escaped into the pinnacles.

The police commissioner ordered that the uprising be allowed to run its course, a policy he had implemented on previous occasions. The new Nauruan president did not agree, and sacked the police commissioner on the spot. Members of the Nauruan community were mobilised into an emergency police force charged with subduing the men. It was a Friday night in Nauru, which meant the majority of emergency policemen were likely to have been drunk. Women and children on the island were told to stay indoors.

There were reported scenes of violence from asylum seekers and against asylum seekers. Asylum seekers were accused of throwing rocks. One man was accused of stabbing a policeman with a butter knife. In response, the Nauruans showed little mercy. Witnesses stated that a group of Nauruans was waiting outside the camp with weapons, including machetes. One account stated that a group of Nauruans boarded a bus full of asylum seekers bound for the jail cells and assaulted them. Witnesses on the night of the event accused some Wilson guards of showing extreme force in their handling of the men; others said that the Wilson guards were being forceful to protect the men from the armed Nauruans waiting outside.

Over one hundred men were arrested and placed in Nauruan jail. Those men were to face charges over the coming days. Every account I heard suggested that the men were not provided with adequate legal representation. They were refused lawyers, instead being served by Nauruan paralegals who merely asked if they would plead guilty or not guilty. They were refused phone calls or any other contact with the outside world.

Many of the asylum seekers had been seriously injured in the riot. Some, like little Devkumar, hadn't been involved in the rioting. Little Devkumar, the man who would always find my hand when I was feeling down, was beaten so badly that he couldn't go to the toilet by himself. It was unclear if the injured men were provided with adequate medical treatment. It was alleged that some of the jailed men were beaten, that they were denied food and water, and some even accused the guards of stripping them naked.

The Nauru Regional Processing Centre had been razed. The accommodation blocks were burnt to the ground, as were the IHMS facilities, the DIAC offices and the Salvation Army offices. Those men not in jail were forced to sleep under open skies on cardboard mattresses. It was reported by Salvo staff that the men were not fed for four days after the riot. When the asylum seekers were returned to the camp they were shocked to see the devastation.

They claimed independently of each other that when they left the camp the night of the riot just one building had been on fire. It turned out that in the days leading up to the riot the authorities had known asylum seekers were planning to set fire to the camp. Salvos claimed they had made reports to DIAC and their reports were ignored. Many of the asylum seekers lost all their paperwork, identity documents, photos of family, clothes, everything. The majority of Salvation Army staff were sent home days later to make way for more security personnel. Only two working groups were left behind, six people to each group. The staff were selected by Salvos and then approved by DIAC. Those left behind were the compliant ones. They were asked to sign new deeds of confidentiality.

It was difficult for all those former workers and current workers who had been sent off the island to get the news of the riot. We feared for the men's safety and we feared for their futures. We were frustrated by their actions because we knew it would affect their processing and their reputation in Australia, but at the same time we could understand exactly how it had happened. Above all we felt helpless to assist. Slowly news emerged that Raj, Dev, Omar and Mustafa were in prison. Raj, the democratically elected President of NRPC in my own head, was now behind bars. My friends were in prison. I couldn't imagine how scared they must have been.

Throughout my work in Nauru I had suppressed the uncomfortable itch of compliance, of culpability. Eventually that itch became a pounding in my head. After the riot I saw public sentiment sway even further against asylum seekers and I decided to speak out. A group of my colleagues had the same thought. We spoke out together as a collective force because we knew the Salvation Army would once again say nothing to support the men. To me it was a sign of the solidarity among the Salvo staff. For too long we had remained silent, forced to swallow our concerns and watch these men suffer. A group of thirty former and current Salvos wrote a press release and issued it to the media. Some of us put our names to it; the majority remained anonymous, fearing for their jobs, fearing for their careers and fearing retribution from the government.

Epilogue

THE RIOT ON Friday 19 July was evidence of the Nauruan Republic's inability to cope with the strains of the Australian government's chaotic and illogical Pacific Solution. In the same time period that the riot occurred both Labor and Liberal parties were making election promises of harsher measures: more people in offshore processing centres with worse conditions. One month after the riot, women and children were transported to Nauru to be housed in tent accommodation. Not long after, unaccompanied minors joined them. Former colleagues of mine told me of limitations to women's sanitary items and underwear. Water restrictions made it difficult to wash, and running water sources in the new centre were hundreds of metres from the tents. I was told of the smell in Manus, an overpowering odour of rubbish that never went away. Salvos informed me that in Manus over one hundred men were housed in one hangar-style room with bunk beds lined up against each other, where sexual assault was not uncommon. The Salvation Army did not have its contract renewed. It appeared that a humanitarian organisation would not be replacing it. By all accounts, conditions are worse than I ever saw them.

Scott Morrison, the new Minister for Immigration, implemented Operation Sovereign Borders, a military-led 'border security operation' headed by Angus Campbell, a senior officer in the Australian Army. The language of the debate had changed once again.

The Australian government donated two patrol boats to the Sri Lankan government to assist it in intercepting asylum seekers fleeing the country by boat. Meanwhile, eleven judges of the Permanent Peoples' Tribunal, an independent assessor of global human rights abuses, unanimously found the Sri Lankan government guilty of ongoing genocide against the Tamil people.[1]

Scott Morrison began to limit the information provided to the press on boat arrivals. The cost of journalist visas for Nauru were raised from $200 to $8000.[2] Boats were towed back to Indonesian waters by the Australian Navy, against the Indonesian government's wishes. It was found that the Australian Navy repeatedly breached Indonesian territorial waters.[3] It was clear that the newly elected Abbott Coalition government was determined to turn back the boats, no matter the costs. I wondered how the Australian government would react if the Indonesian Navy were found to be towing asylum seekers into our waters.

*

The majority of the asylum seekers I worked with were transferred to Curtin Immigration Detention Centre, located in the West Australian desert. Pez, Farid and Salar were among them. A number of the men told me that before they were transferred the government gave them two options: stay on Nauru, or be transferred to Curtin and have their processing start again. A large group of the men were given bridging visas on 12 February 2014 and were released into the community. Almost a year and a half after they first arrived in Australian waters, they are still waiting for their refugee status determinations. They do not have work rights and receive the lowest welfare payments in Australia, which means they live under extreme financial hardship. Upon their release from detention they were expected to sign a code of conduct that allows the government to place them back in detention for acts of 'unsocial behaviour'. Every week the government introduces tighter and more oppressive restrictions on the asylum seekers in the community. The government have begun disappearing asylum seekers from the community, taking them back into detention without any warning.

Many of the men, including Shahab, spent months in hospitals, only to be relocated to detention centres such as Villawood. I was told that Shahab had voluntarily returned home to Iran.

Of the men I knew in Nauru, Atash is the only asylum seeker to have been convicted of a crime and now sits in a prison in Nauru being allowed one visit per week from Salvo staff. Dev, Yaqub, Raj and Mustafa all remain in Nauru accused of being involved in the riot, facing charges that could put them in prison for a long time, and would effectively end any hope they have of reaching Australia. They are adamant that they are innocent and claim they have not had access to legal representation. In January 2014 the Nauruan government sacked and deported its only magistrate, Peter Law, and then denied its Australian Chief Justice a visa to re-enter the country. Mr Law was due to hear the case against Dev, Yaqub, Raj, Mustafa and the other asylum seekers charged after the riots. It was said that Peter Law had fought against holding the court case within the regional processing centre, secreted away from the media, while the investigation into the riot was led by Wilson Security, an organisation that was hardly independent from the incident in question. At the time of publication it was unclear how justice would play out over the coming months for the accused.[4] Yaqub now refers to himself by his boat ID.

Operation Sovereign Borders has marked a steady deterioration in public knowledge about asylum seekers. The government has been determined to restrict information on its asylum seeker policy and the number of asylum seekers arriving by boat, claiming that this approach would frustrate the people smugglers' business models. It has since become obvious, however, that these restrictions were attempts to mask the horrors of the policy from the Australian people. In February 2014, just seven months after the July riots in Nauru, the Manus Island regional processing centre was embroiled in conflict when local Papua New Guinean police, security guards, and civilians reacted to protests by the asylum seekers. The locals entered the camp wielding bats, sticks, and machetes. Australian staff evacuated, leaving the asylum seekers to fend for themselves. According to numerous eyewitness accounts, asylum seekers feared for their lives and innocent bystanders were dragged out of hiding and bashed. Dozens were injured in the conflict, one person was left in a serious condition, another shot and, most tragic of all, one asylum seeker was found dead. These events, which mirror those in Nauru seven months earlier, scream for a need to recalculate our offshore processing policy. What seems more likely is that Scott Morrison and Tony Abbott will demand harsher measures, pushing the blame onto asylum seekers yet again. How many riots have to occur before the Australian public realises the damage we are doing to these vulnerable people? How many more people must die?

I originally recorded these vignettes of life in Nauru to pay homage to the men I worked with and to show the Australian people just how cruel life was in the Nauru Regional Processing Centre. I wanted to tell their stories, detail their characters, show them as the men they are. These people are not statistics, they are not strains on our economy, they are not queue jumpers or rhetoric. These are desperate men sacrificing everything they have for their families' futures.

After the riot I realised I had something more significant than just vignettes of life in Nauru. I had evidence of the ill-treatment these men suffered in the months leading up to the riot. I had a recipe of how to break a man's spirit, how to drive a desperate man so far into the dust that he destroys his own future.

I think back to what the member of the Salvos management team said to me in his office that day. 'What do you hope to achieve with all this?'

This book, that statement—this is a stand, to tell the truth about what is happening, no matter how the government will react. Governments will only be held accountable for their actions if people stand up to them and brave the fierce bullying. If we do not stand up against governments, then they will continue to do anything in their power to demonise asylum seekers and use them as political pawns.

Most of the men I worked with have realised by now that their escape from their countries and boat trips across oceans were just the start of their journeys. Detention marks the longest and most treacherous part of their flight for freedom. There were no bombs in Nauru, no guns, no indiscriminate murders. Just waiting, boredom, insomnia, self-harm, suicide attempts, uncertainty. Uncertainty about their futures, uncertainty about their families' futures, second-guessing, yearning and fear, fear, fear. Their enemies were themselves, their own minds, which may prove to be as trying an opponent as anything their countries can throw at them. How does one battle hatred against oneself?

And yet in such a place there still existed laughter, and momentary happiness. Their optimism and their character give me hope that those remaining in Nauru will endure. Every sunrise the men are getting one day closer to their freedom, one day closer to justice. I think about all my brothers every day. Every day I wonder if they will survive, if they are healthy, if they will be sent home, or if they will voluntarily return home. How many of them will attempt suicide? How many of them will develop mental illnesses? When will they lead safe lives free from oppression and cruelty?

The Pacific Solution goes against every ideal in our nation's self-portrayal. A fair, honest, equitable land. We are travelling down a long dark road that only leads to sadness, for what? This story will only be over when Australia accepts its international responsibility to treat all asylum seekers with the dignity any human being deserves.

---

1   B Haigh, 'Tribunal delivers Sri Lanka's guilty verdict', *The Canberra Times*, 2 January 2014, viewed 2 January 2014, <www.canberratimes.com.au/comment/tribunal-delivers-sri-lankas-guilty-verdict-20140101-305zf.html>.

2   B Jabour & D Hurst, 'Nauru to increase visa cost for journalists from $200 to $8,000', *The Guardian*, 9 January 2014, viewed 20 January, <www.theguardian.com/world/2014/jan/09/nauru-visa-to-cost-8000>.

3   D Wroe & M Bachelard, 'Australian breach of Indonesian territorial waters angers Jakarta', *Sydney Morning Herald*, 18 January 2014, viewed 18 January 2014, <www.smh.com.au/federal-politics/political-news/australian-breach-of-indonesian-territorial-waters-angers-jakarta-20140117-310kk.html

4   M Gordon, 'Courts in crisis as Nauru sacks its only magistrate', *Sydney Morning Herald*, 20 January 2014, viewed 20 January, <www.smh.com.au/federal-politics/political-news/courts-in-crisis-as-nauru-sacks-its-only-magistrate-20140119-312u1.html>.

A brief history of Australia's approach to asylum seekers

As DISCUSSED THROUGHOUT this book, Australia is a signatory to the United Nations Refugee Convention and as such has agreed to certain obligations to process asylum seekers' claims for refugee status. The misconception that seeking asylum is illegal arises from the differing terminology of Australian and international law. Australian law refers to asylum seekers' mode of arrival in Australia without a valid visa, while international law and the UN Refugee Convention state that to arrive in a country that is a signatory to the UN Refugee Convention without identification documents and apply for asylum is not illegal, regardless of the manner in which an asylum seeker comes. There are no international regulations on how asylum seekers can arrive in Australia, and there is no resettlement queue lining up people seeking protection from number one to number fifteen million.

Despite the huge global numbers of displaced people Australia is not being overrun. About 75 to 90 per cent of refugees remain in their region of origin, placing the burden on neighbouring countries to settle them.[1] Only the most desperate flee their homes to get on a dangerous boat to reach an island on the other side of the world from everything they've ever known. The arrival rates of asylum seekers since the start of the Pacific Solution have been much higher than the historical average, but they represent only a few weeks' ordinary population growth.[2] The proportion of refugees we host annually is 0.3 per cent of the world's total refugee population and less than 5 per cent of our immigration intake.[3]

The statistics suggest that the majority of asylum seekers are 'legitimate' refugees and are no threat to our national security. The Australian government website explains that asylum seekers undergo a comprehensive security assessment process. This process includes assessing identities and obtaining formal police clearances from previous countries' of residence.[4] Since 2009, of the 11,168 security assessments completed by ASIO for irregular maritime arrivals, there have been just 63 adverse assessments.[5] According to Department of Immigration statistics, asylum seekers living in the community are 45 times less likely to be a criminal than you or I.[6]

In 2010–11, 93.5 per cent of asylum seekers arriving in Australian migratory zones by boat were found to be refugees and granted protection either in Australia or in another country.[7] This didn't stop Bob Carr claiming that asylum seekers are 'economic refugees' (a defunct term as the very definition of a refugee provides no basis for economic aspiration migration).[8] The public have latched onto this term despite an overwhelming number of statistics that suggest Bob Carr's comments have no basis in fact.

Despite this insistence on 'legitimate' refugees and fitting the definition given in the UN Refugee Convention, there is also a catch-all provision called complementary protection for those people who don't fit into any of the aforementioned categories but face a 'real risk of significant harm'. This is known as the non-refoulement clause. Australia broke this obligation in the Howard era and deported men back to danger. Some of these men were killed when they were returned to Afghanistan.[9]

One of the hypocrisies of the legitimacy argument is the invisibility of 'plane people'. Over the years equal numbers of asylum seekers have arrived by boat and by plane. A higher percentage of those who arrive by boat are granted refugee status than of those who arrive by plane, yet asylum seekers who arrive by plane are not publicly vilified.[10] The public's ignorance of this inequity is indicative of the unjust debate about asylum seekers. Why does Australia have such an issue with 'boat people' in particular? And why does that opposition take so many varied and illogical forms? Looking at the facts, one begins to reveal a skewed view of asylum seekers, but how did such untruths manifest and proliferate in all avenues of the debate?

Australia didn't always have this opinion of asylum seekers who arrive by boat. Between the years of 1976 and 1985 70,000 refugees, mostly Vietnamese, were successfully settled in Australia with good-will and no social meltdown.[11] A peace offering from a country that had sent troops into Vietnam. Then in 1989 the Hawke–Keating Labor government introduced mandatory detention of asylum seekers.[12] This was initially restricted to 48-hour detention. Over subsequent years both Labor and Coalition governments have used bureaucratic and legal discrimination to restrict asylum seekers' rights, slowly broadening powers to mandatorily detain, and removing time restrictions on detention. By 2004 indefinite detention of asylum seekers was ruled legal by the High Court of Australia. The Australian government can now legally detain anyone 'reasonably suspected' of being an 'illegal non-citizen' for an indefinite period of time, with no access to judicial review.[13]

In 1995 the law was changed to reduce Australia's refugee intake. Previously a family application for offshore settlement had been counted as one of 12,000 places granted each year.[14] After the law was changed each person included in a family application was counted as making an individual application for one of the 12,000 places. Then in 1996, Australia became the only country in the world to link its offshore and onshore programs. The 12,000 places previously reserved solely for offshore applications were to be replaced by any successful onshore applications. This meant that the more boats that came, the fewer refugees would be accepted from UNHCR camps and the rest of the world. This is presumably one reason why people use the term 'queue jumper'. Those who came on boats to Australia were identified as stealing places from 'legitimate' refugees. These law changes made it harder for recently resettled refugees to bring their families to Australia. Suddenly we had refugees pitted against each other because of an artificial queue created by Australian policy. Former immigration minister Phillip Ruddock told *The Weekend Australian* in 2007:

> For me, the sight of refugees from the Horn of Africa languishing in the Kakuma camp in northern Kenya without hope of resettlement was disturbing. They were forfeiting [asylum] places to those with money who could pay people-smugglers, and that always loomed large in my consciousness.[15]

One set of refugees more entitled to protection than others. Ruddock identifies money as the differentiating characteristic of a 'legitimate' refugee and an 'illegitimate' refugee, even though a person's financial state has no significance in determining whether they have been persecuted. Furthermore, many of the asylum seekers I met in Nauru had spent all they had on their journey or, worse, they represented an extended family's dream of resettlement and paid for their journey using a collective fund.

In 1998 One Nation MP Pauline Hanson proposed temporary protection visas for asylum seekers.[16] Philip Ruddock refused this proposal as inhumane, stating that the uncertainty in such visas would be unbearable for people trying to build a future. In June 1998 One Nation won 23 per cent of the primary vote in the Queensland election, causing the Coalition to lose its majority in the state parliament. The following year the federal Coalition government introduced temporary visas to people who had arrived in Australia by boat without a valid visa and were found to be refugees. These were repealed under the first Rudd government but it was feared they might be reintroduced.

The Howard government took an aggressive approach to asylum seekers before they had arrived on the mainland. It started with the distribution of videos of sharks, crocodiles and snakes, to countries from which asylum seekers came. Australian islands neighbouring the mainland where asylum seekers landed were excised from the migration zone. The government was withdrawing from its responsibility to protect asylum seekers by preventing them from reaching our shores. Refusals to undergo search expeditions for capsized boats of asylum seekers undoubtedly resulted in deaths. In the infamous *Tampa* saga, a Norwegian freighter that rescued 438 asylum seekers was denied permission to enter Australian territory, and the captain was even threatened with prosecution as a people smuggler. Retrospective legislation legalised John Howard's actions during the *Tampa* incident and permitted boats intercepted at sea to be towed into international waters and their occupants to be held in detention centres on Nauru and Manus Island. The *Tampa* asylum seekers were taken to Nauru in the first incarnation of the Pacific Solution.

Julian Burnside wrote that as John Howard was about to enter the House of Representatives to deliver his speech explaining the government's response to the Tampa, Liberal MP Jackie Kelly approached him in the lobby. She said that she was losing votes to One Nation. Howard waved his speech in front of her and said, 'don't worry, this will fix it'.[17]

The Turn Back the Boats policy came into effect. John Howard uttered the infamous line, 'We will decide who comes to this country, and the circumstances in which they come'. There are countless reports of sinking boats being towed away from safety and into danger. People in distress being kept on those sinking boats, and not provided with medical attention. Then eventually the boats sank while our Navy watched on. Some boats were told they were being taken to Australia, only to find out they had been lied to. The Australian Navy shot at boats. In one instance Special Forces were used to storm a civilian boat. There are accounts from distressed Navy personnel, horrified at what our government was asking them to do, breaking down in front of distressed asylum seekers. On 19 October 2001, despite our extensive surveillance of international waters, 146 children, 142 women and 65 men drowned when a boat sank.

It is highly likely that the Australian government was involved in people smuggling disruption programs in Indonesia that sabotaged boats.[18] Indonesian police encouraged people smugglers to pack more asylum seekers onto already overcrowded boats to increase the chance of failure.

John Howard and Philip Ruddock branded asylum seekers as 'illegals'. In the notorious Children Overboard affair they condemned asylum seekers for throwing their children into the water, an allegation that has since been proven to be untrue.

The People's Inquiry into Detention, published in 2008 under the literary title of *Human Rights Overboard*, was a succinct record of the Department of Immigration's approach to asylum seekers over the previous twenty years.[19] The People's Inquiry was initiated by the Australian Council of Heads of Schools of Social Work (ACHSSW) as open, independent and transparent, asking for anyone with experiences of immigration detention to present any evidence about any aspect of Australia's detention policy. The Inquiry received accounts from a range of sources including lawyers, immigration staff, refugees, advocates and Navy personnel.

The People's Inquiry found that asylum seekers were denied basic human rights within detention. They were denied access to legal advice and representation, and stalling and confusing bureaucracy was used. There were serious doubts as to the legitimacy of all stages of the refugee determination process.

To make a claim for refugee status, an asylum seeker must first present their case to the Department of Immigration. Interpreters used in the interviews were not always of the correct language group, and they sometimes came from a cultural or ethnic group that was prejudiced against that of the asylum seeker being interviewed. The migration agents who reviewed the refugee cases were often undertrained and did not possess adequate research skills. The decisions were proven to be highly subjective and influenced by political pressure. A former case worker for Amnesty told me of immigration staff who gave a homosexual asylum seeker a negative refugee assessment based on lack of credibility because the asylum seeker didn't know the date of the Sydney Mardi Gras or the names of bars on Oxford Street. These agents were not held accountable for their decisions.

Asylum seekers who were not awarded refugee status had twenty-eight days to depart Australia or they risked being deported. Asylum seekers were given the chance to appeal negative refugee status determinations to the Refugee Review Tribunal (RRT). If the claim was rejected by the RRT, asylum seekers could appeal to the Federal Circuit Court (FCC), but the FCC had no power to examine the facts of the case and could only order that the matter be reheard at the RRT.

If an asylum seeker was not awarded refugee status but they were not recognised by a nation-state, and were therefore considered stateless, Australia could not deport them. Nor could Australia deport a person back to their country of origin if that person faced significant harm in returning, even if the person had their refugee claim rejected. These asylum seekers could remain in detention indefinitely unless they voluntarily returned home. That same Amnesty case worker told me of a Tamil who was deported, and upon his return to Sri Lanka was taken by the government and tortured again. When he was finally released he came back to Australia on a second boat.

In 2002 the United Nations Working Group on Arbitrary Detention reported that Australia's 'system combining mandatory, automatic, indiscriminate, and indefinite detention without real access to court challenge is not practiced by any other country in the world.'[20]

I once would have found all this hard to believe. After working in Nauru it all seemed nightmarishly familiar.

There is a perception that Australian asylum seeker policy can stem the flow of boats. Numerous sources, including the Refugee Council of Australia, state that the number of asylum seekers arriving in Australia annually is dependent on global trends and that Australian policy does little to affect it.[21] Despite this, some people who support hardline measures justify their approach using the example of John Howard's Pacific Solution. During Howard's term as prime minister there was a distinct reduction in boat arrivals, from 5516 people and forty-three boats in 2001 to one boat a year for the following three years.[22] The UNHCR reported that during those years applications to developed countries more than halved and countries such as the UK and France recorded their lowest levels of applications in decades.[23] Interestingly, the federal government's own website does not attribute the stopping of boats to Howard's policy but instead states that 'boat arrival numbers in Australia have fluctuated significantly over the last 30 years in response to global events'.[24]

Seven years later, the reintroduction of the Pacific Solution has done very little to stop the boats from coming. Does that mean it needs to be harsher? If Howard's policy was effective, do the ends justify the means? Even if the Howard government's policy was responsible for stopping the boats, it was also responsible for deportations back to countries such as Afghanistan where asylum seekers ended up being killed. The United Nations Convention clearly outlines accepted protocol for the treatment of asylum seekers, protocol which Australia has breached and continues to breach with policies such as the Pacific Solution and No Advantage. According to Human Rights Overboard the purpose of indefinite detention in order to deter is a 'repudiation of the fundamental premise of international human rights law, which is the equal worth of every human being'.[25]

Over the years of bureaucratic discrimination, public attitudes towards asylum seekers have slowly morphed from generosity to suspicion and fear. Public perception and government discrimination have become so intertwined now that it is difficult to identify which influenced the other.

During the reintroduction of the Pacific Solution, the policy debate revolved around 'saving lives at sea' and 'smashing the people smugglers' business model'. It was framed in such a way that our rancour was directed at those who transport asylum seekers across dangerous waters on rickety boats. Those who want to stop boats to save lives are pilloried by the left for supporting an inhumane 'no advantage' policy. Those who want to help all asylum seekers are criticised for being naive and are told that we will be swamped if we have an open door policy. We are at an impasse.

The projected cost to Australia of offshore processing for 2013–2017 is expected to be at least $2.3 billion.[26] That works out to nearly $1 million for each asylum seeker held in Nauru and Manus so far. Rick Towle from the UN High Commission of Refugees said that the UNHCR's global budget for this year is $3.7 billion, a budget that is expected to cover 25 million refugees globally.

---

1   J Phillips, *Asylum Seekers and Refugees: What are the facts?*, Parliament of Australia, 2013, viewed 27 August 2013, <www.aph.gov.au/About_Parliament/Parliamentary_Departments/Parliamentary_Library/pubs/BN/2012-2013/AsylumFacts#_Toc348096466>.
2   J Burnside, 'Alienation to Alien Nation', *The Conversation*, 19 September 2013, viewed 21 September 2013, <http://theconversation.com/julian-burnside-alienation-to-alien-nation-18290>.
3   Phillips, *Asylum Seekers and Refugees: What are the facts?*
4   Phillips, *Asylum Seekers and Refugees: What are the facts?*
5   ASIO, *ASIO Report to Parliament*, Commonwealth of Australia, 2012, viewed 15 September 2013, <www.asio.gov.au/img/files/ASIO-Annual-Report-2011-12_full.pdf>.
6   B Hall, 'Few asylum seekers charged with crime', *Sydney Morning Herald*, March 1 2013, viewed 1 March 2013, <www.smh.com.au/federal-politics/political-news/few-asylum-seekers-charged-with-crime-20130228-2f98h.html>.
7   Williams, 'The Nauru 10: The Habeus Corpus Challenge'.
8   ABC News, 'Fact Check: No evidence to support Foreign Minister Bob Carr's economic migrants claim', 15 August 2013, viewed 24 August 2013, <www.abc.net.au/news/2013-08-14/no-evidence-bob-carr-economic-migrants/4821544>.
9   J Topsfield, 'The asylum seeker we sent home to his death', *The Age*, 3 April 2009, viewed 15 March 2013, <www.theage.com.au/national/the-asylum-seeker-we-sent-home-to-his-death-20090402-9l57.html>.
10 SBS News, 'Asylum seekers: Where Australia stands', 23 August 2013, viewed 24 August 2013, <www.sbs.com.au/news/article/1295782/Asylum-seekers-Where-Australia-stands>
11 L Briskman, C Goddard & S Latham, *Human Rights Overboard*, Scribe Publications, Carlton, 2008, p. 60.
12 Briskman, Goddard & Latham, pp. 59-60.
13 Briskman, Goddard & Latham, p. 63.
14 Briskman, Goddard & Latham, p. 61-62.
15 D Aiton, 'Foreword: 10 Things you didn't know about Phillip Ruddock, Attorney General', *The Weekend Australian Magazine*, 27–28 January 2007, p.10.
16 Briskman, Goddard & Latham, p. 62.
17 Burnside, 'Alienation to Alien Nation'.
18 Briskman, Goddard & Latham, p. 42-54.
19 Briskman, Goddard & Latham, p. 42-54.
20 Working Group on Arbitrary Detention, no. 85 [62] quoted in New South Wales Council for Civil Liberties 2007, *Shadow report prepared for the United Nations Committee Against Torture on the occasion of its review of Australia's Third Periodic Report under the Convention Against Torture and other Cruel, Inhuman or Degrading Treatment or Punishment*, 27 July, par.105, 23 August 2013, <www.nswccl.org.au/docs/pdf/CAT%20shadow%20report.pdf>.
21 Refugee Council of Australia, 'Myths about refugees and asylum seekers', 2011.
22 Department of Immigration and Citizenship, *Asylum Trends: 2011–2012 Annual Publication*, Commonwealth of Australia, 2012, 23 August 2013, <www.immi.gov.au/media/publications/statistics/asylum/_files/asylum-trends-aus-annual-2011-12.pdf>.
23 Briskman, Goddard & Latham, p. 110.
24 Phillips & Spinks 2011, *Boat arrivals in Australia since 1976*.
25 Briskman, Goddard & Latham.
26 ABC Television, 'No Advantage'.

Acknowledgements

THROUGHOUT THIS JOURNEY there have been many people who have supported me, my writing and my endeavours, without whom none of this would have been possible.

To Fabia and Ariana, thank you for unwittingly setting me on this path, which has irrevocably changed my life.

To Amanda, Catherine, Joel, Ash, Jack, Jacko, Tilbo, Pat, Jelly, Martin, Nicole, Chris Cohen, ATB, and my colleagues in Nauru, for your support and your unfailing care for the underprivileged of the world in the hardest and most trying of conditions.

To Julian Burnside, for his unfailing commitment to the cause and his support for all those who were courageous enough to speak out.

To Donna Mulhearn, for guiding a naive young man through the publishing world and pointing him in the right direction.

To Lyn Tranter, for pushing me to the limit to make this book the best it could be. To Tim, for your tireless hours of editing. Alice Whitmore de Yanis and Louis Bottom-Robertson, for your friendship that meant reading through a lot of tripe over the years. Julian, Pippa, Bel, Owen and Zuri, for the essential Brisbane debriefs. To Fran Berry and the Hardie Grant crew, for believing in this vision, and to my editor Penelope Goodes, for taking this book to the next level.

To my dear parents, David and Carmel, and all my family and friends, thank you for your unconditional love.

And most importantly, to those who have suffered and are still suffering the traumas of Australia's Pacific Solution: thank you for giving me insight into your world, and allowing me to share your stories. You are people. We do care. And one day I hope you may have justice.